Say "Thank You" and See Miracles

The Garden of Miracles

190 True Stories about the Power of Gratitude

By

Shalom Arush

D1250279

In all matters relating to this book, please contact:

Chut Shel Chessed Institutions

Shmuel HaNavi St. 13

POB 50226, Jerusalem, Israel

Telephone 972-2-581-2210

Distribution:
Tel: 972-52-224-0696

www.myemuna.com

Printed in Israel

ISBN 978-965-92613-0-7

Say "Thank You" and See Miracles

The Garden of Miracles

**190 True Stories about
the Power of Gratitude by**

Shalom Arush
Director of Chut Shel Chessed Institutions

Author of:

The Garden of Emuna

The Garden of Peace

The Garden of Yearning

In Forest Fields

Women's Wisdom

The Garden of Riches

The Garden of Gratitude

The Universal Garden of Emuna

The Garden of Wisdom

The Garden of Education

The Garden of Knowledge

The Garden of Purity

The Garden of Emuna for Young People

and other books

Translated by:
Lazer Brody

"Enter His gates
with gratitude,
His courts with praise."
(Psalm 100:4)

"If everyone heeded the true tzaddikim, and walked in the path of their advice, always believing that everything Hashem does is for the good, and constantly thanked Hashem for the good and for the seemingly opposite, then all suffering and exile would be totally nullified, and the full redemption of our people would arrive."

Rebbe Natan of Breslev

Table of Contents

Foreword – In the Garden of Miracles and Wonders

With Hashem's loving grace, we have had the privilege of spreading the wonderful way of gratitude the world over by means of our book, "The Garden of Gratitude" and by way of our emuna CDs and pamphlets that talk about the power of gratitude.

With my own eyes, I have witnessed so many miracles happen to people in every facet of life. As soon as they decided to live their lives with gratitude and thank Hashem for everything, they benefitted outright miracles and their lives turned around for the best. Childless mothers are suddenly expecting. Debtors no longer owe people money. Unmarried people are suddenly finding their soul mates. Sick people with no hope in sight suddenly recover. How? They say "thank You" and see miracles.

King David says in Psalm 105, "Thank Hashem and call His Name – inform the nations of His wonders." The Zohar says, "We are obligated to tell the world about the miracles that Hashem does." By doing so, we sanctify Hashem's Name and His honor is magnified both in the spiritual and in the physical realms.

Rebbe Elimelech of Lizhensk teaches that when we tell about the wonders and miracles that Hashem performs, we invoke more wonders and miracles. But, if a person attributes the amazing things that happen in life to natural phenomena, he no longer sees miracles. Even worse, he is left to the mercy of natural phenomena.

A person who has merited miracles is obligated to tell about them. This is similar to the gratitude offering in the

Holy Temple, where a person donates a special sacrificial animal and ceremonial bread, and subsequently holds a thanksgiving meal where he would publicly thank Hashem for the miracle that he benefitted.

Since one must say "thank You" for the privilege of saying "thank You" to Hashem, we have compiled 190 stories of miracles that people have brought to our attention. They have seen miraculous salvations by expressing their gratitude to Hashem and by clinging to the belief that everything He does is for the very best.

We really don't need to say a word all day long except "thank You" to Hashem. Rebbe Natan of Breslev says, "Truly, if people heeded the true tzaddikim and followed the path of believing in Hashem always, that everything is for the best; and if they thanked Hashem always for the good and for the troubles, as it is written, 'I'll praise Hashem and I'll praise Elokim' (Hashem being the Name of Divine compassion and Elokim the Name of Divine judgment), then all troubles, exile and diaspora would be null and void, and we'd have the Geula, the full redemption!" By thanking Hashem in any situation – for the seemingly bad as well as for the good – not only would our troubles be nullified but we'd see the complete redemption with tremendous mercy.

We want the way of gratitude to be public property, available to anyone. The more gratitude spreads in the world, the quicker and easier we'll see the Geula, with no push-button wars or bloodshed and with a big smile. When will that happen? It will happen when we all stop whining and complaining and start singing songs of gratitude. This will invoke a huge measure of Divine compassion for the world.

Everyone must know that whatever one lacks – whether

income, health, a soul-mate or anything else – the solution is to turn to Hashem for thirty minutes a day and thank Him wholeheartedly for the deficiency. Make gratitude notebooks and write down the things that you're thankful for and the miracles you see by saying thank You. That way, the full redemption will surely come.

The more people say thank You the more the light of the redemption will shine. Every week, we hear new miracles: "I said thank You and I got a great job." "I said thank You for a half hour a day and I found my soul-mate." "I said thank You and I became a mother". Everyone must write these types of things down, so that people will see that it's for real and not just theoretical or nice rhetoric. Do you harbor negative thoughts? Do you suffer from tribulations? Whatever it is, say thank You for a half hour daily: "Thank You, Hashem for my depression." "Thank You, Hashem for my negative thoughts." When you thank Hashem for the seemingly bad as well as for the good, you'll surely see miracles.

We would like periodically to publish additional volumes of stories about people who saw miracles by way of gratitude. We'd be happy to hear your story too, so feel free to write it down and send it to us.

I heard most of the stories that appear in this volume from the first-hand source. Because of editing and privacy considerations, we have omitted personal and private details of the people behind the stories. Yet, this is only a drop in the sea of letters, emails, conversations and other things that come to my attention about the power of saying thank You and seeing miracles that defy nature in every sense of the word. And, what we hear is only a miniscule part of the amazing things that are happening to people who have learned the power of gratitude.

A portion of the stories in this volume have already appeared in our other books, pamphlets and CDs, but because of their significance, we have compiled them together with new stories to make up this volume. We hope that you will derive encouragement and joy from reading them. If by virtue of this book, one additional person becomes spiritually stimulated enough to begin thanking the Creator for a half hour daily for all of life's blessings, then the efforts of publishing this book are worthwhile. What's more, every person who expresses gratitude to the Creator expedites the full redemption of our people!

May it be Hashem's will that everyone see miracles by way of gratitude, thereby enhancing the light of gratitude in the world, making life here a virtual heaven on earth. May we merit seeing the Geula, the full redemption of our people in peace and mercy, and may the Divine Monarchy and honor be revealed in our days, speedily, amen!

Now smile – everything's for the best!

Rabbi Shalom Arush

Send your stories for the coming volume of

"Say Thank You and See Miracles"

to: amartitoda@gmail.com

1. Double Winner

I heard this story directly from a couple whom I personally know. Before his wedding, the groom knew that he was not able to have children, a fact he had hidden from his bride-to-be. He knew this wasn't the right thing to do, but he was afraid that she wouldn't want to marry him and so he opted to hide the truth. The bride also knew before the wedding that she had problems with conceiving and for the same reasons, decided not to tell her groom-to-be. But the Creator makes matches, so by exacting Divine providence, He paired them together and they were married.

After the wedding they could no longer keep such secrets, so they revealed the truth to each other. They came to me after having met with several doctors who all told them that they would never have children. I told them to say, "Thank You." I explained that the Creator sees them and what they're going through and knows that it is only through this deficiency that they can attain their ultimate perfection. In other words, this deficiency is actually a gift. I said, "You must spend a half hour every day saying 'Thank You,' strengthening your emuna and remaining happy with your lot. This gratitude will guard you from all sadness, depression, heresy and negative thoughts – especially from thinking that the Creator is doing something horrible to you, Heaven forbid."

This couple already knew they couldn't have children, so they had no choice but to subjugate their will to the will of the Creator. This was easy since the only way to avoid misery was to accept their lot in life and be happy with it. And so, they truly thanked the Creator with joy and nullified their will to His. Every day they would say to the Creator, "Master of the Universe, You created us this way, with these problems, with these deficiencies – this is our lot in life. This is how You want it to be. And we, therefore, gracefully accept your will and wholeheartedly bind our will with Yours. Thank You for making us this way. Thank You for our fertility problems and for giving us full emuna that this is coming from You and is for our benefit. Thank You for bringing us close to You. We have no idea what the future holds but we'll face it with full emuna." This couple succeeded in realizing the purpose of gratitude – to nullify and unify one's will with the will of the Creator, lovingly accepting that all that He does is for the very best.

They were happy with their lot in life because they believed that their deficiencies were for their very best; they said thank You to the Creator for their difficulties. The very reason that they were given these deficiencies in the first place was to build true emuna, knowing that everything the Creator does is for the very best. Therefore, the moment that they arrived at this point of true emuna, they were healed. Thank G-d, today they have two children!

"This is the gate of Hashem through which the righteous, holy ones shall enter. I thank You, for You have answered me and become my salvation." (Psalm 118:19-20). We learn from this line that when someone lives his life with gratitude, he is called 'a holy, righteous one'. And, when someone is thankful, all the gates of salvation and solutions are open to him.

We must emphasize the great responsibility that comes with this. Many learn about being grateful and saying 'thank you' but they don't understand just how much of a basic obligation this is. They think that it's just a nice idea and a positive character trait to work on or part of proper etiquette. But that's not so! Gratitude is the first step in having a true connection with the Creator. We are obligated to contemplate every day the goodness that the Creator does for us. It is not only our duty to sing His praises, but also the responsibility of every created being to give thanks, to praise, to glorify, to magnify and to exalt His Holy Name.

This is not merely a good piece of advice – it's codified in Halacha, Jewish Law, just like the laws that govern other aspects of daily life. One is obligated by law to thank his Creator and lovingly accept everything Hashem does, for better or for worse (see Shulchan Aruch, Orach Chaim, 230:5). The Rambam, in his conclusion of the Laws of Blessings, says that one must "ask for mercy in the future yet thank Hashem for everything in the past – the more one thanks Hashem, the more it is praiseworthy."

The *Shulchan Aruch* (Code of Jewish Law) states further that a person must gladly thank Hashem for the seemingly bad in the same manner that he thanks for the good, for the servants of G-d know that the seemingly bad is intrinsically good, for their ultimate benefit" (ibid, 222:3).

2. You Rescued Me from the Depths of the Sea

One of my students told me the story about when he and his friends went to the beach. The Mediterranean was rough that day and the waves were powerful. Even though they swam close to the shore in a shallow area, the strong waves repeatedly washed over them. Suddenly, my student felt his artificial tooth – a gold crown - drop into the water. He was upset about this because this crown had cost him a lot of money. If he had at least caught it, he could have it reattached at the dentist, sparing the time, expense and trouble of getting a whole new tooth made. But now that it fell into the water, even if the waves calmed down, he'd have no chance of finding some tiny tooth on the sandy floor of the sea. All the more so with the stormy conditions and high waves – there was just no way he would find it.

He was sorely disappointed. But suddenly, he remembered hearing my classes on giving thanks. He said to himself, "The first thing I need to do is say 'thank You'. I don't understand anything. And, surely, everything is for the best. Therefore, I need to let go of my will and accept the will of the Creator to receive this with love. I must surrender to what has obviously been decreed upon me from Above – as it is for my very best – and show my gratitude for it."

The young man began to thank the Creator sincerely that his tooth fell. He was standing in the water and thanking the Creator for about twenty minutes when, suddenly, the waves calmed down. He looked down and there was his tooth, resting atop the sandy sea floor! He was shocked by the power of gratitude. He didn't understand how this was possible, after so much time had passed. What's more, he had moved from where he had originally had lost the tooth, not even remembering where exactly that place was. Now, suddenly, he sees his tooth, resting on the sea floor in plain sight. To him, this was a revealed miracle – outside of the realms of rational logic. Through giving thanks and receiving the Creator's will for us with absolute love, we can evoke miracles and wonders way beyond by the limitations of nature.

Rebbe Nachman of Breslev says, "Nature is bound by limitations, but prayer changes nature" (Likutei Moharan I:7). Rebbe Nachman's mention of prayer is synonymous to gratitude.

I always say, "If you believe, you pray." **Gratitude constitutes complete emuna.** A person should live with an awareness of gratitude, because if you don't say "thank You," you are lacking an essential element of emuna – "This is what the Creator wants." The Creator is doing what He does to bring you closer to Him.

My student told this story in the middle of a class I was giving on Shabbat. At the time, it was really hard to believe it. But, his friends that were with him that day at the beach verified the story, declaring – right in the middle of my class - "We were with him and we saw it with our own eyes."

That initial feeling of remorse that he had when he first discovered that his tooth was missing showed a lack of emuna. He didn't yet believe that whatever was happening to him was from Hashem and for his ultimate good. He thought that he didn't deserve to lose an expensive tooth and therefore he was upset because of it. But, after he strengthened himself and nullified his will to the Creator's, he connected to true emuna. He no longer cared whether he found his tooth or not – the essence of his salvation lay in the fact that he was saved from living a life of heresy and falsehood, which are the source of all suffering. By way of gratitude, one internalizes the truth that everything Hashem does is for the very best; miracles that come from gratitude reinforce this point. Even without the miracle that my student witnessed, he should have rejoiced in the strengthening of emuna that enabled him to accept a painful situation with joy, thus saving him from a life of denial, trouble and sorrow.

Why do we say, "Say thank You and see miracles"? Why is it that when a man says "thank You" to the Creator he sees miraculous salvations?

There are many reasons given in the course of this book, but the essential reasoning is that there are no tribulations without prior transgressions. Then, any difficulty that a person experiences in life is an indication that he still lacks complete emuna. Life's challenges are designed to prod us into seeking more emuna, for learning and attaining emuna is our very purpose on earth.

Therefore, when a person thanks Hashem for his or her problem for half an hour every day, they will soon realize that their difficulty is all for the best, earning them stronger emuna. When a person attains the level of emuna where he believes that everything is good, then his difficulty in life becomes superfluous and miraculously turns around for the better.

Any feeling of lack comes from a deficiency in spiritual awareness, and a deficiency in spiritual awareness is a deficiency in emuna. Once a person attains spiritual awareness, he no longer feels that anything is lacking. With complete emuna, one lacks nothing.

3. The Diamond Dealer's Gift

A diamond dealer once told me that for some time he had been corresponding through mail with a supplier in Africa in order to close a good business deal with him, buying quality diamonds at a good price. He consulted with me whether or not he should go there to close the deal. I blessed him with a safe trip and success. Contained within his tale below is a lesson for everyone:

Hello,

My name is A.G. and my business is in importing gemstones and diamonds.

It is important to note that I feel connected to Rabbi Arush with all of my heart and soul. As a result, for many years I have been engaging in personal prayer with the Creator in my own words for an hour every day – every now and then even six hours.

My story begins with a big business deal regarding the purchase of some diamonds from Mozambique, Africa. This was my first time dealing with this particular supplier, as he was new to the scene. At the beginning of the deal, he demanded down-payment of a third of the value of the stones – a standard in the industry. At first, I refused to give him the money, but he won me over by constantly speaking of emuna in the Creator and saying that he belonged to a group of individuals that believed that Jews were the chosen nation – so I gave him 30% of the sum.

I travelled to him and prepared the full amount in advance – a great sum of cash. When I arrived in Mozambique, I checked out the stones. The supplier demanded that I give him the rest of the sum in order to close the deal. I determinedly refused on the grounds that the agreement was that he would receive the rest of the money once all the stones were in my possession. He wouldn't agree and wanted to void the deal, which would mean I would lose out on the amount I had already paid him.

I tried to reach Rabbi Arush to get his advice, but he wouldn't answer me. I then did an hour of personal prayer with the Creator, after which the rabbi answered me and advised me not to give him the rest of the money.

In the morning, after much deliberation, I knew that the supplier and I needed to find common ground so that I wouldn't lose the advance. We agreed that I would give him another sum of money to enable him to get the export confirmation he needed. We travelled together to the capital city, Maputo, in order to expedite the process.

At this point I had already given him tens of thousands of dollars. We finally got to Maputo after it was already very dark and arrived at a dilapidated hotel. The supplier said that this place was very cheap and that the owners were connected to his family. Later on that same night, when we sat down to eat, the supplier suddenly informed me that he had to go to the border of South Africa (a distance of an hour and a half from where we were), in order to take care of the bank transfer at his branch, and that he would return immediately in the morning.

I forcefully refused, demanding to at least ride with him. Upon realizing that my visa would not allow such a trip, he begged, prodded and pleaded, giving me his solemn promise that he would never lie to a Jew and that I needed to trust him. I had no choice, and so he left for the border.

In the morning I went out into the street and my heart sunk – I saw that the hotel was actually very far from the city in a scary area. I found myself in the middle of an impoverished village – and was frightened. I immediately ran back inside and called the supplier only to discover his phone was disconnected. I decided that there was nothing for me to do but to accept what had been decreed upon me. I put on my prayer shawl and tefillin, and said my morning prayers. Then, I had my daily, personal-prayer session with the Creator. Finally, while whispering nonstop prayers, I made a quick escape from the hotel so as not to be robbed or killed. By way of a miracle I found a suitable hotel in the center of the city of Maputo and went out to have a long, six-hour conversation with my Creator. I begged Him for signs showing me what I should do. Near the end of the six hours, I saw a building with writing on it in Portuguese. Suddenly, an important and reasonable looking man passed in front of me, and for some reason I told him I was a Jew. Shocked, he turned to look at me and said, "If you are a Jew, you are the son of the Lord."

I told him my whole story and he took out his cell phone. He said to me, "If the Lord sent you to me, I am obligated to help you." I was a little bit concerned that he was planning to swindle me. The man sensed my trepidation so he took out his documentation proving him to be an Honorary Consul of the Congo. I thanked the Creator! He assured me that he would help and make sure the supplier returned to Mozambique.

I began speaking with the Creator again and called Rabbi Arush in shame to tell him the unfortunate series of events that had transpired. I promised the Creator that I would do exactly as the rabbi told me. Rabbi Arush told me that from now until I returned home, I must thank the Creator every day for every little thing that happened to me while in Africa, and – most importantly – not to ask for a single thing! The rabbi warned me another time not to request anything of the Creator, not even once, only to thank Him.

At first, when I finished speaking with the rabbi, I was really broken-hearted, because I understood that I must now resign myself to the fact that I lost over a hundred twenty thousand dollars and that there was nothing to do about it. But a few seconds later, I stopped myself and thought, "Up until this point in my life, the Creator has shown me just how much He loves me, sending me help every time I asked for it."

I remembered the lessons taught by Rabbi Arush about the power of saying "thank You". I had even read the book "The Garden of Gratitude". Therefore, I had no doubt about the power of one word to help me, even in my current situation. I decided to thank Hashem for six hours straight! After just a half hour of expressing my gratitude, I had a fleeting thought that maybe there was a synagogue in the neighborhood that I could go to and pray in solitude.

I determined that this was no passing thought, so I ran to my computer to Google "Synagogue, Maputo"; lo and behold there was a synagogue less than two minutes' walking distance from my hotel. I made contact with someone from the congregation and he came to give me the key. Once I got there, my heart was bursting with unending joy – I felt as if I had come home. I began to laugh and cry and call out to the Creator from a place of deep, unbounded bliss.

I spoke with the Creator for six hours – only I couldn't just speak – I sang, danced, and clapped my hands with gratitude for all of the good that the Creator had done for me up until this point in my life. As the end of the six hours neared, I was feeling exalted happiness from the depths of my soul. I sensed that I was on the right path to nullifying my own will and lovingly accepting Hashem's Divine providence – the way He was handling my life.

(In the words of Rav Arush: "If we were to write a whole book on the subject, we still would not be able to describe what one receives when he spends six, consecutive hours saying "thank You." When a person thanks the Creator for six, consecutive hours, he experiences an enormous elevation of his soul and is able to clear away any negative spiritual debris from his being, giving him incredible joy and emuna, to the extent that the problem no longer "bothers" him.)

The following day I returned to the synagogue. It was a few days before my return flight. I sat in the synagogue for ten hours…and I didn't ask for a thing – I only said "Thank

You." Over the course of these two days I realized I didn't want to be making deals with the Creator. I wanted only to thank Him for whatever was happening in my life. If I could but stand in front of the Creator and thank Him for many, long hours every single day, how could I possibly be ungrateful? Why be sad and disappointed, reacting like a heretic? Everything that goes on in the world is the result of Hashem's will, and all for the good!

I told the Creator, "Now I know what all of this was for. You gave me an enormous gift – the gift of emuna, the gift of coming closer to You. Now I understand why I had to go through what I went through – to come closer to You." I decided to book the next flight home. Neither the money nor the diamonds were interesting to me any longer.

I gave one last shout to the Creator: "THANK YOU!" I suddenly felt an intense, spiritual awakening within me. I felt the Creator right there with me – as if I were touching His throne of glory. And then I began to laugh a wild, redeeming laugh over which I had no control. And then I began sobbing from a place of sheer joy, the likes of which I have never before experienced. I sang to Him, danced for Him, cried out to Him – all in the name of my deep love and gratitude for His presence in my life. Once my excitement calmed down, I began to think how irrational this all was. Why would the Creator of the Universe bestow His Divine presence on a lowlife like me? Who am I anyway? It didn't make any sense. What had overcome me? So I asked the Creator, and the moment that I asked, He instilled me with the understanding that every person is worthy of a deep, blissful connection with Him – even more than I felt at that moment – all by simply expressing his gratitude without wanting nor requesting anything in return.

That night, before my flight home, the supplier called

me. He promised me he was coming back the next day. I immediately saw that the Creator had returned him to me and I couldn't stop laughing and thanking the Creator for the incredible kindness He was doing for me. Needless to say, this whole deal was no longer my main goal. I said to the Creator, "If You don't want me to be successful in closing this deal that's fine by me. And if You want me to close the deal, then I'd love Your help. I already thank You for whatever turns out!"

I started thanking the Creator for everything – for my life, for water, for shoes, for food, for my left hand to wear tefillin on and for my right hand to wrap the tefillin. I thanked Him for all the ways in which I am able to connect with Him. Of course this was all a product of the insights I gained from Rabbi Arush's classes – words that I had heard but never implemented in my life nor really understood, but which had now all fallen into place.

I won't describe the details of all that transpired, but the supplier returned; the Consul, together with the police, apprehended him. The whole story is long and spans over many weeks, but I saw the hand of G-d throughout the entire experience. Incredible miracles took place before my eyes. In the end, I closed the deal directly with the ones who owned the stones, with whom my newfound connection would open up the doors to greater profits and lower prices, eliminating my need for a supplier. Mysterious are the ways of the Creator.

Upon returning home, I asked Rabbi Arush: "Why did you tell me not to make requests of the Creator?"

He said to me that my test was very hard. "We are talking about a large sum, so your investment needed to be equally as large. You flew to Africa, you had the expense of the flight and the time. I knew that whenever someone begins to ask for things, he tends to feel sorry for himself and he starts whining – everything looks bad. In this way, he ends up losing everything. And so, you needed emuna that everything was good! **The bigger the test, the more careful you need to be in refraining from making requests – only to thank.**"

That is the diamond dealer's story in brief, even though there's more to the original letter he wrote. We learn here that every person goes through difficult tests of faith – some have been desperately searching for their soul-mate for a long time, some are sick with terminal illnesses, some couples don't have children – everyone has something that they are waiting for or hoping for or desperately wanting. If only we said "thank You" and not ask for a thing! Because when we make requests, we fall into whining and self-pity, making life even more difficult.

As everyone can see, we're on the verge of Redemption and the Messianic Age. We really should ask ourselves, if the prodigious righteous and pious spiritual leaders of yesteryear failed to usher in the Messiah, how are we so presumptuous to expect that we can? How can this seemingly low and dark generation overturn all of the suffering and bring about the Geula, the full redemption of our people?

Hashem has enabled me to understand that the Geula will arrive by virtue of gratitude. And, with His loving help and guidance, the awareness and practice of expressing gratitude to the Almighty is spreading around the world. People are praying, organizations are encouraging people to give thanks, and millions of copies of books, CDs and pamphlets on the subject are being distributed around the world in a variety of languages. Additionally, we see through the stories included in this book that people are realizing, implementing, and reaping benefits from the power of gratitude. With the help of the Creator, this message will spread even further.

How can I claim that it is this generation that will bring the light like no other generation before?

The answer is that the essence of the darkness we find ourselves in is a lack of spiritual awareness– a lack of emuna. This tells us that people in earlier generations did not accept what the Creator did for them with song and dance, with love and gratitude. Rather, it was with disappointment and self-pity. The reason for the continuing exile and generation after generation of sorrow and suffering is that we continue to cry and complain, to the extent that things just get worse.

A person may have, at one point, been a completely righteous person, but the moment that he is no longer appreciative – and therefore no longer says "Thank You" – he is called 'an incompletely righteous person'. A 'completely righteous person' is always grateful for what he has and never complains about what he doesn't. An incompletely righteous person is unhappy and ungrateful when things don't go his way. Such a person must come back another time to work on himself in order to become a completely righteous individual. If a person is grateful and always giving thanks, he merits tasting paradise.

The moment a person begins to be grateful, he fixes everything. For example, a person desperately searching for his or her soul-mate who engages in half an hour of thanking the Creator for not yet finding what he or she seeks – every single day – fixes the painful self-pity of every person in every generation in every incarnation who was hoping for their soul-mate. He who doesn't have children and says "thank You" for half an hour every day for the fact that he doesn't have children, fixes the painful self-pity of every person in every generation in every incarnation of those bereft of children in previous lives. This is the case with every lack. Especially in the spiritual realm, when a person says "Thank You" for half an hour every day for the fact that he isn't spiritually progressing, he fixes the painful self-pity of every person in every generation in every incarnation of those lacking in spiritual refinement in previous lives.

The Gemara tells that Hashem wanted to make King Hezekiah *Moshiach* (Messiah). The angel of stern judgment objected: "Master of the World! King David sang endless songs of praise to You, and You didn't make him Moshiach. You did wonderful miracles for Hezekiah, and he didn't sing any songs of praise. How can he be Moshiach?"

There was no one in all of history who spread the knowledge of Torah like King Hezekiah did. In his generation, everyone was a Torah scholar. And, he did praise Hashem for the miraculous salvation against the marauding army of Sannherib. So why was there the destruction of the two Holy Temples and the Diaspora and exile that followed?

The answer is that King Hezekiah's thanks to Hashem for the salvation was not enough to qualify him as Moshiach. Yet, he didn't thank Hashem for the trouble itself! To be Moshiach, he should have accepted everything with joy. And to prevent exile and destruction, his generation should have learned to thank Hashem as well.

It's a wonderful thing to be a good person and praise the Creator. But it is even a higher level to be able to *thank* the Creator for *everything*.

4. The Dream and the Cancelled Lawsuit

The headmaster of a prestigious school was in big trouble. Many years ago, he owed a large sum of money to someone and then finally paid him back. But the lender never destroyed the check he was holding as security and one day decided he would cash it for almost $10,000! The headmaster called me sad, dejected and completely broken. He said to me, "I already paid him! And he won't give me back the check, and now he wants to take me to court saying that I owe him that amount – plus interest!" I told him to go to the beach and for an entire hour just say, "Thank You" - only "thank You". Not to ask for a single thing! "The Creator wants you to pay $10,000? Whatever the Creator does is good. Tell Him, 'Thank You'!"

He went to the beach and spoke to the Creator in his own language, thanking Him for everything for an entire hour. Instead of lamenting his situation, he strengthened his resolve and instead said, "Creator of the Universe, I know I don't owe this man anything, but if You want me to pay him $10,000, then I trust You. Thank You! Everything You do is for my very best. I don't understand the Divine accountings You keep and maybe I owe him from a past life or something. The only thing I do know is that if this is what You want, then it is all for my good. Thank You so much, Master of the Universe! I believe that this is all coming from You! And that this man is only a messenger for whatever You are trying to tell me or give me – a stick in Your hand. Thank You, for You know what You are doing." And he thanked and praised the Creator.

In the morning, the man demanding the money called the headmaster and said he had such a strange dream after which he knew he must return the check and cancel the lawsuit. And he did just that.

One hour of giving thanks and he was saved!

Everyone needs to learn from this how important it is to strengthen one's emuna. If we truly understood everything the Creator does, there would be no room for emuna! **One who knows the Creator's deeds has no emuna – he has information.** When we know, we have no free choice and therefore no chance for reward. But emuna is to believe even when we don't understand anything – even when all is dark and confusing. And even when everything seems upside down, if we believe that there is no such thing as 'bad' – if we can see the darkness and still call it 'good' – we are enacting our free will. For this is our free will in this world – to believe or not to believe. He who has emuna and believes, lives a good and successful life always dancing and singing to the Creator. But when something doesn't go his way, the one who has no emuna and does not believe that everything that happens is for his good, enters into a state of depression, whining and complaining, resulting in pushing himself even farther away from emuna, his life's purpose, and from light itself.

We can end our current exile easily and simply through gratitude. And once we do this, true knowledge – the knowledge that everything is good and that there is no bad – will permeate the entire world. Therefore, through using this tool of "thank You", everyone will come to know the Creator, which will bring great light, redeeming us from a dark exile. For the essence of the knowledge of redemption is gratitude. Rebbe Nachman of Breslev tells us that the essence of the pleasure of the World to Come is to thank and praise the Creator, getting to know Him, and ultimately coming closer to Him and His greatness.

He also wrote that, **"All trials and tribulations and darkness are nothing but a lack of spiritual awareness and understanding."** Why does a person suffer? It's because he has no spiritual awareness. He lacks understanding and is devoid of emuna. Why is a person in a state of exile? For the same reason – he has no spiritual awareness. "When one attains spiritual awareness, he fills any void," for "If he acquires spiritual awareness, what can he lack?" When one is able to have emuna that everything is for the good, he then attains the wisdom that everything really *is* good, and through this, he is able to come to know his Creator, which grants him eternal life – because knowing the Creator means being connected to infinitude.

Once every single person is able to thank the Creator for the bad just as he would for the good, then the whole world will be united, as one – and the Creator will be one. Rather than some tyrant who chooses when to be good and when to do bad – everyone will know that the Creator only does good and then He will be one – with only one name – a name of good. Then we will have true spiritual awareness – the knowledge that not only is everything good, but that there never was such a thing as 'bad' nor such a thing as 'lack' – there will be no more darkness nor exile.

5. The "Garden of Gratitude" Changed Their Lives

There was a woman in one of my classes who asked to speak with me before the lecture. She presented herself as a teacher in a secular school and told me that after reading a book I had written – "The Garden of Gratitude" – she began to teach her students to say "thank You." Every day, she would begin her classes by having every student write an entire page just giving thanks. She had brought all of their notebooks to show me.

I read them and was very impressed – just to see the pure innocence of children and all the different ways they came up with to give thanks; all of the beautiful and wonderful things they felt they had to be grateful for…it was very moving to read and brought tears to my eyes. She told me that the parents of these children began to notice their sons and daughters changing – suddenly saying "thank You". They not only became happy but disciplined as well. Their manners even improved – it was so strange! Their parents began to investigate what was behind this change and came to speak with the teacher, after which they understood what was happening. Once the school principle got wind of all of this, she declared that the entire school would learn the book "The Garden of Gratitude"!

If only every school and every university learned this book and the invaluable lessons within. If only every degree earned required such a text! If only every person in the entire world learned the importance of just saying "thank You"…

Every book I have been privileged to write contains within it a vital message. Every CD lesson I recorded is important. But the book whose message stands out above the rest is "The Garden of Gratitude". The most important CDs I recorded like "Stop Crying" and the pamphlets that I have had the privilege to write and disseminate, like "Kisses to the Creator" are all on one subject – expressing gratitude.

This is not a novel concept I suddenly discovered. Our sages say that in the future, any method of atonement for wrongdoing will no longer be effective except for the tool of gratitude – of saying "Thank You". They even say that prayer itself will no longer be effective – only giving thanks – for no one will need a thing as they will see that everything is good. The main mode of connection to the Creator will be merely thanking Him for everything He does! That's why everyone must learn "The Garden of Gratitude".

When a person says "thank You" he merits both his personal salvation and a life of emuna. Therefore, everyone should have a "Thank You" notebook and write down every day all that he or she has to be thankful for. And every day he should learn from "The Garden of Gratitude". This is especially important for someone who seeks to refine his character traits and make a positive change in his life. No matter what trait he's working on, gratitude will help him improve himself, especially in the area of strengthening emuna. **Emuna means saying "thank You"!**

The light of gratitude is the way to a life of inner meaning and emuna. It rectifies the reasonless whining of our forefathers and solves the problems of our current generation. Everyone must read our "Gems of Gratitude" pamphlet series and distribute them to others as well. Although I'm not unaccustomed to making promises, I do promise that whoever learns the gratitude book and pamphlets and listens to the gratitude CDs – doing his best to live by their lessons – will see face to face how he merits solutions to his problems and amazing salvations, as so many people testify in this book.

6. When the Worst Becomes the Best

There was a woman who was suffering from an abusive husband and a terrible marriage. She told me about all of her troubles at home – I can personally tell you she was suffering beyond description or imagination. I told her that she should say "thank You" every day for half an hour for all of her problems and she would be rescued. This woman was very honest and innocent and so every day she sincerely and joyfully thanked the Creator for all of her problems, accepting them with love. The issues between her and her husband worsened beyond repair so they divorced. She was a lonely and single mother with several children to care for.

A relative of hers involved in the whole story knew she had received advice from me and what I had advised her to do. He, too, began strengthening his gratitude and saying "thank You". But, when he saw how difficult her life was as a single mother with no help or support, he began to have many, hard-hitting questions as well as doubts about my judgment. "She listened to the advice of the rabbi and did what he told her to do, so why - instead of things working out - did they only get worse? Why must she be alone and stranded with her children?" Due to his agitation at the outcome of things, he resented me and the whole concept of giving thanks. Soon, he stopped his own daily "thank You" session almost as quickly as he had picked it up.

Despite the fact that everything seems to be going downhill, in reality, we don't understand what's good and what's not. This woman believed that her divorce was a miracle and that the Creator had freed her from the terrible torment that her marriage had caused her; as such, she continued to thank the Creator with sincerity. It took time, but thank God, despite the fact that she was a divorcee with children, she met a very special and wonderful man by way of a miracle. They are now married and continue to have a fulfilling and deep relationship. This is the young man's first marriage – he cherishes her and loves her children, taking care of them as if they were his own. The children themselves are thriving fantastically.

When her relative with the doubts and resentment saw all of this, he understood that while a man has many thoughts in his heart, the Creator directs the world and conducts it in the best way possible according to Divine logic. The relative realized that the single mother's thank Yous had earned big dividends in the form of amazing Divine blessings.

This relative realized he had been mistaken and came to me asking for forgiveness: "Respectfully and with utmost honesty, after the divorce I thought badly about you and completely discarded the whole gratitude deal. I knew that my relative was clinging to her daily gratitude sessions but everything in her life looked terrible. Yet now, I see the favors that the Creator did for her in freeing her from her first husband who abused her terribly. And recently, she landed a special young man who has never been married! On top of all of that, they are truly in love and have a wonderful, healthy marriage. He's a great father to the kids as well. Who could dream of something so good for her? So, I came to ask for your forgiveness. I am so sorry that I ever thought badly about you and your advice, rabbi. I now realize the tremendous power of saying 'Thank You' and what true emuna really is."

What was this man's mistake?

He wanted to see the Creator act according to what *he* thought was good for his relative, the single mother. He refused to either nullify himself to the will of the Creator or to accept that the Creator knows what 'good' actually is, that He alone knows when and how it will be revealed as such. Gratitude is the point at which you nullify your intellect to the Creator. You simply say "thank You" and "There is no bad in the world at all". If things get worse, say "thank You" again, because there is no such thing as 'worse' as there is no such thing as 'bad' – and for everything we say "thank You".

Sometimes saying "thank You" can fix things on the spot. But other times a person must lovingly accept his circumstances as his soul correction and say, "This is what the Creator wants and this is what I must endure to rectify myself!" Sometimes there are solutions that take time until they come into fruition. If you can say "thank You" in the meantime, you are guarding yourself from negative thought patterns and blatant denial. Gratitude grants the patience to endure whatever you must go through, the strength to be happy with your lot in life and protection from sadness and depression.

The Creator decides what hardships we must endure, but we decide whether or not we will suffer as a result. With emuna, we don't suffer at all!

7. The Painted Black Mercedes

This story was sent to me by one of my students:

In April I got married and I moved near Rabbi Arush to learn in his married men's seminary.

Before I became observant I had bought a brand new, red Mercedes sports car. My new wife asked to sell it and instead buy a car that's much less flashy. A buyer arrived and wanted to check out the car. He checked everything in the car – under the hood, behind the seats, the lights, the windshield wipers – everything. Finally, he said he had 'one more thing to check' – he took out a white piece of cloth, went around to the exhaust pipe, and asked me to give the car a little gas. I laughed at him and said, "This is a Mercedes, not a Subaru with a million miles on it. This engine will last a long time!" He insisted, so I obliged. After a few revs of the engine he said, "This is not good…switch with me and

I'll show you." Totally naïve of crooks and schemes, I went around to the exhaust; he jumped in the driver's seat and steeped on the gas, darting off in my expensive car! I chased after him yelling, "Thief! Thief! Stop him! Help me!"

This man had just stolen my incredibly valuable sports car! I ran after him for four, long streets after finally losing him and my breath. My wife fainted when she saw this and people began to gather around us. I called for the police and desperately tried to elicit their help. They didn't know what to do. I realized that there was no person to speak to about this – it was all from the Creator.

I didn't have insurance because car insurance on such a car was very expensive. I had just had the car checked out and outfitted with new tires and a new battery. What's more, I had just washed it and the gas tank was full.

Rabbi Arush once asked, "If a man is beaten with a stick, to whom should he complain? Should he confront the stick, or the one wielding the stick?" It is important for me to note that in my first few months of learning at the Rabbi's seminar, I had not only read, but practically memorized every single one of his books. That's why I was able to see my situation with clarity – I knew that everything that was happening to me was coming straight from the Creator – and so I simply danced and accepted it with utter joy. Everyone thought I had lost my mind. I explained to them that I believe that everything the Creator does is for my very best. I must thank Him and lovingly accept that He took my car, for this is His will. If it is also His will for me to have it back, He'll return it to me! If not – this too is for the very best. Of course, I did my basic efforts and filled out all the necessary forms with the police. Afterwards, I forgot the whole matter…

A few days passed. The police called me and told me that

they had found my car. I asked them if it was still intact. The officer answered, "There is an engine and a gear…just come and see it." I came with very low expectations, but what follows is nothing short of a miracle. Not only was my car returned to me, but the thief had painted it black, making it look very nice and new (which would have cost me a few thousand dollars). I have pictures of the car from before and after and it is clear that after the paint job, the car looked much more impressive and valuable, meaning I could sell it for much more than I had originally thought. How great is the Creator?! He took my car, improved it, and then returned it to me! It is so important to say "thank You". And with that, I must say 'thanks' to my teacher, the righteous Rabbi Shalom Arush, may Hashem bless him, who taught me how to thank the Creator, and of course to the merciful and compassionate Creator.

***

How important it is to thank Hashem and to hold on with emuna! We must put logic completely aside. In their limited perception, logic and intellect tell us, "This isn't good". But emuna says, "Everything is good". Say "thank You" for *everything*. Our first reaction in any situation must be, "Thank You! There is no 'bad' in the world. Hashem, this is what You want? Then it's all for the good – thank You!"

Our outlook on things must always begin with emuna. A person might seem to be righteous, but if he lacks emuna, he cannot turn a bleak situation into a bright one or exile into redemption. For that, you need emuna. Rebbe Nachman of Breslev says that the essence of exile is a lack of emuna. This 'lack of emuna' is one's failure to believe that everything the Almighty does is good and to thank Him for it. So, if you believe that everything is for the good, then say "thank You"! There is no other way. You can't say it? Then you don't believe that it is good, which means you don't believe in the Creator – because the Creator does only good!

8. The Hole in the Heart Disappears

Days after the birth of their baby boy, the parents found out that there was a serious problem with their baby's heart; the doctors told them that there appeared to be a hole in one of the ventricles, Heaven forbid. The doctors continued to perform tests and were convinced that open-heart surgery was the only viable solution, despite the great risks for a tiny, newborn baby. They informed the parents that there wasn't much time to hesitate, for it appeared that the hole was growing.

The parents, although stricken with grief, turned to emuna. They began going from one spiritual leader to another, asking for advice and blessings. They prayed fervently, begging for mercy for their son. But with every passing moment, the baby's condition was worsening; the doctors exerted tremendous pressure on the young couple to agree to the surgery before the situation got any worse.

I was one of the people the couple came to, seeking advice. I instructed them to go to the holy gravesite of Rebbe Shimon Bar Yochai in Meron in the Upper Galilee and each do six hours of thanking the Creator for their son's condition. They listened and did as I said, but after only two hours, they had no strength to continue and so they returned home.

Upon returning home, they received a call from the hospital that the hole had grown to a dangerous size and that surgery was a must. With heavy hearts, they returned to the hospital and again underwent intense pressure to consent to immediate surgery. The doctors said that the alternative was something they'd rather not think about...

Distressed, the wife sobbed uncontrollably. Her husband comforted her, saying, "Look, after all, we are students of Rabbi Shalom Arush, and he says that we need to be thankful for this trying situation. We have one hour before the surgery. Let's use this hour to say "Thank You" to the Creator for this difficulty."

"But how can we say 'thank You'?" the sobbing wife protested.

"It doesn't matter how," her husband answered her. "At this point, there is nothing we can do. We must make an effort and say 'thank You' any way we can and leave the rest up to the Creator." The couple sat in the waiting room with tears in their eyes and a murmur of gratitude on their lips; in their silent recitation, they literally doled up words of gratitude from the depth of their souls. For a whole hour they poured every last ounce of their emotional, spiritual and even physical energy into their prayers of gratitude that everything Hashem is doing is surely for the best – not *probably*, but *surely*!

Their baby was wheeled into the operating room where he was about to undergo his surgery. A short while later, the attending cardiologist came out from the operating room and asked to speak with the exhausted parents in his office. He sat them down; with joy diluted in tears he said to them, "I completely apologize for all of the needless trouble you have endured. Just before starting the surgery I decided to catheterize your son and, after doing so, we saw that there was no hole in his heart at all. Nothing. He is completely healthy. As soon as he recovers from his anesthetization you may take him home. On behalf of the administration and staff here at the hospital, I apologize for any pain or hardship."

What?!?

How could this be? The baby clearly had a hole in his heart!

Sure, the parents prayed and visited many spiritual leaders and teachers. They asked for blessings. But who would ever dream of a miraculous salvation like this?

When they came to thank me, I explained, "When a person prays and pleads for something with all of his heart, his prayers are not necessarily answered. Also, when he depends on charms or ploys, or other people's prayers and blessings, he nonetheless lacks emuna. Thus, his prayers lack the power to redeem him from his trying predicament.

They questioned me: "You're saying that a person who prays and believes in the blessings and prayers of his teachers and spiritual guides doesn't have emuna?"

"Of course he does!" I answered them, "True, such a person has emuna that there is a Creator of the Universe. And he has emuna that the only solution is to increase his prayers. He even has emuna that the Creator listens to his prayers; even stronger still, he believes that only the Creator can help him. But, such a person does not have the emuna that whatever the Creator does is for his very best. Therefore, he suffers when something 'bad' happens to him. He doesn't have emuna! **The essence of genuine emuna is to believe that everything that the Creator does is good.**"

What does a person sound like before he decides to be grateful? He says to the Creator: "Listen, Father in Heaven, I'm not satisfied with the deal You are handing me. I'm not satisfied with the way You're running my life. It's not good! It's bad! Therefore, I'm asking you, Master of the Universe, answer me…do what I want. Nullify Your will to my will!" That tone doesn't exactly invoke Divine compassion. No wonder such a prayer is not accepted!

When a person says "thank You" he is saying to the Creator: "First of all, I believe that whatever You do must be for my very best. And I nullify my will to Yours, Hashem. I am indeed happy with the way You run my life. I accept Your will with love and say to You, 'thank You' with all of my heart. I accept everything You do for me."

If a person suffers, it's due to a lack of emuna. If he believed that his circumstances were for his ultimate good, he would not suffer nor ever be disappointed. Good things don't disappoint people. Lottery winners don't say, "Oh no! I won the lottery!" If you are disappointed, it means that you think the Creator is acting unfairly with you or tormenting you for no reason. That's heresy! Therefore, every single person must learn to live a life of emuna and gratitude, thanking the Creator for every single thing. Gratitude is not only for the good, but also for what appears to be 'not good'. And, if you see that you are still far from this level of emuna, implore the Creator to give it to you; don't let up!

9. The CD Babies

One of our readers sent us the following story:

When we got married, people were congratulating us right and left and blessing us that we should soon have children. Our marriage was wonderful; we had everything – marital bliss, a great relationship and anything a young couple could dream of. Everything, except children…

People who never experienced the anguish of childlessness – not being able to become a parent when you want to so badly – can't understand what a difficult tribulation this is. Days of anticipation and hope turn into weeks; weeks turn into months and months turn into years.

Like turtles, we introverted into our shells. Without telling anyone, we tried all types of treatments – painful ones at that. Weekly, we went to pray at the Western Wall begging our Father in Heaven for salvation and a child.

Once, late at night at the Wall, we each went to our respective corners in the men's and women's side to pour our hearts out to the Creator. Having said my prayers, I turned to leave with a look of anguish on my face.

A Breslever Chassid sat at the exit from the Western Wall Plaza. He looked at my face and handed me a CD. I looked at the CD; it was titled, "Stop Crying". The Breslever didn't ask for a thing, neither charity nor payment for the disc. He didn't say a word.

I'm not the type of person that listens to CDs, but I couldn't be an ingrate. I thanked him, took the CD, gave him a few coins and walked away.

I met my wife and we left the Western Wall area. I completely forgot about the CD, having put it in the glove compartment without listening to it. My CD player was acting up anyway so I didn't even try to listen to it.

We were back to our routine. Once, while on a drive, we were searching for something to listen to. The radio was a bore and the news was even worse. We wanted something uplifting to listen to. I opened the glove compartment and saw the CD. I inserted it into the player, which up till now hadn't been working, and it began to play!

…and it changed our lives.

From the outset, we were hearing something new – pure, holy and a pleasure to listen to. The words of the soothing voice went straight to our hearts. They were easy to understand and amazingly logical. A CD that cost a few shekels enabled us to grasp concepts that eluded us even after years of reading and hours of listening to lectures.

We listened to that CD over and over. Every time we heard it, we seemed to glean additional messages and a deeper understanding. We were shocked at the simple yet miracle-invoking advice of avoiding all whining and complaining while choosing the path of gratitude instead. We had heard of these concepts, but now, they were delivered to us in a practical and readily adaptable way at our own eye level. Expressing our gratitude and singing songs of praise became an integral part of our daily lives. The CD played over and over, and we always joined in the singing with the rabbi.

During that time, we were about to undergo more fertility procedures, difficult and painful at that. But this time was different. We were full of emuna and gratitude to Hashem. Our lexicon changed. Instead of talking about pain and anxiety, we were singing all the way to the clinic, "Whatever was, was! The important thing is to start anew!"

My courageous wife, her body shattered from so many chemicals and treatments, started singing and thanking the Creator. Her trust in Him was awe-inspiring. She gave me strength. She was sure that things would be good now. And guess what – nine months later, she gave birth to a sweet baby girl…

We decided that all our children would learn gratitude.

Rabbi Shalom Arush explains in the CD that the special attribute of King David was the way he always sang songs of praise and gratitude. Today, we have three children. We don't know how to thank You, beloved Father in Heaven. **Thank You!**

PS: Some babies are called "test-tube babies". Our children are "CD babies."

10. Totally Grateful

A new student in our seminary told me that he finally came to understand the concept of total gratitude. Here's what happened:

His life was a mess; he owed money everywhere and his marriage was falling apart. Now, with a restraining order, he appeared to be on the verge of oblivion. Once, while driving his jalopy, he merited Divine compassion and it broke down right next to the holy gravesite of Dan the son of Jacob, in the forest near Bet Shemesh. He had been hurrying to an important meeting, so he was really frustrated and upset.

With no alternative, he entered our seminary that used to be adjacent to the gravesite and asked for help. Our young men helped him in a different way than what he was seeking and gave him emuna books and CDs. Hashem saved him! He returned to his wife and his entire life turned around for the better. To this day, he thanks Hashem that his car broke down back then, because that's when his salvation began.

There are thousands of examples of miraculous salvations sprouting from seemingly terrible circumstances. I tell those who come to me with their troubles, "**From an emuna standpoint, your troubles are your salvation**. But, without emuna, you see only bad. If you cling to emuna and to gratitude, everything will soon turn around for the very best. Be thankful to Hashem and you'll be happy – you'll see miracles. Your current difficulty is only temporary, for it's a test of your emuna. You might not see how it's all for the best, so believe that it's all for the best."

In retrospect, if you asked our abovementioned student if he'd be willing to have his car break down again, he'd say, "For sure! Heaven on earth! Master of the World, for all I care, send the car to the junk pile; just bring me close to You!"

We learn here that during trying times, we must hold on with emuna. Don't think that Hashem is giving you a rough time for the sake of tormenting you. Thank Him even if you don't understand what's going on and how everything is for the best. Don't forget that whatever the Creator is doing in your life is the product of His love for you.

11. When Things Go Wrong

My same student with the jalopy told me another story with an important moral to it.

His father was supposed to be his Passover guest, but the night before the Seder, his father suffered a stroke and was rushed to the hospital. My student's family was in turmoil, not knowing what to do about Seder night. How could he leave his dad alone in the hospital? But if he did, who would make Seder night for his wife and children? They finally decided that the whole family would spend Seder night at the hospital – whatever would be, would be…

A volunteer charitable society organized Seder night for the hospitalized patients and their families. They informed my student that he wouldn't have to bring anything, for they'd be serving a complete meal with meat, wine, matza and everything else. That was a bit of bright news.

The family thought that they'd arrive at the big hospital auditorium to find a set table reserved for them. Their expectations were one thing, but the reality they found was something entirely different. The Seder was in a tiny room that was already jammed with patients in wheelchairs and their families. Everybody was pushing, children and old people were yelling and there was pandemonium. People pounced on the food as if there were no tomorrow. The family had nowhere for their sick father to sit, much less for themselves. They consoled themselves that the food was gone, at least they'd have matza and wine for the four cups, but the supply of wine and matza turned out to be finished as well.

Needless to say, the evil inclination was about to have a field day, with negative thoughts such as, "Now what are you going to do? It's the most important evening of the year, and you're left with nothing – no Seder, chaos, a sick father…"

My student had listened many times to my CD, "Stop Crying". He had also heard my lecture about spiritually preparing oneself for Seder night. I had taught my students that the Seder begins with emuna, for many times, things happen that weren't planned, like guests coming late, food getting burned or the children losing patience and disrupting everything. At that point, one must remember that this is what Hashem wants. The core of emuna is accepting Hashem's will, believing that whatever's happening is for the very best and not to lose composure; on the contrary, one must be happy! Instead, one must say to himself, "Sure, I wanted to make a Passover Seder according to the letter of the law. But obviously, Hashem has His good reasons for wanting things differently. Please Hashem, help me accept Your will with unblemished joy and self-composure."

My student decided to implement what he learned. Instead of whining and complaining, he began to thank Hashem that his Seder was ruined. He thanked Hashem over and over. He was filled with happiness and he decided that he'd perform his Seder obligation this year by helping the patients and their families make their Seder. Even though he saw that no food, wine or matza was left, he began clearing tables and making room for others to sit, for many of the patients simply made brief Seders and returned to their rooms.

His thank Yous and his cheery attitude had a profound effect on his family. His wife and children also began cleaning and setting tables, helping the sick and preparing as if they had a whole stock of food waiting to be served. Suddenly, as if out of the blue, volunteers from another organization appeared with baskets of hot food, wine and matza!

"Our hearts filled with such indescribable joy, like you can't imagine," my student told me, "as if Hashem's Divine illumination filled the room. We had the Seder of our lives! The patients and their families were overjoyed." They merited such a Seder because they withstood a difficult test of emuna.

What's more, my student's father – now hospitalized – finally had the chance to read "The Garden of Peace." When he recuperated – miraculously, even in a manner that the doctors couldn't grasp – he came home earlier than expected. My student's mother said, "I don't know what they did to your father in the hospital, but he came home a new, much more likeable man." After seeing how his marriage had improved so dramatically, the father said, "That's probably why I was hospitalized in the first place – to learn "The Garden of Peace"!

12. The Aquatic Seder

I learned that the main preparation for Seder night is emuna, not only from my rabbis and teachers, but from personal experience.

Years ago, I told my wife: "This year, we'll pray early so that we can conduct a complete and leisurely Seder and finish by midnight. Inform our guests that we'll be praying early and starting early." That didn't help much, because one of the couples arrived an hour and a half later. Patiently, we waited for them. I told my family, "This is what Hashem wants." In the end, I had to rush through the Seder, not as I had planned, but as Hashem had planned...

Another year, we invited a non-observant family to our home for Seder night. We arranged a separate guest apartment for them so they could have their privacy. When the evening of the Seder arrived, they lost their key. They felt like they couldn't come to the Seder table because they hadn't changed into their holiday clothes and they lost their self-composure. Meanwhile, we tried to find them an alternate key and it was taking a long time. I told my family, "This is what Hashem wants – He wants us to start late."

Another one of my students who heard my lecture that the Passover Seder begins with emuna came home from the Passover evening prayers, enthusiastic about beginning the Seder. While he was in the synagogue, his exhausted wife decided to lie down and rest until he came home. In the meanwhile, one of the faucets in the house was left running and their whole apartment was flooded with water. The wife woke up suddenly and found herself ankle-deep in water. She was terrified at how her husband might react. She was broken-hearted, having worked so hard to prepare for Seder night, and now this. But, her husband had Divine assistance; he understood that this was a test of his emuna, so he didn't lose his temper. He figured that Hashem wants him to begin his Seder with a mop in hand.

The wife was amazed when she saw her husband calmly take the mop in hand, and as if he were merrily playing hockey, he was mopping the water out the front door. Meanwhile, he was singing and dancing the whole time. Later, he found out that one of his small children had opened the faucet to the washing machine in the laundry room while his wife was sleeping. He closed the faucet and continued mopping water for another two hours. Then, he and his wife sat down to Seder. He told me that they never had such a meaningful Seder their entire lives.

One doesn't merit spiritual gain without being tested first; this is a fact of life. By withstanding a difficult beginning in any situation, whether it is unexpected mishaps, delays or whatever, a person ultimately merits the light of redemption. This is something we must remember all year long, not just at Passover. Activating our emuna insures success.

Emuna must come first, before our own plans and desires. Emuna means gladly and lovingly accepting Hashem's plans and desires. Anyone who appraises a difficult situation with eyes of emuna will smoothly and successfully overcome the difficulty.

We never know how Shabbat, the Passover Seder, the wedding or anything else will begin. Sure, we do our best that everything goes according to plan. But, when it doesn't, we automatically must switch off logic – which tells us that things aren't good – and activate emuna, which tells us that everything is for the best, for this is what Hashem wants. With an emuna attitude, a person sees tangible salvation.

Whenever you encounter a challenging situation, tell yourself, "Hashem is running my life and it's all for the best. I'll be happy and I'll even thank Him for what seems to be difficult, for whatever He does, it's great, for it is giving me the light of emuna and redemption."

13. Children by Virtue of Gratitude

A couple who had been trying to have children for nine or ten years came to me after they had seen many doctors and spiritual guides to no avail. I told them that I'd bless them but they asked for advice: "What can we take upon ourselves in order to merit children?" I told them that they wouldn't succeed in implementing my advice. The wife declared, "We'll do whatever the Rabbi tells us to!" I told them to thank Hashem for thirty minutes a day that they have not yet been blessed with children.

The husband protested: "How in the world can we thank Hashem for the most painful thing in our lives?"

"I told you that you wouldn't succeed in implementing my advice," I said.

The woman then said to her husband, "What do we have to lose? We've tried everything else with no success. Let's try this." I gave them copies of "The Garden of Gratitude" and my CD "Stop Crying." They took my advice, and they were blessed with children.

Without a doubt – a person says "thank You" and his troubles are over. I prayed that Hashem would enable me to share this principle with the entire world; people don't readily accept this advice because it sounds so weird.

Let's understand this on a deeper level: until this moment, everything that has occurred in your life has been the outcome of Hashem's will. And, if it's Hashem's will, it's the best thing in the world for you. We're not talking about levels of spirituality for the select few – this is simple emuna, for everyone. As such, the first step in the direction of salvation is to accept whatever's happening in your life with emuna.

This is the basis of the advice that I gave to the childless couple. Hashem put us on earth to learn emuna and He knows how to prod each of us into seeking emuna. So, as soon as we realize that whatever He is doing is for our ultimate good, we should sincerely thank Him. Once we strengthen our emuna and our feelings of gratitude, Hashem discards the prod and we soon see salvation.

14. Anyone Can

On Chanuka, I was invited to hang mezuzot in the home of one of my students. A young man came up to me and said, "Rabbi, do you remember me? I came to you several months ago and told you that the doctors said that my wife and I can't have children. You told us to say 'thank You" for a half hour every day. We read 'The Garden of Gratitude' and listened to the CDs about gratitude. For three months, we thanked Hashem for not blessing us with children just as you told us to. We thanked Him in a dozen different ways. We became truly happy and we never once asked for children, yet now, my wife is expecting!"

Where did I get the power to promise people that gratitude will bring them miraculous salvations? I base this on Rebbe Natan's promise that if people thank Hashem for everything, all their troubles will be nullified; not "almost" all their troubles, but **all** their troubles. In Rebbe Natan's own words, "for sure…all their troubles and all their exiles will be nullified," meaning that we could have brought the Geula – the full redemption of our people - long ago.

Anyone can make this same promise. Anyone can give a person a "Gem" gratitude booklet, a CD about gratitude or a copy of "The Garden of Gratitude." Once they do, they can say, "I promise you! Learn this book, read this pamphlet and listen to these CDs and thank Hashem for half an hour a day and you'll have children, a good income or whatever else you want. Just say thank You!" You can say emphatically, "I promise!"

Trust in Rebbe Natan and you'll see miracles. Tell everyone, "Learn this book - this is the light of Moshiach!" An indication that Messianic times have arrived is when everyone begins to say, "Thank You."

Rebbe Nachman explains that the Israelites in Egypt didn't listen to Moses because of their "impatience and difficult toil". He explains that impatience is a lack of emuna. They didn't believe that their redemption could come easily. They said to themselves, "How can the Geula possibly come from saying thank You? If Moses had asked us to fast for sixty days straight, to make a hole in the ice and immerse ourselves or to walk on a path of knife blades, we'd believe that our redemption cold come. But how can thank You bring it?!?" Even today, people don't believe in the true tzaddik Rebbe Nachman of Breslev or in his protégé Rebbe Natan who say that the Geula can come easily if we only spread the emuna that everything is for the best.

15. I Was Accepted to a Prestigious Seminary

Shalom!

I wanted to tell you what happened to me last year – it was a big miracle that defies the course of nature. I am a student in a girls' school and come from a very good family, thank G-d. About to graduate, I applied for acceptance to a prestigious teachers' seminary, where out of thousands of applicants, only a few dozen girls are accepted.

Every day, I'd ask my parents, "Did any letter arrive from the seminary?"

One day, I asked my father the same question that I'd ask daily and he avoided me. I felt in my heart that he was hiding something from me, which probably was a letter that I hadn't been accepted. He probably didn't want to sadden me, and maybe he thought that in the meanwhile, he'd try to pull strings to get me accepted.

I understood that I too had to pull strings, not by the dean of the seminary but by the Dean of all deans. For several hours, I began to thank Hashem: "Hashem, thank You that I wasn't accepted. That's the best thing in the world for me. Master of the World, I understand that You want me to depend on You only, and not on connections or pulling strings with seemingly influential people." I told my father that I know I was turned down and that's the best thing in the world for me. My father agreed. I told him that I depend on Hashem only, for He will always do what's best for me.

Less than a day passed and we received a phone call from the seminary inviting me for an interview, as the final step before being accepted to the seminary…

That's impossible! What about the rejection letter? No one could explain what happened. I can – my thank Yous to Hashem opened up all the locked doors. Nothing can stand in the way of gratitude.

Thank You, Hashem, for the privilege of thanking You.

16. Saying Thank You for Everything

I was in an elevator in Bnei Brak, when another person there turned to me and said, "Excuse me – I want to ask for your forgiveness."

I always forgive immediately when anyone asks. Without even knowing what people say about me, I forgive them and wish them the best. It turned out that this person spoke slander about me. Fine! If that makes him happy, I have no problem with that.

Our sages teach that if one person speaks slander about another person, the speaker's merit gets transferred to the victim while the victim's transgressions get transferred to the speaker. So, if people speak badly about us, it's as if they gave us a check for a million dollars, at least! Our sages even said that the great wise men used to send gifts to those who slandered them.

For some reason, I don't know why, this time I didn't say anything to the person in the elevator. The man started talking and I listened. "The reason I want you to forgive me is because I always used to say that it's easy for Rabbi Shalom Arush to say 'thank You' because he's rich, famous and he has no troubles in life…he lacks nothing in life so it's easy for him to preach to others about gratitude. But now, I heard that you lost your baby granddaughter Feigie Chana bat Yael in a car accident and that her parents – your son and daughter in-law – were almost killed too. I'm so embarrassed. Please forgive me."

At Feigie Chana's funeral, I thanked Hashem for the gift of our lovely baby granddaughter for the duration that we had her in our midst.

Why am I writing this? No one can know the difficulties, tribulation and challenges that other people suffer. But a person in this world must live a life of emuna, knowing that emuna is the greatest gift Hashem can bestow upon us. Emuna is the sweet life. There is no bad in the world! Hashem is totally good and everything He does is good.

Intrinsically, a person's disadvantage is really an advantage, for it is conducive to humility. One's disadvantages thrust him or her closer to Hashem. Yet, an advantage is liable to be a disadvantage, for strength, wealth, beauty, intelligence and power frequently inflate a person with arrogance, thus distancing him or her from the Creator.

One must not only thank Hashem for life's difficulties, but especially thank Him when those problems and difficulties are resolved.

Once, a righteous wise man had a dream. He ascended to the upper spiritual realm and he saw a great hall with much commotion. There seemed to be thousands of angels who looked like they were sorting mail. "What's going on here?" he asked one of the angels.

The angel answered, "This is the Hall of Prayers, where all the requests for salvation come. Here, they get sorted and passed on."

The man entered a second hall, where there too was a great commotion with myriads of angels at work. After inquiring what was happening, an angel told him, "This is the Hall of Prayers that were answered, and we're preparing the respective salvations to be delivered to those who prayed for them."

The righteous man visited a third hall in his dream. Here, there was no commotion, only a few angels quietly working as if they had all the time in the world. After asking about what was happening in this hall, one of the yawning angels told him, "This is the Hall of Gratitude, where we sort the expressions of gratitude from those people who received salvations. We should have been the busiest department in Heaven, but to our dismay, you see what's going on – we're pretty bored with not much to do. Our colleagues who handle the prayers and the screams for salvation are much busier than we are. People down on earth forget to say thank You once the pressure goes away. They forget the most basic principle of ethics – acknowledging a favor and saying thank You."

Gratitude is the ultimate purpose of all of creation, in both the material and the spiritual realms. Man was created for the purpose of recognizing his Creator and thanking Him.

The entire purpose of houses of worship is for people to get together and publicly thank the Creator. In fact, the word in Hebrew for "Jew" – *Yehudi* – comes from the word "to thank" – *lehodot*. That's why we should thank Hashem constantly, taking nothing for granted.

Our sages tell us, in keeping with the above principle, that the reason man received his powers of speech was to enable him to sing songs of praises and gratitude to the Creator. As such, when we do, we are fulfilling the very purpose of creation.

17. By Virtue of My Debts

A previously secular person came to me and told me that by virtue of his debts he started to pray. He fell in love with prayer and soon began observing all the Torah's commandments. This shows, as we previously stated, that one's disadvantages are truly advantages.

One person spends years searching for his or her soul mate. Someone else has a health challenge. A third person has lost his job. Each person has his or her own challenges, all of which are designed to bring us to our own personal perfection. That's why we each must express our gratitude for our own individual difficulties in life.

A person who lives with emuna that everything is the product of the Almighty's precision Divine providence over each individual and all for the best, he or she has no doubts about the Creator. They're like relaxed passengers in an airliner who trust the pilot – they're not worried about flying the plane.

On the other hand, a person who lacks emuna is like a nervous passenger who is worried whether the pilot is flying in the right direction or whether he is qualified to fly an airliner at all. Every few minutes, he's buzzing the stewardess and complaining about anything and everything. He lives a life of needless worry and anxiety, because he doesn't believe in the pilot. Even worse, as in the case of many people's agnosticism, they don't believe that anyone's in the cockpit at all, not realizing that Hashem is the Captain Who is taking us all exactly where we need to go.

One of my students was having tremendous grief from neighbors; that's how he found his way to Jerusalem and to our yeshiva. He had no intention of learning in a yeshiva, but his troubles chased him here. He discovered a new world and he became a new person. Profusely, he thanked Hashem for the troubles that brought him here. Yet, from time to time, he'd slip back into bitterness about his old neighbors who made him miserable.

I said to him, "Without those neighbors, would you be here today? These aren't troubles, they're salvations! By virtue of them, you're here in the Yeshiva today – you've begun to live." Rebbe Nachman says that when a person is persecuted by others, it's really a favor from Hashem to bring that person closer to Him. Getting closer to Hashem is the ultimate success.

18. Winner of the Lottery

Here's another example to reinforce the above principle:

A young student of mine was supposed to travel with his family from Tiberias to Jerusalem, a hot and exhausting two-hour drive by car. There wasn't enough room in the car for the whole family so some of the children would have to take the bus, an even longer and more tiring trip. The parents put the children's names in a hat and the lucky two siblings would get to ride in the car. The other five would have to take the bus. My student, who had recently joined our high-school yeshiva but had already heard some of my lectures on gratitude, prayed and thanked Hashem in his heart and won the privilege of remaining in the car.

This young student realized the power of emuna and prayer in bringing a person closer to Hashem. This seemingly trivial lottery win strengthened his emuna in seeing how his prayer was answered. Seeing Hashem's Divine Providence brought him to thank Hashem profusely and to realize that every small detail in life is a reason for prayer and gratitude.

Each person can see the above principle in endless seemingly mundane events that occur in his or her life. We should search for Hashem's guiding hand in everything and never stop thanking Him, taking nothing for granted.

In the above example, we see that Hashem gave the young lad a reason to pray – he wanted something badly, to travel in the car and to avoid the bus ride. By translating this desire into prayer, he added another building block to the wall of emuna that fortifies his soul. Every person should translate all his desires, problems and challenges into prayer, for this strengthens his emuna and his connection to Hashem. All the stimuli in a person's life and in his environment are calling him to get close to Hashem.

19. Hashem Gives Emuna

A person came to me with a lot of worries and anxiety. I told him that these negative emotions stem from a lack of emuna. He said, "Emuna? I have plenty of emuna."

I responded, "Sure, you believe in Hashem but you don't believe in His precision Divine Providence, otherwise you'd realize that you're in good hands and you'd gladly accept whatever happens in your life. You'd believe that everything's for the very best. When a person feels like that, he has no worries or anxiety. Negative emotions stem from the feeling that things are bad and that the future is bleak. They also come from phobia that all types of things can hurt you. This is the result of a person's feeling that he's not in Hashem's hands and of doubting that all Hashem does is for the very best.

"So what do I do?" the person asked.

"Get copies of "The Garden of Emuna", "The Garden of Gratitude" and "In Forest Fields" – read the Gems series pamphlets and listen to emuna CDs. Once you learn emuna, you can start living emuna. Ask Hashem to give you emuna – you can't obtain emuna from the department store or the pharmacy, only from Hashem. Ask Hashem to help you believe that there's no bad in the world and that everything is for the best."

"Do you mean that I can ask Hashem for emuna?"

"Do you have a better address?" I answered. "Everything comes from Hashem, particularly emuna. If you lack emuna, ask for it. As soon as you feel the slightest negative emotion, turn to Hashem right away and ask for emuna. Wait and see the profound effect it has on you."

Even King David acknowledged that his emuna came from Hashem, and he in turn thanked Him accordingly. Any other person must know that if he or she has merited any level of emuna, this comes from Hashem and they too are obligated to express their gratitude. Emuna is the greatest gift Hashem can bestow on a person. Gratitude therefore is not enough; we must sing songs of praise to Hashem for giving us emuna.

The mitzvah of emuna is the first of the Ten Commandments: "I am the Lord your G-d that took you out of Egypt"; not "Who created the world" but Who "took you out of Egypt", to show that emuna is revealed in the miracles and wonders that Hashem did for us in Egypt.

Whenever a person feels weak in emuna, he should call out to Hashem and beg for emuna. As we wrote in "The Garden of Emuna", all of the suffering that a person feels stems from insufficient emuna. Sadness and depression come from weak or a total lack of emuna. Anger, worries, jealousy are all manifestations of emuna deficiency. Anxiety is borderline heresy, when a person fears that Hashem is nowhere to be found. Emuna says that Hashem is right here with us.

What can a person do to fortify emuna that's weak?

First, he must thank Hashem for putting him in the situation where he needs Him. Recognizing that we need Hashem is for our ultimate good; therefore, whatever deficiency in our lives that brought us to this awareness is intrinsically for the very best.

Every creation has a spark of emuna, even if it's a tiny one. With constant prayer and gratitude where we maintain contact with Hashem constantly, we fan this spark into a big flame of emuna that warms the soul and illuminates our lives.

When we take a closer look at Likutei Tefillot, the compendium of prayers that Rebbe Natan of Breslev wrote, we're amazed. He never looked at what he wasn't supposed to, he was the son of righteous parents and he was a genius in Torah who never lifted his eyes from a holy book. He earned the highest rabbinical ordinations at a tender age. He was the prime disciple of Rebbe Nachman who wrote and disseminated Rebbe Nachman's teachings. Despite all of this, he never stopped begging Hashem for emuna. From here, we should all learn that until we haven't reached levels of absolute inner peace, patience and happiness, we haven't yet attained full emuna.

Know full well – if you believe, it's because Hashem enables you to believe. Don't blame yourself for any lack of emuna. Simply, ask Hashem over and over to give you emuna. The more you realize that Hashem is the only address and that everything comes from Him, the more you'll ask.

Hashem enabled me to understand that emuna – like everything else – comes from Him. Therefore, if a person has emuna, he certainly shouldn't brag about, for it's a gift from Above. Emuna is everything – happiness, fulfillment and peace of mind. With emuna, you have a good marriage and wonderful personal relationships, for emuna is the basis of everything good.

A passerby in a car once saw me in personal prayer. He stopped the car, got out and walked over to me. He told me that he's the head of a yeshiva. "Rabbi Arush, without your emuna CDs, I wouldn't have had a life. Ever since I listen to them, I have much more positive influence on my students."

20. A Six-Year Wait

Before we completed the final draft of this book, a man came to me and told me that he and his wife had been childless for six years after their wedding; he came to me for a blessing and for advice. I told him back then not to ask Hashem for a thing, simply to say thank You. Now, he came to inform me that he and his wife had been blessed with a baby girl. I asked him to write his story down and here it is:

My wife and I were in our seventh year of marriage and still childless. Not a day passed without us praying for children; many of our friends and relatives prayed for us too. We tried everything – Psalms, spiritual ploys – you name it. We also invested much effort in doctors and treatments of all types.

I was well aware of Rabbi Arush's teachings and often attended his lectures, but it was hard for me to express gratitude for something so painful. I couldn't internalize his advice on gratitude. I said to myself, all our patriarchs and matriarchs saw salvation through prayer. Moses too, for this has tied the Jewish People to Hashem since the beginning of our history. So why should I stop praying for what I need and simply thank Hashem for my deficiency?

I travelled to Uman on Rosh Hashana of 5775 and prayed on Rebbe Nachman's holy gravesite for the blessing of children. I came back to Israel and during Succoth, while sitting in my Succa, I read a copy of the weekly "Chut Shel Chessed" Torah portion sheet that Rabbi Arush's yeshiva publishes. In the weekly sheet, the Rabbi answered my questions as if he were personally talking to me.

But, I hadn't started to thank Hashem properly.

Later, during Chanuka, I went to Rabbi Arush's home to seek his advice and blessing. He said, "From this moment on, you and your wife stop praying for children – say 'thank You' to Hashem and nothing more. What? Stop praying? The Rabbi said once more, "No prayer – just gratitude. I promise you that within a year, you'll be blessed with a child." I couldn't believe it – the Rabbi was giving me a promise! He reiterated, "Yes, I promise; but, you may not ask for a thing – only say thank You to Hashem for not having children."

I felt a sense of relief when I left Rabbi Arush's home. Asking for something for so long seemed to weigh heavily on us. The move over to the gratitude mode was relieving. I started to express my thanks to Hashem. When I came home and told my wife what the Rabbi said, she started thanking too.

In time, we both saw the hidden blessing of not having children. We felt that Hashem was bringing us closer to Him and this filled us with joy, to the extent that our thanks were more and more sincere.

Several weeks passed. My wife came home from the doctor's office with a giant smile on her face and tears of joy in her eyes: "Thank G-d, we're expecting a child!"

Now, we couldn't stop saying thank You. We decide to name the baby, "Odeya", which is Hebrew for "I shall thank Hashem".

Thank You Hashem, thank you Rebbe Nachman and thanks to your disciples from bring the light of gratitude to the world. Rabbi Arush, we love you and pray for your good health and continued strength in spreading this Divine light in the world.

Most sincerely, A.A."

Since A.A. received a lot of spiritual reinforcement from what I wrote in the Parsha newsletter of Succoth 5775, here it is in a nutshell:

"The epitome of good is closeness with the Creator. Likewise, the opposite – being far away from Him – is the epitome of anything negative in this world. If a person has wonderful talents and attributes, but he's arrogant about them, then they are detrimental for they distance him from Hashem. Yet, if a person's troubles and deficiencies stimulate him to seek Hashem, they are intrinsically good for they serve the best ultimate purpose, helping a person to strengthen their emuna and connect with Hashem. That's why a person must thank Hashem for his deficiencies, for everything is for his very best benefit.

How then can one pray for salvation if deficiencies are all for the best? We know that prayer creates vessels for abundance.

The answer is that everything that happened in your life up until now has all been for the best. If you had been successful in whatever you were seeking, maybe you'd have become terribly arrogant. Hashem didn't let that happen. You must develop the cognizance that you are powerless without Hashem – this is a spiritually healthy feeling that we all must have.

Therefore, our job is twofold. We must thank Hashem for the past and express our desires and yearning for the future. Rebbe Nachman explains that prayer has two sides to it – praising Hashem and asking for our needs. It's the prime tool a person has in life and it's based on gratitude for the past and expressing our yearning and desire in requesting for the future.

In my experience, I've seen that although people understand that they should thank Hashem for what causes them pain, they are unable to joyously and sincerely do it. The light of emuna has not yet illuminated their hearts.

Hashem enabled me to understand that in times when a person finds difficulty in expressing gratitude, he should express his desire and yearning. "Heavenly Father, I want to believe that everything is for the best, that there's no power on earth but You and that everything goes according to Your will. Please instill in my heart the knowledge that You are a loving Father and that You love me, so I'll always be sure that everything You do is for my ultimate welfare with no exceptions. That way, I can be happy always, no matter what. This is the emuna I ask for; please help me attain it."

With my own eyes, I've seen how prayers of yearning and desire like the one above can pull a person out of the deepest emotional abyss and bring him/her to a state of genuine joy. The desire leads to emuna and emuna leads to lasting joy, all in a beautiful upward cycle.

Another critical point to learn and remember is to know when to simply say thank You and when to pray and make requests. In the case of a difficult, long tribulation – like a person who has been searching in vain for a soul-mate for years or a couple that has been waiting for children for a long time – it's better to simply say thank You and not to make any prayer requests. Why? A person who longs for a particular salvation won't likely be able to pray without slipping into a tone of complaining, sadness or self-pity.

But for other things, especially spiritual needs such as emuna and personal holiness, one should devote thirty minutes a day to pray for this one thing, to seek Hashem's help, as we elaborate in our books "In Forest Fields" and "The Garden of Purity."

21. Gratitude Alters Reality

An individual from an observant background began listening to my CD lessons and reading my books. He started to devote a daily hour to personal prayer and his life became a heaven on earth. He told me that he said to his wife, "On the surface, our lives haven't changed. We still have the same problems and the same debts. But, there's one major difference: before we learned Rabbi Arush's teachings, every tiny crisis would knock us down. But now, with emuna, we are happy and grateful no matter what."

Frequently, a person loses heart from saying "Thank You" because he doesn't see results. But one must understand that saying "Thank You" in itself is a salvation. Gratitude is truth, and the closer a person hones in on the truth, the more he sees miraculous salvations.

Gratitude is the manifestation of emuna and joyful acceptance of Divine will. It consequently invokes miracles. Yet, gratitude isn't instant coffee – no one promises immediate results. Furthermore, the salvation that's right for the person i not necessarily what the person wants. The main salvation is in the gratitude itself, for the grateful person is acting in a way that Hashem wants – the way of emuna. As a result, the individual attains true happiness.

22. The Gift that Hashem Gave Me

I learned the lesson that thanking Hashem is the gate of salvation on my own flesh – that's why I don't stop thanking Him. About thirty years ago, I received a "gift" from Above of heavy debts. I owed tens of thousands of dollars and there was no rational way that I could ever repay my debts, even if I worked around the clock for double the money that I was earning. I composed myself and thought that there are no tribulations without prior transgressions, so I took stock in myself: what did I do wrong to trigger all those debts? I began a serious process of teshuva.

I received encouragement from a friend who was in a similar predicament. Like me, he was learning in a rabbinical seminary. His rabbi told him that according to religious law, he must leave the seminary and get a job to repay the debts. My friend had simple and innocent faith. He decided to go to work for Hashem! He said to Hashem in one of his personal prayer sessions, "Hashem, why should I work in a store or a factory, forfeiting so much time of prayer and Torah learning, when I can work for You?" He decided to spend eight hours a day thanking Hashem, praising His Name and praying for the whole world. Miraculously, he wiped his slate of debts clean in virtually no time!

In all fairness, my friend's debts were a fraction of what mine were, but his mode of action and his outlook were a source of inspiration and encouragement for me. I decided to go to work for Hashem too! When people told me that I should be travelling around ringing doorbells and asking for charity, I didn't argue. I started ringing Hashem's doorbell and asking Him for charity. It was clear to me that only Hashem could help me, especially when it came to the amount of money I owed.

I began to engage in daily personal prayer devoted exclusively to my debts. The first thing I did was to thank Hashem every single day for the debts. It was apparent that they were a gift, for they were bringing me closer to Hashem. Within the tribulations of owing money were two hidden blessings:

First, I began to pray much longer with deeper fervor, something I don't think I could have attained without the severe challenge of the debts. Hashem was personally awakening me and bringing me closer to Him. What a gift!

Second, while I was praying and thanking Hashem for the debts, He was showing me other aspects in my personality and behavior that needed rectification, so that my teshuva became much more comprehensive. This gave me the greatest joy, for it was another gift that was hidden within the debts.

I was thanking Hashem for so many hours every day that my spiritual life was really improving. Never did I pray and do teshuva so much. I used to sing for hours in the field, "What a joy it is to have such a great problem and to turn to Hashem. Thank You for the debts! What a pleasure it is to do teshuva!"

Nothing makes a person happier than getting close to Hashem. What else gives lasting joy in this world? Many people are fabulously rich but they're bitter and miserable, with worries and anxieties of all sorts. Is there any true joy in this world other than emuna? For sure, not! So, I strengthened my emuna, spoke to Hashem and thanked Him for hours on end, every day.

Since I viewed my predicament through eyes of emuna, I was happy about the debts. People were amazed at me and that I had perhaps lost my senses or my connection to reality, Heaven forbid…

I used to answer them by paraphrasing one Rebbe Nachman's characters in the Tale of the Seven Beggars, "I live the good life; what is my good life? I owe money! I'm deep in debt! Thanks to Hashem for all the gifts He gives me."

The debts truly did not cause me to lose my self-composure in the slightest. I believe wholeheartedly that there was no mistake in Divine Providence – these debts were all for my ultimate benefit. I called them "kisses from Hashem". I would also encourage my wife not to worry, for salvation was surely on the way. Meanwhile, we were building spiritual vessels to hold greater emuna and trust in Hashem, assets that would stay with us for our entire lives.

After thanking Hashem, I'd plead with Him to reveal to me why I had fallen into debt. What was it that I needed to rectify? A person's troubles in life are simply the stern judgments that he has incurred, which now torment him in any number of ways. Teshuva wipes away the stern judgments. Hashem had pity on me and showed me what I needed to correct. Meanwhile – inexplicably – I was seeing fantastic miracles and salvations. Hashem helped me rid myself of debt within one calendar year!

All a person's troubles are simply wake-up calls from Above calling him or her to correct something. My debts were no exception. Those who attribute their difficulties in life to natural causes are missing the message entirely. What's more, ignoring the spiritual messages invokes even more stern judgments from Above, to the extent where a person's predicament gets even worse.

Uncorrected misdeeds lead to stern judgments that manifest themselves in all types of difficulties in life. That's why the Gemara says that that there are no tribulations without prior transgression. But, as soon as a person begins the process of sincere teshuva, the stern judgments disappear. When they disappear, so does sorrow! The consequence is far-reaching: even if a person's economic or health situation is far from favorable, if he or she is engaged in self-assessment and teshuva, they won't feel any sorrow. Emuna will illuminate their lives and once it does, the individual will feel joyous.

When it comes to debts, there's another important point to remember: don't cause more anguish to those whom you owe money to. Ask Hashem to help you repay the debts fast so that others won't have ill feelings toward you. With steadfast, earnest prayer and teshuva, Hashem will help you repay the debts easily and within a short period of time.

If I had fallen into the blame trap – blaming myself or others - I'd have fallen into a pit of despair, self-pity and self-persecution. I'd have wanted people to have pity on me and I'd have shirked all responsibility. What's more, I'd have never repaid the debts. What's more, I'd have never written my emuna series of books, including "The Garden of Emuna", "The Garden of Riches", "In Forest Fields", "The Garden of Peace", "The Garden of Wisdom" and others, which now appear in millions of copies around the world in over a dozen languages. I'd have never started my own yeshiva or be able to devote so much to emuna outreach.

My debts triggered my massive efforts to strengthen emuna and my connection with Hashem, especially to attain the level of faith where I could believe that everything is for the best and to truly thank Hashem for the most seemingly terrible situations. Rather than breaking down, by virtue of my debts, I strengthened myself in emuna and in gratitude, seeing with my own eyes how Hashem performs magnificent miracles.

We can now understand the purpose of every person's difficulties in life; they're all designed to bring the person closer to Hashem. Life's difficulties are catalysts for teshuva and strengthening emuna. They're intrinsically good for they bring us closer to Hashem, and that's our ultimate purpose on earth! Hashem wants only the best for each of us, so that we'll enhance our emuna and get to know Him better. So, when we look at life's ultimate purpose, there are no tribulations, suffering or difficulties. We can thank Hashem with all our hearts.

Without my challenges in life, I'd have wasted my time on this earth. As such, we all must thank Hashem for giving us life and the opportunity to get close to Him.

23. He Said Thank You and Received Reparations

A person called out to me, "Rabbi, I finally get to meet you! You don't know me, but I'm your student from all your books and CD lessons. I have to tell you about a miracle that happened to me." He told me that he owed a tremendous sum of money, which he could never logically repay. But, he heard a CD lesson of mine and he began to work on his emuna that everything is for the best. He'd sing all the time, like he heard me singing on the CD, "I don't understand a thing; I only believe that everything is for the very best.

Thank You, Hashem, for the debts You have given me."

Logically, he was in big trouble. But from an emuna standpoint, everything was great. So he kept on singing, over and over. His wife heard him thanking Hashem for his debts. She thought he lost his mind. He told her, "Dearest wife - true, our situation looks horrible. But I want you to listen to this CD, 'Stop Crying' – it will completely change your outlook. Only Hashem can help us."

He continued to strengthen himself. Many years ago, his father was incarcerated in Syria. He learned that his father was entitled to receive reparations. After filing the necessary papers, his father received a tremendous sum of money. He called his son and said, "Here, my son – take the money and repay your debts." His singing to Hashem and his saying "Thank You" really did the job!

As I wrote in "In Forest Fields", singing to Hashem is priceless. It's a beautiful way to express one's love and gratitude to Hashem and it invokes tremendous Divine compassion.

Song gladdens an individual and stimulates one's heart. Rebbe Natan would utilize his travel time by learning Torah and praying to Hashem. Once, while in a wagon with his students, the time for morning prayers arrived. At first, his prayers were heavy, as if weighed down with unhappiness. Rebbe Natan began to hum a joyful melody, which became stronger and stronger until he was praying with enthusiastic fervor while singing his prayers. As the wagon passed through a village, the locals started to run after it to hear more of the beautiful song that Rebbe Natan was singing.

By the time Rebbe Natan reached the "Shmona Esrei" prayer, he was so engrossed in prayer and impervious to his surroundings that his students had to lift him off the wagon and stand him in a quiet pace where he could pray with no interruptions.

When they continued on their way, the students asked Rebbe Natan why he was so sad at the beginning of his prayers and how he attained such fervor. He replied, "Negative thoughts overcame me, until I remembered Rebbe Nachman's teaching that a joyful melody can revitalize a person. "

It's amazing how so many people say our prayers, many of which come from songs of praise that King David wrote, in such a boring, fast and monotonous manner. They don't realize what they're saying! For example, when they recite Psalm 148, which is a part of our morning prayers that calls the entire universe to sing songs of praise to Hashem, they mumble and don't even think about what they're saying. That can't possibly be prayer. True prayer must be full of "heart" – in other words, sincerity, desire and heartfelt intent. Such prayer has the power to purify the entire universe.

If people engaged in songs of gratitude and praise to Hashem, troubles and suffering would be rendered null and void and we'd soon see the full redemption of our people. The Zohar says that the main spiritual accusations against people are that they fail to express gratitude to the Creator. It's time that we rectify this!

24. From Iran to Israel

Many stories show that a person's only true difficulties in life are his or her lack of emuna. Here is one of them, about an individual who came to see me especially from Iran to

Israel. With tremendous excitement, he told this story at one of my lectures while one of my Persian-speaking students translated:

This man was a wealthy real estate dealer in Iran who lost all his assets and became terribly depressed. He was deep in debt. His aunt, who lives in Israel, sent him a copy of "The Garden of Emuna" in Persian. He read the book carefully and began to apply its lessons to his everyday life. Among other things, he began to thank Hashem.

In "The Garden of Emuna", we write that anyone who devotes an hour a day to personal prayer for forty days consecutively will surely see salvations. He did, speaking to Hashem in his native Persian tongue and local dialect. We also wrote that sometimes a person sees salvations even before the forty days are up. He reached day fourteen, but nothing yet happened.

The evil inclination bombarded him with doubt, discouragement and disappointment. He overcame and kept going. Days twenty and thirty rolled around, but still, there was no change. He finally hit day thirty-nine...

Suddenly, he received a phone call from his mother. This person had closed his cellphone because of all the people he owed money to who were chasing him. His mother called his house and told him that someone was looking for him, but hadn't been able to establish contact. The individual wants to do a major transaction with him...

He told his mother to have the individual call him at home. This was late in the afternoon of the thirty-ninth day. The individual called and offered a deal that would not only enable him to repay half of his debts but to put him back on his feet.

The Iranian told, "At that moment, I was so embarrassed for all the times I doubted Hashem and became discouraged."

He did a second and a third daily string of forty consecutive days of personal prayer and saw more miracles. He prayed to be able to come to Israel so that he could meet me, thank me and tell me his story. He finally came to Israel by way of Turkey. In Israel, he met one of my students who brought him to my lecture, where he told his amazing story in first person.

Can you imagine the risk that this man took? Israel and Iran have no diplomatic relations! He endangered himself just to come here, to kiss my hand and to get a blessing from me! It took him 48 hours to make the roundabout return journey to Iran by way of Turkey.

This story is only one of many. We see over and over how a person strengthens emuna, begins to thank Hashem and sees miraculous salvations. Troubles evaporate! It turns out that one's only trouble was the lack of emuna.

A person asked me when Moshiach would come. I told him that we need Moshiach to reveal and publicize Hashem's monarchy, and not for our own personal benefit. It's not Moshiach's task to solve our personal problems. Indeed, when we learn what to do about our problems, Moshiach will come. Once we learn emuna, our problems disappear. Remember the popular expression: Don't tell Hashem that you have problems, tell your problems that you have Hashem…

Nevertheless, it's even a good thing to tell Hashem about your problems. But, don't do it in a way that sounds like whining and complaining, for that's not emuna but just the opposite. Instead, why not tell yourself that no matter what, you have Hashem and He does everything for the best. As such, thank Him! Once you do, you get a shot of encouragement and strength – nothing frightens you anymore. Say thanks and see miracles. Hashem is always with you; the stronger your emuna, the more you'll feel that Hashem is right there with you.

25. Gratitude Opened the Gates

A rabbinical student told me that he fell into a debt of 1.2 million NIS, about $300,000. He didn't know what to do so he went out to the field to speak to Hashem. On the way, he met Rabbi Brizel shlit'a, who asked him how he was feeling.

The young man whined, "My troubles are great! I owe 1.2 million NIS…"

Rabbi Brizel asked, "Are you headed to the field to cry to Hashem?"

The young man answered, "Is there anyone else to cry to?"

Rabbi Brizel asked him how long he'd been complaining to Hashem and the young man answered that it's been a long time already, but nothing yet has helped. "If you listen to me," said the rabbi, "stop crying and simply thank Hashem for the debts." The young man heeded the rabbi's advice; although it sounded weird, he had nothing else to lose.

A few weeks later, he received a windfall gift of one million shekels! He was left with a mere sixth of his debt, which he was able to deal with. These are not just fairy tales, but real stories with real people.

The Zohar says that anyone who learns to thank the Creator properly, merits that the Creator does his will.

26. No One Can Touch that which Belongs to Someone Else

A merchant had a profitable store in Jerusalem's Machane Yehuda market. The rent was extremely high but so were the profits and the traffic, so it was worth it.

Hashem decided to do this merchant a favor. One day, a competitor opened up a similar store right across the street, exactly opposite his store. The merchant's profits dropped and dropped. Yet, the rent stayed the same. He finally hit the point where his expenses were greater than his sales. If this slide continued, he'd lose everything.

The merchant went to Rabbi Biniyahu Shmueli shlit'a and told him about his predicament. He told the rabbi how angry he was that the competitor was robbing him of his income. He said that if he hadn't become an observant Jew, he'd have murdered his competitor. Yet, if he even contemplated such a crime, the merchant had not yet learned what observant Judaism is…

At any rate, the rabbi told him, "What's got into you? It's not your competitor across the street, it's Hashem, and He does everything for the best!"

The merchant had difficulty in accepting the rabbi's comment and said with irritation: "It's not Hashem – it's my competitor!" Yet, he caught himself and remembered that he was talking to one of Israel's foremost rabbis and Kabbalists, who has more than a slight inkling about emuna and the ways of Hashem. "So what do I do, Rabbi?"

Rabbi Shmueli replied, "Everything's for the best. Close the store and reopen in a new location, where the rent is much less. Maybe you won't earn what you have been earning, but at least you'll have an income. Accept this decree with love."

The merchant, disgruntled and frustrated, left the rabbi. He had no choice but to listen to the rabbi's advice. A few weeks later, he reopened his store in Mea Shearim.

In the apartment above his store, lived an elderly widow who was all alone with no children or relatives. The merchant took pity on her and began bringing her food at no charge. In time, he began helping her financially too, paying her bills and acting just like a son.

One day, the elderly woman asked the merchant to devote her an hour of his time. Weary after a day's work, he felt like refusing but he didn't. She started to tell him her life's story. He squirmed in his chair and looked at his watch. The woman said, "Stop looking at your watch. Have just a bit more patience. You've given me so much already – I only ask for one more hour."

Then she got to the point. Her rich uncle died and left her an inheritance of five million dollars. She had no heir. Since he had helped her for several years, she is bequeathing everything to him in her will. She just asked one favor, that he should purchase a room in a yeshiva where Torah students will learn for her constantly…

This story was revealed when the merchant returned to Rabbi Shmueli and told him that he wants to purchase a room in the rabbi's yeshiva and dedicate it to the woman who had since passed away. Rabbi Shmueli asked, "Aren't you the merchant who complained about losing his income?" It was then that the merchant told his entire story.

The rabbi said to him, "I told you that everything Hashem does is for the best. The Almighty saw that a large sum was awaiting you, and He maneuvered your life around so that you'd not only get it, but that you'd strengthen your emuna and do charitable deeds on the way. What you thought was a tragedy in the beginning, turned out to be the best thing that ever happened to you."

This is just another example of how Hashem does everything for the best. During a test of emuna, things appear to be terrible. That's why we must cast logic aside and simply thank Hashem, for whatever is going on is certainly for the good. Knowing this, we can be happy all the time, no matter what. A person must trust Hashem and nullify his will to Hashem's will, accepting whatever Hashem does with love and thanking Him always, whether a situation seems good or the opposite, Heaven forbid.

27. The Loser who became a Winner

Why should we thank Hashem for a situation that appears to be unfavorable? Let me tell you a story about a billionaire who didn't even know how to write his name. One day, his secretary asked him, "Sir, how did you amass such fortune and success without knowing how to read and write?"

The billionaire answered, "Indeed, had I known how to read and write, I wouldn't have been a billionaire today. Here's the story:"

He grew up in a broken, dysfunctional family. He never went to school and never learned to read and write. From a tender age, he scraped out a living as a menial factory worker. One day, the company administration decided to arbitrarily fire any illiterate workers. They gave him a bit of severance pay and he was out the door, jobless. Yet, he had emuna that Hashem would never forsake him and that everything was for the best.

With his severance pay, he opened up a market stall selling tobacco and enjoyed immediate success. He opened up retail outlets all over town and eventually bought a tobacco factory whose products became international hits on the worldwide market. "You see, if they hadn't fired me back then, I would have never gone out on my own; it's doubtful, even ridiculous, to think that I could ever become wealthy as a menial worker. By virtue of losing my job, Hashem made me a billionaire."

The vital message here is that a person can't possibly see what Hashem sees. So in the meanwhile, he should be calm, confident and believe in Hashem. Hashem does only good, whether or not we understand how. There truly is no bad in the world.

What happens to the unfortunate individual who lacks emuna? He gets angry and worried: 'The nasty boss fired me! What's going to be?' Not only is he denying Hashem's Divine Providence, but on the way, he's transgressing other sins like anger, slander and even physical violence, Heaven forbid. The news is full of stories about people who lost their composure and ended up committing murder because of anger, jealousy, honor or financial disputes.

On the other hand, a person with emuna garners a harvest-full of mitzvoth when he or she accepts a difficult situation with emuna. Besides the main mitzvah of emuna, which is one's main objective in the world, the emuna-filled person makes others happy, serves Hashem in the best way and mitigates stern judgments for the entire world, earning a greater portion of Divine light and getting even closer to Hashem. And that's not all…

The Rambam writes in his commentary on the Mishna in tractate Berachot, "One is obligated to make a blessing on the [seemingly] bad just as he makes a blessing on the good". The Rambam explains that a person, when confronting a difficult situation, must overcome negative emotions such as anger and accept it lovingly. He benefits his soul by making the blessing *Baruch Dayan Ha'emet* over a bad tiding just as he benefits by making the blessing *Baruch Hatov Vehametiv* when he hears joyous news. Rebbe Akiva would always say, "Everything Hashem does is for the very best." Since we are not privy to Divine considerations and we cannot see the entire picture of whatever is happening, we should accept with simple faith that Hashem is doing everything for the best.

The Talmud Yerushalmi tells the story about a man named Judah, whose ox broke its leg while plowing. As he tried to prod the ox out of the mud, he discovered a buried strong box with a treasure inside. Judah said, "It was for my own good that the ox broke its leg."

28. The Divorcee's Salvation

A divorced woman with several children endured a nasty divorce and suffered tremendous difficulties after the divorce. Her husband left her and the children penniless with the entire burden of making a living on her shoulders. Not only that, but she was left with prodigious debts. The woman sank into severe depression and her household ceased to function. Hashem had pity on her and she received the CD, "Stop Crying." For several weeks, she thanked Hashem that she was all alone, and before long, she found an ideal soul-mate.

When a person regards any tribulation in life as Hashem's way of bringing him closer to Him, he can pray and thank Hashem properly and weather the challenge with joy. Indeed, he uses the challenge or tribulation as a catapult to propel him upwards closer to Hashem and he certainly doesn't allow the evil inclination to spoil his thoughts and mood. Many people would wallow away in spiritual slumber were it not for the difficult situations that stimulated them to seek Hashem, by way of prayer, penitence and self-assessment.

As I explained in many of my CDs as well as in "The Garden of Emuna" and in "The Garden of Gratitude", the objective of any suffering and deficiency is to cleanse us of sin and to bring us closer to Hashem. When a person looks at the ultimate purpose of life, tribulations are not tribulations at all because they serve the purpose of bringing us closer to Hashem.

Tribulations aren't designed to sink a person into sadness and depression, for everything Hashem is doing is all for the best. Rebbe Nachman writes explicitly (Likutei Moharan I:65) that tribulations are all from Hashem for a person's ultimate benefit, for Hashem's intent is only for the good.

A person who begins to live his life with emuna begins to taste the sweetness of this world. Emuna, in addition to being the answer to every question, is the solution to every problem in this world! When there's emuna, everything is good and there's no bad in the world.

As soon as a person begins to live with emuna and seeks Hashem's guidance, asking Hashem to help him/her find the path to objective truth and clarity, suddenly he/she discovers a new world. They see things that they never paid attention to before. Everything turns into a beautiful conduit of getting close to Hashem. Suddenly, life becomes wonderful.

All a person must do is to put his intellect and logic aside and turn to Hashem, like this: "Hashem, You know what's best for me and what I need to attain my soul correction. Guard me down the path that You desire, and not necessarily what I desire, for my subjectivity gets in the way of Your truth, which is absolute truth. Give me the emuna that everything is under Your control and there are no mistakes in Your precision Divine Providence. Enable me to internalize Your desire and make them mine, and bring me closer to You."

Internalizing Hashem's desire and thanking Him neutralize all severe judgments. How? Rabbi Chaim of Volozhin explains that as soon as a person tells himself that there is no one but Hashem, and he nullifies himself to Hashem, no forces of evil or stern judgments can affect him, for by nullifying himself to Hashem, he becomes one with Hashem. From here, we can understand why our sages in the Mishna said, "Nullify your will to His will, so that He will nullify others' will (stern judgments) to your will (Avot 2:4).

There's an important principle here to learn: before Hashem gives a person a gift, his faith is tested. Rabbi Moshe Chaim Luzzatto teaches that in this world, sorrow is often the forerunner of extreme good. Our sages say that wonderful gifts often arrive while cloaked in suffering.

29. He Heard the CD Thousands of Times

A young man from our rabbinical seminary entered a new store that recently opened. He said to the proprietor, "Congratulations on your new store. I have a good piece of advice for you – every time a customer enters the store, thank Hashem. You'll see big blessings if you do."

The proprietor looked at him askew and said, "You come to teach *me* about gratitude to Hashem?! Let me tell you what it means to thank Hashem…" He began telling about the miracles he personally experienced from thanking Hashem…

The store owner was deep in debt and he fell into depression. With Hashem's mercy, someone gave him the "Stop Crying" CD, which became his oxygen. He listened to it over and over: "I heard it thousands of time – I'm not exaggerating!" He played the CD from morning till night – in his house, in his car, at work, even when he was sleeping. He internalized every word and upheld its advice to the letter. He didn't stop thanking Hashem for his debts.

The store owner continued, "You see the result yourself. Thanks to Hashem, I saw miracles. My debts not only vanished but I began to earn respectable sums too that enabled me to open this new store. This whole store was born out of thank Yous to Hashem." My student came in the store with the intent of encouraging the proprietor, but he was the one who received the encouragement.

The owner said that people would yell at him: "Hey, change that CD already!" He'd refuse of course, saying that he lived by that CD – it's not going anywhere. He'd sing along with it and thank Hashem all day long.

One of the odd phenomena of this generation is that the observant community is so far away from gratitude and personal prayer. The entire purpose of putting man on this earth and teaching him Torah is to bring him to the recognition of Hashem, so that he praises Him and thanks Him. Even when the Holy Temple is rebuilt - soon and in our days, amen – the only ritual sacrifice that will remain will be the *korban toda*, the gratitude offering. A person is obligated to thank Hashem incessantly, his or her entire life.

We could bring endless passages from Torah sources that support the above idea. The Torah explains the reason behind all the terrible curses in the Book of Deuteronomy when it says, "...because you didn't serve Hashem with joy." Joy means gratitude – singing, dancing and expressing one's appreciation of all the good that Hashem does.

Nothing invokes severe judgments like disgruntlement and a lack of gratitude. Hashem judges people fairly; He knows that they have an evil inclination and they sometimes get tripped up and sin. This He forgives. But, when a person lacks gratitude and lacks joy, especially when he whines and complains "with a loaf of bread under each arm," Hashem doesn't forgive and stern judgments prevail over that person.

30. He Said Thank You and Received a Loan

In continuation of the above story, when another one of my students heard the story about the store owner, he went to visit the store himself. He wanted to hear the story from the proprietor first-hand. The owner said, "It's all true what you heard – everything you see here, the store and all its contents are all by virtue of saying thanks to Hashem."

This student of mine was in such deep debt that the cellular phone company disconnected his phone. He could neither call out nor receive calls. For an hour, he thanked Hashem for his debts and for his disconnected phone. He had the desire to call everyone he owed money to and thank them, but now, he couldn't do that anymore. Yet, one number was open to him – that of the cell-phone company. He called the number.

A customer service representative (csr) answered the phone. He said, "I called to thank you for disconnecting my phone service."

The csr thought he was crazy. "Are you OK?" she asked.

He answered, "I'm fine and clear-headed. I thanked Hashem for my misfortune and I simply felt that it was befitting to thank you folks too. That's why I called, to tell you that I'm not upset with your company – I'm grateful to you."

"Wait a second," the csr said. "If I reconnect your phone, will you be able to call a few people and organize a loan to pay your phone bill?"

"I don't know," he answered innocently.

"I'll tell you what," she continued, "I'll give you another week of service where you can have both incoming and outgoing calls." This was a total miracle!

The first call my student made yielded a loan of $12,500 at wonderful terms, enough to clear him of his debts. That's the power of gratitude.

Many say that they can't say thank You to Hashem for their suffering. They'd be insincere, even lying. They don't realize what they're saying: "Oh yes, I want to get out of debt; I want to find my soul-mate; I want to be healthy, etc., but I can't say thank You in my current predicament…"

A person must thank Hashem not because he wants to see miracles and salvations, but to show that he accepts Hashem's will. Once he realizes this, he'll be able to thank Hashem sincerely and to feel happiness. In doing so, he dispels the stern judgments that are triggering the difficulties in the first place.

Emuna never changes, no matter what's happening in our lives. Emuna means that everything is from Hashem and that it's all for the good. That is an eternal truth. Hashem's Divine Providence is always for your ultimate benefit.

Hashem wants everything good for you, many times more than you want for yourself. Therefore, believe that if Hashem is withholding something from you, it's for your very best. Believe that Hashem loves you and He wants to do everything good for you. Therefore, say, "Hashem, this is what You want for me? I'm delighted and I thank You!"

King Solomon tells us in Ecclesiastes that everything has its appointed time. It doesn't matter when salvation arrives; meanwhile, we must hold on with emuna. No one can attain his or her personal perfection without having to deal with life's challenges.

Any person who is dealing with a challenge or difficulty should devote thirty minutes a day to thanking Hashem. Here's what he or she will gain:

1.   They pass the test of emuna;

2.   They become happy with their lot in life;

3.   Without thanks, they'd succumb to depression and self-pity as well as heresy; the thirty minutes of gratitude protect a person from heresy and questioning the Almighty;

4.   They bring salvation to the entire world. Rebbe Yehoshua ben Levi says in tractate Taanit that he who lovingly accepts his tribulations brings salvation to the world!

More than anything, thirty minutes of daily thanks to Hashem for whatever is painful to you will protect you and help you attain genuine emuna. Not only that, but you'll be helping others too, even the whole world!

As I wrote in "The Garden of Gratitude", gratitude unlocks gates. Surely, the Gemara says that the gates of tears are never locked, but with gratitude, there are no gates at all!

31. Escape from Million-Dollar Debt

A person came to me and told me that he owed a million dollars. I told him that he needed a strong spiritual antidote and I recommended that he do six hours of daily personal prayer for thirty days straight. He did, following my advice to the letter. He succeeded in understanding that this severe debt was Hashem's way of bringing him closer. He loved talking to Hashem so much that he continued the six-hour sessions even after the thirty days were over. He escaped his million-dollar debt in less than a year and today, he doesn't owe a cent! That's the power of gratitude and teshuva.

These are miracles beyond miracles that we can't fathom, as I merited seeing in my own life when I owed so much money. Every day, I'd go out to the field to sing, dance and thank Hashem. People thought I was deranged. But, I did teshuva and developed an amazing personal relationship with Hashem, all by virtue of my debts. I was therefore truly joyous and thankful for them, for they brought me so much closer to Hashem.

We all must believe that whatever challenge we have is entirely for the best. They are catalysts that bring us to real emuna and closer to Hashem.

The Gemara tells about two merchants on their way to the port, planning to sail to an important city of commerce. One received a thorn in his shoe and couldn't continue on the way. Disappointed and angry, he cursed his misfortune. A few days later, he found out that his friend had lost his life, for the ship was wrecked in a storm. Then, his curses turned into songs of praise and thanks.

32. A Lease on Life

A women asked me, "Why didn't the Creator ask me if I want to come into the world or not?" From her question, I understood that she was miserable and that she can't see or feel the beauty of the world around her. She obviously doesn't taste the sweetness of emuna or Shabbat, for she hasn't yet learned the mindset of gratitude. My heart felt for her.

For anyone who lacks emuna, this world is one big pit of non-stop suffering. She hasn't yet learned how to pray and express gratitude, so she does what she knows – she frowns and complains. Too bad there are so many people like her. That shows us how critically important it is to spread the light of emuna and gratitude, for they are a lease on life in every sense of the word.

People frequently complain to me that Hashem hates them, Heaven forbid. They use their tribulations as proof of this skewed notion.

Why do they think like that?

People tend to forget the good that Hashem does for them every moment of the day, including every breath and every heartbeat. As soon as they encounter or feel the slightest deficiency, they focus on it and forget all the good in their lives. It's the "What has Hashem done for me lately" attitude. If they engaged in daily personal prayer and self-assessment, they'd see that Hashem has done magnificent things for them lately. That's why they should be saying thank You to Him.

Try carrying around a pocket notepad and ballpoint pen; write down every favor that Hashem does for you and don't ignore a thing. How about that car that nearly cut you off on the highway this morning? How about the fantastic dinner you had last night? What about your eyesight that's enabling you to read these very lines? And how about the fact that you don't have a headache right now? They are all big reasons to thank Hashem. When you contemplate every detail of your life, you'll discover so many reasons to thank Hashem that you'll fill up an entire notepad every day. Once you reach your daily personal prayer session, go down the current day's list of favors in your notepad and thank Hashem for each detail.

As soon as a person opens his eyes in the morning, he should thank Hashem for another day of life. Everything else is an additional bonus. Remember, there's no bad in the world – Hashem does only good.

How does a person reach the point where he can say that Hashem hates him? It's because he takes things for granted and has a sense of entitlement. He hasn't learned to thank Hashem for what he has and he certainly hasn't learned emuna. That's why the gratitude notepad is so important, for it teaches a person both to recognize Hashem's favors and to thank Him for them.

We all are obligated to open our eyes and pay attention to all the good that Hashem does for each of us, thanking Hashem for every little blessing in our lives. The more we thank Hashem, the more He'll give us reasons to thank Him.

33. Paradise on Earth

A young lady told me that she started a gratitude diary and began thanking Hashem for all His favors. Her gratitude diary quickly ran out of pages. She wrote, "I'm writing everything down so that I don't forget the favors that Hashem does for me every day." She told me that her life became a paradise on earth and she felt happy all the time.

No angel has the license of obstructing words of gratitude to Hashem. They rise directly to the Heavenly Throne. If a person enjoys thanking Hashem, He gives him plenty of reasons to continue thanking.

Any person who pays attention to Hashem's acts of loving-kindness and writes them down – both big and small - will feel tremendous happiness. He'll begin to realize that life is full of Hashem's endless acts of loving-kindness. He'll laugh at his gratitude notepad, thinking that he'll need to write something as big as Encyclopedia Britannica to list all of Hashem's wonders, favors and miracles that he sees every day.

The Slonimer Rebbe writes in "Netivot Olam" that Hashem forgives all the sins of anyone who accepts whatever happens to him with joy. This is measure-for-measure: it's as if Hashem is saying, "If you accept whatever I do with joy, I'll accept whatever you do with joy."

Start your own gratitude notebook and you too will taste paradise on earth. Join the wonderful select group of people who joyfully accept their lot in life and thank Hashem for everything. Not only does Hashem forgive them of their sins, but their sins become merits, since gratitude leads them on the path of complete teshuva.

34. 20,000,000 Thanks

Avi Hershko from Brooklyn tells this story: "I print and distribute gratitude booklets with blank pages where a person must write down 100 thank Yous every day, one page per day. This way, people become aware of all the good that Hashem is doing for them. There are 40 pages in each book, which means once the book is filled, it contains 4,000 thank Yous.

"The last printing, which I paid for out of my own pocket, we printed 5,000 booklets. You know what that means? **20 million thank Yous to Hashem!!!**

"How did it all start? I work as an investment broker in a well-known New York financial institution. My close friend and coworker told me that he writes a long daily list of 100 thank Yous to Hashem. At first, I made fun of him. I said to myself that he must be some space cowboy that believes in anything. I also said to myself that I too say thank You to Hashem several times a day during my prescribed prayers, so what's the big deal?

One day, my friend told me what happened to him. Every day he writes 99 thank Yous, and then leaves the 100th for something very special that he ponders on until the next day. The day before, he couldn't think of a proper 100th thank You; he finally said to himself, "I was born in Argentina. I'm going to thank Hashem that I know fluent Spanish."

The next day, our company's CEO called him and asked him to contact and meet a prospective client with a huge investment portfolio who's willing to work with our company on condition that he gets an account manager who knows perfect Spanish. My friend was the only qualified individual in our company! He landed the account – his largest by far - and is now reaping tremendous commissions.

When my friend told me the story, I thought that if gratitude will fatten my bank account, I too am willing to invest in more thank Yous. My friend coached me and I also read the fantastic book "The Garden of Gratitude." The first day, I only came up with twelve thank Yous – boy, did I have a long way to go!

Gradually, I began paying closer attention to Hashem's many acts of loving-kindness. I started with all my amenities in life – the car, the family vacation and the fact that I am employed. Then, I started adding life's basic blessings and necessities that we take for granted – our health, eyesight, spouse and children. I started thanking Hashem for each part of my body. Finally, I started to thank Hashem for the things that don't go according to my desire, as I learned in the "Garden of Gratitude." Once I started thanking for the painful and unpleasant things in life, I became much happier and felt so much closer to the Creator.

Yet, I don't keep good things to myself. I share them with others. Now, thousands of people around the world are saying their 100 thank Yous every day. How about you?

35. The Supernatural Kidney

Our dear friend Avi Hershko tells two other thank You stories:

"I have a friend who underwent a kidney transplant at the age of 12. One day recently, he woke up with swollen eyes. It was the first time that his transplanted kidney malfunctioned. He immediately checked himself into the hospital. Once hospitalized and undergoing tests, he promised himself that if it turns out that his kidney is OK, he'd thank Hashem for a whole hour.

"The next day, the attending physician visited my friend and told him that he never saw a transplanted kidney functioning so wonderfully in all his 26-year medical career. My friend saw with his own eyes just how powerful the commitment of gratitude is, even before he said the actual thank Yous. Gratitude virtually overrides nature!"

36. Forty Days of Thanks

Here's the second story that Avi told (of the many that he has personally witnessed):

"I have a friend that writes 100 thank Yous every day but he never told his mother that he does so. One day, she complained about her 28-year old daughter who hasn't yet found a soul-mate. So far, nothing has helped including the many prayers she prayed and the spiritual ploys she tried.

"The family belongs to one of the biggest Chassidic groups in the USA, where most of the girls are married by nineteen and mothers by twenty. They consider an unmarried 28-year old to be a withered old maid. **Rabbi Shalom Arush told me that I can promise in his name that if they thank Hashem for 40 days in a row, they'll surely see salvation**. I therefore told them to write thank Yous for 40 days straight.

"Rav Arush really meant for me to tell them to thank Hashem for 30 minutes a day in personal prayer for 40 consecutive days, but I knew that the mother wouldn't take upon herself a commitment to perform personal prayer every day, so I told her to write the thank Yous instead. She did. When I told this story to Rav Arush, the young lady got married that same night."

37. Dancing and Gratitude at King David's Tomb

The young men of our rabbinical seminary saw the tremendous reviving powers of gratitude in a "live broadcast"; one of our students tells the story:

"One night, when returning from personal prayer in the woods, I passed by a supermarket. One of the workers saw me with my beard and sidecurls and ran up to me in a panic. He told me that his 12-year old sister was deathly ill because she accidentally swallowed poison. She was hospitalized in ICU and all her bodily functions were collapsing. She and her brother are orphans, and while he is on his own, she is being raised by their aunt.

"The young man had just been informed that his sister didn't have long to live. He was hysteric with a frustrating feeling of futility. I told him to get in the car – we're driving to King David's tomb on Mount Zion in Jerusalem.

"Once we arrived, at midnight, the young man burst out crying and screaming. I calmed him down and suggested that we read together Psalm 100, the Psalm of gratitude. We did, and I sang and danced too. The young man thought I was crazy. I forced him to join me and explained to him the power of gratitude. While we were dancing, he got a text message that his sister's condition was worsening. I forced him to ignore it."

A few minutes later, he got a call from the hospital. The doctors weren't giving the girl any chance of surviving and his aunt wanted him to sign a paper to disconnect her from the respirator, which was needed for a new patient that was also deathly ill.

The young man didn't agree under any circumstance. The doctors and his aunt did everything to persuade him. He finally begged them to give him a few more minutes. The aunt said, "If whatever you're doing succeeds in working, I'll commit to pray every day!"

"Meanwhile," our student continued, "a few other people joined us in singing Psalm 100 and dancing, while praying for the miraculous recovery of the young girl, who was hospitalized outside of Israel in Paris, France where the aunt lived. I wouldn't let the brother stop dancing and thanking Hashem."

All of a sudden, the young man stopped dancing; he received a text message that the Israeli Consul was visiting the hospital…

The consul heard about the 12-year old girl from Israel who was also an orphan. He decided to visit her room. When he got there, he heard yelling and arguing; he heard that the medical staff wanted to discontinue life support. The Israeli consul approached the chief physician of the department and asked if there was something else that could be done.

The doctor said, "There is one option, but the chances of success are close to nil – surgery."

The consul personally contacted the brother in Israel who was with all of us at King David's tomb. The brother immediately agreed to the surgery. In eighteen minutes, they'd know if the emergency surgery succeeded or not.

At first, it appeared to the surgeon that the young girl's life was about to terminate. Suddenly, in the eighteenth minute, she began to come out of her coma.

The group at King David's tomb was delirious with joy. They sang and danced like never before. Our student told the girl's brother, "Call your aunt now – she has a promise to keep!"

The brother's phone rang again. This time, it was the doctor from France, an Arab. The doctor asked, "What did you do over there?"

The brother answered, "We turned to the Creator."

The doctor said, "I know that you turned to Him, but you did something else that you're concealing from me. The miracle was too great – that little girl was finished. I saw it with my own eyes. The consul arriving at the hospital, the unexpected surgery – nothing makes sense. It's just not logical."

The brother said, "We thanked the Creator that my sister was about to die, telling Him that we believe in His mercy and that He does everything for the very best. We sang songs of praise and danced to the Creator."

The French doctor was silent for several moments. "I'm thoroughly moved by what you are telling me and I know it's the truth. I'm an Arab, but I have feelings for the Jews. I'll share a secret with you – my mother is Jewish." In that case, the French-Arab doctor is a Jew!

The whole cycle of events was less than two hours.

In the end, the girl was in a convalescent facility for two weeks and then discharged to go home.

Today, the aunt prays every day. And, the doctor knows he's Jewish.

38. Gratitude Lengthens Lives

I heard a Midrash that was quoted in the name of Rabbi Chaim Kanievski shlit'a. Two people were walking down a road and meanwhile, the angel of death was summoned to take their lives. Suddenly, a blind man walked by and one of the two gave him a few coins of charity. He said to his companion, "Give the blind man some charity, too."

The companion answered, "I don't know that blind man, but you did a good thing by giving some money to him."

Just then, the angel of death arrived on the scene. The angel told the charity giver that the few coins he gave to the blind man saved his life; he told the companion that he was obligated to take his life. The companion begged to the angel, asking him to wait a minute and to give him another chance to give charity to the blind man. "Sorry, pal – it's too late," said the angel. "You missed your chance."

The companion said, "I understand; but, I just ask for two minutes to thank Hashem, because I thank Him every day for two minutes and I haven't done so yet today." The angel had to comply to this request.

The companion stood by the side of the road and said: "Master of the World, thank You for the life You gave me. Thank You for everything else You gave me. Thank You for Your decision to take my life now, to enable my soul to really be close to You…" He continued like this for two minutes.

The angel of death said, "Now, I can't touch you anymore. Not only am I prohibited from taking your life, but you've received added years to your original allotment."

This wonderful story shows the live-saving power of gratitude, even greater than charity. Charity saves lives but gratitude lengthens lives!

39. Say Thank You and See Miracles

Here's what I call a "katanchik" (tiny) miracle story, and it happened to me:

I had a lingering cut on my finger that just wouldn't heal. It bled from time to time and didn't close. I thought to myself, how can it possibly heal by natural means when I'm periodically washing my hands all day long?

During my next personal prayer session, it occurred to me to thank Hashem for the cut on my finger. I thanked Him for about a minute, no longer than that. The next day, the cut disappeared as if I never had it, and all I did was to say thank You to Hashem for barely a minute…

This was a miracle that defied nature. For weeks, I suffered from that lingering cut that refused to heal. But once I realized that I must thank Hashem for this too, it disappeared!

Hashem wants us to believe in His perfect Divine Providence, never taking the small things for granted. Gratitude is emuna, and it works better than Band-Aids…

40. The Wound that Disappeared

I've seen many miracles in the area of health and healing, but the following story really reinforced my emuna. I heard the story from a seminary student who is studying to become a religious-court judge in the kollel of Rabbi Ovadia Yosef, osb"m. The same young man also attends my emuna lectures. When he heard about my story (above, #39) about the cut on my finger that healed, he told me about the miracle that happened to him:

The student had a terrible cut along the entire width of his heel. It was so deep that he could see the flesh; needless to say, he couldn't stand on the foot. If he had to walk somewhere, a 3-minute distance would take him a half hour and the pain was unbearable.

He heard my lessons on gratitude; one evening, he began to thank Hashem for the wound on his foot. He thanked Hashem for each painful step and for the tribulations that he could barely stand. He apologized that up till now, he didn't believe that this too was for the very best. He tanked Hashem for a half hour straight. When he woke up the next morning, the wound was closed, healed completely! This was a miracle above nature that defied comprehension.

The cut was so deep that it's hard to believe it healed without stitches or special medical treatment. The skin on his foot was new like a baby's. And, this story was told to me by a very serious young scholar with two feet on the ground.

Hashem is teaching us that gratitude is the solution to any problem! Gratitude is in effect penitence for lack of emuna. With gratitude, everything turns around for the very best. What's more, gratitude overrides nature.

41. Root-Canal Treatment on Shabbat

I'll tell you a story that exemplifies how gratitude overrides nature; this is a story I've told repeatedly over the years, how on Shabbat, Hashem gave me a swollen jaw and an excruciating toothache. I did a "root treatment". How? On Shabbat? I went out for a personal prayer session! Why did I get the toothache and swollen jaw in the first place? I obviously did something wrong. So, if I did teshuva and rectify the root of the problem, there'd be no reason for the pain and swelling anymore.

I went out to speak to Hashem for nearly two hours. First I thanked Him for sending me the "wakeup call" of the toothache. After that, I asked Him to show me what misdeed I did that triggered the toothache. Maybe I said something that violated the laws of wholesome speech. Maybe I ate something that wasn't strictly kosher. I searched and I searched. Finally, Hashem illuminated my heart. I found something that I did wrong and I did teshuva on the spot. The swelling in my jaw went down almost immediately. By the time I walked home, there was no more swelling and no more toothache! Miracles like that have happened to me in many different circumstances; I do teshuva and I see miracles right away.

The entire purpose of tribulations is to bring us to teshuva. Once a person does teshuva, Hashem releases him from the prison of tribulations. Not only that, but he gets rewarded too, for teshuva is a positive mitzvah that is worth more than its weight in gold. In this world, a person is rewarded for doing teshuva by receiving enhanced happiness and emuna. He gains a belief in teshuva and in the power of his prayers and penitence. He attains a higher spiritual level. And even more, his income, health and marriage improve, because if a person fails to do daily teshuva, his outstanding spiritual debts frequently manifest themselves as problems in the areas of income, health and marriage. As far as his rewards in the next world go, they are both inestimable and infinite.

People remain in darkness because they think that it's too hard to speak to Hashem. That's not true. All we must do is to ask Hashem to give us the right words. What's the big deal? A person doesn't need any talent, ability or qualifications of his own. To talk to Hashem, all he needs in Hashem's help! It's that easy.

If we were expected to speak to Hashem on our own ability, that would be hard. But since it's all up to Hashem, it's easy! Just say, "Father in Heaven, give me true emuna and give me the right words to speak to You. Give me the right thoughts and bring me close to You."

We must realize in our hearts that everything that happens in life is a gift from Hashem, a love letter to make us run to Him. There is no greater achievement in the world that to get close to Hashem. Therefore, since tribulations are a vehicle for bringing us closer to Hashem, they are intrinsically good and we must thank Hashem for them.

A young lady was diagnosed with cancer. She was miserable, so her friends suggested that she seek my advice. I told her how much Hashem loves her and that he wants to arouse her from her spiritual slumber. I told her that if she begins to speak to Hashem daily, including gratitude and teshuva in her daily talk with Him, she'll not only get close to Hashem but she'll become healthy again.

At any rate, we all leave this world by the time we reach our 120th birthday. Life in this world is full of bitterness, hate, jealousy, competition, stress, anxiety and hatred. As soon as a person comes close to Hashem, he rises above all the purgatory of this world. He lives a life of meaning and succeeds in fulfilling his mission on earth. **The conclusion: If a person does teshuva, what does he lose? Nothing! What does he gain? Everything!** Why? The benefit of getting close to Hashem is for posterity. That's why it's wonderful to get a "love Letter" from Hashem before it's too late.

The Creator does everything for a purpose. If He gives us tribulations, it's for triggering us into making teshuva and rectifying whatever it is that we've done wrong. It could also be that He wants us to strengthen our performance of a certain mitzvah or that He simply wants us to wake up from the coma of a material-oriented life that we're in pursuit of. Also, if arrogance gets the upper hand over a person, Hashem sends tribulations to deflate the arrogance and to bring the person back to normal proportions. Each one of us must try to understand the reason behind our tribulations so that we can do teshuva, rectify and get closer to Hashem.

By way of everything that happens in a person's life, Hashem is teaching him emuna. A person must look at the intrinsic wisdom within any creation of event he encounters, for by way of that wisdom, he can enhance his emuna.

The matter of searching for the intrinsic wisdom in everything is very deep. But in order to merit the spiritual level where he can discern the intrinsic wisdom within every event or creation, he must believe that there are no tribulations without prior transgression.

There is no fate or coincidence. The basis of our emuna is that everything comes from Hashem by way of His super-precise Divine Providence. Sometimes, Hashem brings you closer by giving you a book or CD. Other times, He sends a friend or a teacher to say something to you that helps you learn emuna. Then, there's the love letter of tribulations, when Hashem is saying to you, "Beloved son/beloved daughter, I love you so much! Why are you ignoring Me? Why aren't you looking for Me?" There's no such thing as chance. Once a person begins to believe that there are no tribulations without prior transgression, he begins to make a thorough correction of himself and mitigates all stern judgments.

42. A Cure for the "Nasty Big C"

A man who suffered from "the nasty big C" (cancer – we don't like to say words like this) was lying in the hospital. The doctors said that he only had a few more days to live, Heaven forbid. One of my students visited the sick man, encouraging him and his family to thank Hashem for everything that's happening. They began thanking Hashem profusely and before long, the tumor disappeared completely. The doctors couldn't believe their eyes! They thought that perhaps there was some mistaken diagnosis, but that couldn't be because the man was bald and emaciated from the damages of the disease and the treatments. He almost died but he was cured by way of emuna.

Rebbe Nachman writes (Likutei Moharan II:5) that there are incurable diseases that can be cured by way of emuna. For that reason, strengthening emuna enhances longevity as well. On the other hand, as Rebbe Nachman continues, there are diseases that result from a lack of emuna that no medicines or treatments are capable of curing. The only thing that helps in such cases is emuna.

We see that many illnesses can be traced back to spiritual causes. In such cases, as soon as the sick person rectifies the core reason that triggered the sickness, he becomes healthy again. Strengthening our emuna is therefore one of the best things we can do to guard our health.

Thanking Hashem for our tribulations is certainly a wonderful strengthening of emuna. When a person thanks Hashem for his tribulations, it means that he is joyfully accepting them. When – despite the tribulations – a person remains joyful, he merits the Divine Presence. The Doctor of all Flesh is right there with him! Of course he'll be healthy again!

Gratitude is something deep and internal. It's not a bumper sticker that says, "Give me a smile, my brother!" It's not a rabbit's foot. It's the deepest expression of emuna, which accompanies a person all the days of his life.

43. Ten Days Left to Live

A man came to Rabbi Brizel shlit'a and told him that the doctors told him that he only has another ten days to live. The Rabbi taught him to repeat Psalm 136 over and over which says, "Give thanks to Hashem for He is good." He told him to rejoice in every additional moment that he's alive and not to pay attention to the doctors' doomsday forecasts.

A person must say, "Master of the World, thank You for all the tribulations that You give me. Whatever You do is certainly for the good. Not only do You do good, but You love me immensely and You suffer when I suffer. I know that it hurts You to give me these tribulations, but that You must because You see that I need them in order to accomplish my mission on earth."

One who thanks Hashem for his tribulations and for all the seemingly bad turns the measure of stern judgment into absolute Divine mercy. How? This person is making a statement that Heavenly justice is good! He's acting as if it's mercy. In measure-for-measure fashion, Hashem takes the severe judgment and actually converts it to mercy and loving-kindness. This is a magnificent concept; what's more, it invokes abundance for the whole world, as we said previously in the name of the holy Rabbi Yehoshua ben Levi. As long as there is one person in the world who is thanking the Almighty for his tribulations, he is bringing salvation to the whole world.

As soon as a person lovingly accepts Hashem's will, he no longer suffers. Our sages say that the cure for tribulations is the acceptance of them with love; that means thanking Hashem for them with all your heart. Rejoice in them. There's no problem in the world that a person can't overcome if he accepts his tribulations with love. He brings salvation to himself and to the whole world.

One other thing – gratitude leads to joy. I heard about several patients in critical condition who saw miracles as soon as they started saying Psalm 136; they invoked Divine compassion on themselves and they were healed.

44. Gem of Gratitude

A rabbi from Bnei Brak who follows my teachings had a terrible problem. I taught him to thank Hashem for his problem in daily personal prayer. Since then, he distributes my CDs and emuna booklets.

Sometime later he met me and told me about a couple who came to him with their only son. The boy was sick with the nasty big C, Heaven forbid. The doctors said that there was no hope for a cure.

The rabbi told the parents to say thank You for an hour a day that their son has a terminal illness. He told the boy to do the same. The rabbi was more stringent than me, because I usually tell people to do a half-hour a day in such cases. At any rate, both the parents and the son did what the rabbi told them to. Of course, he explained to them the rationale behind the daily hour of thanking Hashem for their troubles. He gave them my book, "The Garden of Gratitude" and told them that even when according to nature there is no cure, gratitude for tribulations is high-level emuna that overrides nature. It wasn't long before the boy was released from the hospital, completely healthy. A medical miracle!

45. Gratitude Game-Changer

Rabbi David Elkayam recounted the principles of gratitude that he learned from me in one of his lectures. After the lecture, a well-known Rebbetzen approached him and said, "You saved my life! I never heard such an arousing lecture. For me, tonight's lecture is a game-changer!"

A week later, the same Rebbetzen phoned Rabbi Elkayam and told him that she had been sick with the nasty big C and that she was scheduled to undergo a CT scan. All week long, she had been thanking Hashem for the disease.

The time came for the CT scan. After the examination, the doctors were reviewing the results; lo and behold, the tumor vanished! The doctors couldn't believe their eyes. In the previous exam, they had clearly found a malignant tumor. They asked, "Did you undergo any treatments in the meanwhile?" She said no. "What, you didn't take any medicines?" asked the doctor.

"I didn't take anything," the Rebbetzen said.

"That can't be," the doctor remarked. "Are you sure you didn't take any natural medicine or the like?"

"100%," she said. What else could she tell him, that she was thanking Hashem for her sickness? She was afraid he'd have her admitted to a psychiatric hospital…

The more we spread the light of gratitude, the more we'll see salvations. People all over are reading the Gem series of gratitude booklets, listening to our gratitude CDs and reading "The Garden of Gratitude." More and more people are telling us about the miracles and salvations they've been seeing. Go with gratitude, and you too will see miracles and salvations in every facet of life.

46. Recovery from a Serious Sickness

When I lectured in Bet El, a man approached me and told me that his wife had been stricken with the most severe of sicknesses – it affected her in her blood. The doctors didn't give her much time to live. The man and his wife listened to the gratitude CDs, implemented the advice they learned and she recovered completely.

Hashem illuminated my brain with a one-liner that I presented in one of the Gem-series gratitude booklets: **"If you lovingly accept Hashem's will, He will do your will."**

A person must lovingly accept what Hashem wants with joy and emuna. If he's not happy, it's an expression that he doesn't like what Hashem is doing. Why? Everything comes from Hashem. A person should therefore never blame himself or anyone else. He shouldn't attribute his troubles to anything or to anyone. We should therefore be happy with whatever happens in our lives, for it's all from Hashem and all for the very best. We can therefore thank Him for everything!

Suppose things are difficult or not going according to our plans or desire. We should say, "Thank You, Hashem, that things aren't going the way I want them to." This way, we crown Hashem as King over us every minute of the day. To be able to do this with a whole heart, we must pray profusely for emuna and totally nullify ourselves to Hashem.

Why do people suffer? Why do they whine and complain? Why do they lose their will to live? It's all because they don't believe that everything is from Hashem and all for their ultimate good. As such, they refuse to accept Hashem's decrees and the way He handles their life. People like that have a sense of entitlement, as if he deserves everything he wants and is adamant when things don't go according to his will. They should know one thing: **nobody deserves anything and Hashem owes nothing to no one**. Therefore, we are obligated to thank Hashem for everything He gives us, no matter what. That way, we're always happy and always striving to rectify ourselves, never forgetting that there are no tribulations without prior transgression.

47. Against all Logic

One of my students was diagnosed with the nasty big C. The doctors told him that he'd need chemotherapy, which he did not want. He heard that chemo wrecks a person, weakens him and makes him lose his hair. He said to himself, "I believe in the power of personal prayer – I'll turn to Hashem."

For an hour a day in personal prayer, he thanked Hashem for sending him the disease. In addition to the hour of gratitude, he did an hour of teshuva and soul-searching, adding Psalms and Rebbe Natan's prayers from "Lekutei Tefillot". He also did a "pidyon nefesh", a "redemption of the soul", which is charity money given to a righteous individual that's aimed at mitigating severe judgments. He also prayed by the holy gravesites of tzaddim, praying for forty days straight at the Machpela Cave in Hevron.

Chemotherapy weakens the body to the extent that a person is virtually incapacitated. It doesn't do much good for the mind and soul either, for the weakening effects of it render a person prone to sadness and deep depression. My student decided to devote his power to personal prayer rather than lose it in chemo.

This young man was putting all his hope and trust in prayer and teshuva. He even asked the oncologist that would have been treating him to speak to him periodically about the dangers of the disease so that he'd know what to pray for. When he'd hear about his deteriorating health and the unfavorable test results, he'd be aroused to pray with even more fervor and for longer periods of time. He'd also thank Hashem for the new tumors and for the older ones that had grown larger and more dangerous.

A difficult test of faith like this is dangerous. A sick person is liable to fall into despair and to have doubts about Hashem, Heaven forbid. But, my student merited in sincerely thanking Hashem, which brought him to joy and inner peace. He truly believed that Hashem was doing everything for his ultimate good, for by virtue of the disease, he came so much closer to Hashem. He continued to thank Hashem daily and at length.

Weeks passed. His prayers became a full-time job. He spent hours on end in personal prayer, traveled to the gravesites of our patriarchs. Before long, all of his tumors vanished.

That's the way it is when a person throws all his weight into emuna and prayer, especially when expressing his gratitude. Gratitude indicates that the individual has nullified himself to Hashem. Such a person calls out with glee, "Master of the World! I love You and Your Divine Providence. Thank You!"

48. Everything Disappeared

To reinforce the point that gratitude leads to miracles and salvation, as well as strengthening in emuna, we are sharing the following letter with you:

Thank you, Honorable Rabbi – you saved my life.

My name is K.T. and I'm a 25-year-old woman. For six months, I suffered from terrible headaches. Not a single medicine gave me any relief. My mother took me to Wolfson Hospital in Bat Yam to undergo all the relevant examinations.

The MRI revealed that I had a malignant tumor and hemorrhaging in my brain. I was immediately hospitalized in the oncology ward. When first hospitalized, I saw an ad on the Breslev Israel website about how to get a blessing from Rabbi Arush. I sent a request to be blessed for recovery and good health. Several days later, M. from the Breslev Israel office phoned me and said that the Rabbi wanted me to thank Hashem for thirty minutes a day for my sickness.

I bought three books: "Garden of Gratitude", "Garden of Healing" and "Women's Wisdom." They really reinforced my emuna. I began to thank Hashem for 30 minutes a day. I had been in the hospital for a month already; at first, they gave me pills, but they didn't do any good. I decided to stop taking the pills and to put my hopes in prayer. Meanwhile, I was released from the hospital. Several months later, I went back for examinations, and the results that came back said that the hemorrhaging had stopped and the tumor had disappeared. The doctors had no explanations for this medical miracle that happened before their very eyes. The sickness vanished with no medications or treatments.

I thank Hashem so much for strengthening me in emuna. I go everywhere with the "Gems" series booklets and I especially love "Miracles Above Nature." I read it every day. In my purse, you can also find "Kisses to the Creator", "I Said Thank You and I Saw Miracles" and "Say Thank You".

At the time I wasn't at all observant, but gratitude has brought me to observing Shabbat, dressing modestly and living with emuna. I have also been a positive influence on my girlfriends, teaching them that gratitude brings salvations. Everything is from Hashem, and He gives us tribulations so that we'll get close to Him.

Thank you so very much, K.T.

49. The Disease that Disappeared

One of our new students at our yeshiva had been suffering from a painful disease for many years. Nothing he tried eased the situation. Finally, he heard a lecture teaching about the power of sincerely saying "Thank You" for life's difficulties.

The new student began devoting his entire daily hour of personal prayer to expressing his gratitude to Hashem for his sickness. He thanked Hashem for giving him all the years of pain and tribulation, for helping him to become a *baal teshuva* (a newly-observant Jew) and for bringing him to our yeshiva so that he could learn all about emuna and gratitude.

He never asked for a cure or relief; he only said thank You. Within two weeks, his disease disappeared without the help of medicine, doctors, treatments or anything else.

Clearly, we must thank Hashem for the apparent good things in life. But since everything comes from Him, when we express our gratitude for the difficulties and tribulations, we are making the greatest statement of emuna. We are saying that we not only believe in Hashem but that everything He does is for the very best. This invokes phenomenal Divine compassion.

There are three stages to the Divine service of gratitude:

1. **Believe that everything is for the best**. We put our own logic aside and rejoice in whatever pain and difficulty we encounter, because it's all a product of our loving Father in Heaven's Divine Providence and all for the best.

2. **Express gratitude – say thank You!** It's not enough just to believe that everything is for the best; we must thank Hashem as well.

3. **Do teshuva**. We realize that Hashem wants to bring us close to Him and that our suffering could very well be because of some misdeed that we have failed to correct. We therefore look for the Divine message within our suffering and do teshuva accordingly.

50. Gratitude in Payments

A useful principle to know is that one can thank Hashem ahead of time for the salvation he anticipates. What's more, a person can promise Hashem that when his salvation does arrive, he'll thank Hashem for a certain number of days and for a certain time period each day. In that way, he can make gratitude payments for whatever he wants!

We had a student in the yeshiva who had such a lust for sleep that he couldn't get out of bed in the morning. He had no hope of changing until he heard my lesson on gratitude.

He decided to try his hand in gratitude, so he changed his approach in his daily personal prayer. He asked Hashem that if He woke him up at midnight, he'd thank Him for half an hour. Lo and behold, he got up that night at midnight with no problem.

The student kept his end of the deal and thanked Hashem for half an hour. Then he thought: maybe it was by happenstance that I got up? He made the same deal with Hashem for the next night, and again, he got up at midnight. Again, he thanked Hashem for half an hour.

The third night, he was really tired because he lacked sleep from the two previous nights. Against his nature, the deal worked again the third night. Since then, he asks Hashem to wake him up, pays with a half hour of gratitude, and gets up whenever he needs to.

Many people worry about the future. What will be? Will I be healthy? Will there be peace? In short, they have a bleak view of the future. What's the solution? Say thank You! Gratitude calms the soul and dispels worry.

A person expresses his level of trust in Hashem by thanking ahead of time for the salvations that are on the way. In other words, if someone wants to invoke future salvations, he should thank Hashem for them ahead of time. "Beloved Creator, thank You for the favor You are about to do for me." Keep doing that until the salvation is realized. Of the two ways of requesting something from Hashem – simply requesting or thanking ahead of time – thanking ahead of time works much better. Why? Whereas the accusing angels filter requests and possibly say that the person doesn't deserve what he requested, they are not allowed to interfere with or obstruct expressions of gratitude, which reach the

Heavenly Throne directly. But, the expressions of gratitude must be sincere and not a mere ploy. Without emuna, believing that Hashem does everything for the best, the expressions of gratitude said ahead of time won't work.

Hashem is always quicker than we are. We can't put up a mezuzah until He gives us a house. We can't make a blessing over our food until He puts food on our table.

The above principle is true with everything except for gratitude. We can thank Hashem for something before He gives it to us.

This is an amazing principle. If a person is childless, he should thank Hashem for the children he's about to receive. He should be profuse in his thanks, expressing his gratitude for an hour or two. Hashem promises, "Whoever shall anticipate Me, I shall reward him" (Job 41:3). In other words, with gratitude, a person can "anticipate" Hashem and thank Him ahead of time, thus earning the promised reward.

Rabbi Yitzchak, the son of Rebbe Natan of Breslev, once became seriously ill. When he asked Hashem for health and recovery, he said, "Master of the World, what can I promise You? If I promise that I'll be completely upright if You cure me, I won't be able to keep such a promise. But I will promise that if You give me good health, I'll always thank You for your loving-kindness." He soon recovered.

51. Spiritual Perfection

Once, at the end of one of my lectures, I asked the audience, "Who is willing to commit to a daily hour of personal prayer?" A few scattered people raised their hand. A lady approached me after the lesson and told me that after a previous lecture of mine, she committed to a daily hour of personal prayer. She even does one six-hour session every month. Two of her daughters were off the path of observant Judaism, yet since she started daily personal prayer, one of the daughters had begun to dress modestly and to accompany her to Torah lectures.

Such is the power of prayer.

Here's a concrete spiritual law: when a person lacks something, it's due to his lack of emuna in the power of his prayer, namely, that he can attain what he seeks by way of prayer and gratitude. Why? If a person really believed that his prayers were effective, he'd pray until his wish would be fulfilled and never give up. We're not talking about great tzaddikim, but about simple people. With my own eyes, I've seen how our new students in the yeshiva – brand new *baalei teshuva* who don't even observe all the mitzvoth yet or have barely begun to learn Torah – have seen miraculous salvations in every area of life. We're talking about things that defy nature.

Now we can understand what Rebbe Nachman says: "By way of gratitude to Hashem, blessed be His Name, one is rescued from all calamity" (Likutei Moharan II:2).

52. The Good News: "You're Fired!"

A person from the USA phoned me and said, "I heard that if someone learns a page a day from the book, "The Garden of Gratitude", he'll have paradise in this world – it's true! I can testify to that!"

A young man who regularly attends my lectures approached me and said, "Rabbi, I've got good news – my boss fired me. Now, I'll have more time for personal prayer. I thank Hashem for His loving-kindness. I firmly believe that He'll give me whatever is allotted to me with or without the job."

This happened when the young man was just beginning to become observant and listen to Torah lectures. Here, already, he's thanking Hashem for losing his job. If he hadn't learned emuna and gratitude, he would have come to me whining and complaining…

With a mindset of emuna and gratitude, everything is good. That's what will be when Moshiach comes; then, everyone will understand that it's all good. Here's a sample phone conversation from the future, once Moshiach arrives:

The phone rings and Alan answers.

"Hello?"

"Hello."

"How can I help you?"

"Is your name Alan Ames?"

"Yes, that's me."

"We wanted to inform you that the merchant ship you own has just sunk at sea."

"Really? Thank You, Hashem! Thank you, sir, for passing the good news on to me."

Alan Ames then starts to dance and he blesses the Creator: "Blessed are You, the Lord our G-d, King of the world, Who is good and does good."

Afterwards, with his last hundred thousand dollars, he rents a wedding hall, hires the best caterer and the best orchestra, and invites the entire community to a big banquet to celebrate the loss of all his assets. His friends and neighbors don't think that he's crazy, for this is a natural reaction. They are happy to participate in his "celebration" and all congratulate him on the loss of his assets. They all dance gleefully with Alan, for everyone *knows* that this is all for the best.

Does the above scenario sound delusional? It is delusional to a person who believes that there is bad in the world. But once Moshiach arrives, everyone will know that there is no bad in the world. Alan's celebration will be perfectly normal.

We don't have wait until Moshiach arrives; with the mindset of emuna and gratitude, we can all realize right now that everything comes from our loving Father in Heaven Who only does what's best for each of us. The things that today appear to be troubles and tribulations will tomorrow be reasons to rejoice. This is the light of Moshiach. Since everything is for the best, we can surely thank Hashem for everything! When we lack happiness, it's simply because we lack emuna.

53. The Strange Talmudic Passage

The students of the Maggid of Mezeritch osb"m asked him to clarify a passage from tractate Berachot in the Talmud that says, "A person is obliged to make a benediction over the bad just as he is obliged to make a benediction over the good". The Maggid referred them to his disciple Rebbe Zusha.

The Maggid's students approached Rebbe Zusha, who was destitute beyond description. He would even give away to other people the money people gave him when he blessed them. The students saw his old dilapidated shack with holes in the roof and in the walls, a dirt floor and a few broken boards for furniture. There were buckets in the middle of the floor to catch the rainwater that leaked through the roof. Rebbe Zusha wore rags; he sat on a block of wood and learned Talmud. His face was aglow with joy.

The students said, "Our holy master the Maggid asked that you explain us the passage from the Talmud that says, "A person is obliged to make a benediction over the bad just as he is obliged to make a benediction over the good".

Rebbe Zusha was baffled by their request. "Are you sure the Maggid sent you to me? I never understood this passage myself, for I never understood how anything can be bad in the world. Nothing bad ever happened to me. Everything in my life is good. How can I possibly clarify such a passage for you? It's a riddle I haven't yet solved."

54. The Thanks that led to Salvation

I receive letters from Israel and from all over the world. Here is one of them that bears an important message:

Shalom!

I live in Toronto, Canada. I grew up in a religious home and married at age 20. I had everything – my own home, a good job and three children. I thought that I was on top of the world and a success story at that. I looked down at other people. I had my own theory as to how people should behave.

Overnight, my husband came down with a sickness that also damaged him emotionally. We entered a difficult period of doctors and medical treatments. At this time of crisis, I received a phone call from a girl whom I was friends with at school who married one of Rabbi Arush's students. After I tearfully told her about my husband's health problems and the shame of his being committed to a mental hospital, she told me that lately, Rabbi Shalom Arush has been speaking about the amazing power of gratitude – 'Say thank You and see salvations.'

I said to her, "Are you nuts? What should I say thank You for, for torture in purgatory? For nightmares? For not being able to make a decent living? For being bedridden?"

She said, "Yes – thank Hashem for all the hardships in your life and everything will turn around for the best."

I started to thank Hashem for all my tribulations. I was also finding positive reasons to thank Hashem, like for the good caretaker He sent my husband. While I was thanking Him, my phone rang: someone had organized a very large sum of money to aid us.

A year later, my husband's condition further deteriorated and the rabbis suggested that I get divorced. I accepted their Halachic opinion, that if I didn't accept a *gett* soon, he would soon be in condition where he couldn't have the mental faculties to give one. I found myself in the religious court hearing my husband say the words, "You are hereby divorced."

Only my prayers of gratitude prevented me from having a nervous breakdown then and there. That year, I flowered. I learned new things and received a marvelous promotion at work. By virtue of gratitude, I blossomed when otherwise I'd have withered. My tribulations were a gift in disguise. I wouldn't have things any other way.

Two years passed and I was tired of being alone. I wrote a letter to Rav Arush. He answered, "Say thank You for the hardship and learn two pages a day from "The Garden of Gratitude." I cast my brains aside and did just what the rabbi told me to. The rabbi said not to ask for a thing, just to say thank You. A few months later, I sent a similar letter again to the rabbi; he said to be patient and to continue expressing gratitude for being alone.

I increased my hours of daily gratitude, some days thanking Hashem for as much as three hours a day. I received what looked like a wonderful suggestion for a match, but at the last minute, it fell through. I was so disappointed. Impatient once more, I called my girlfriend who introduced me to Rabbi Arush's teachings in the first place. I asked her, "How is it that I haven't found a soul mate yet? Why is Hashem doing this to me?"

My girlfriend said, "Now thank Hashem for the shidduch that fell through. It's the best thing in the world. Believe that Hashem was doing the very best for you."

I went back to my prayers of gratitude and thanked Hashem for the unsuccessful shidduch. My emuna became much stronger; I really was sincere in thanking Hashem because I truly believed that everything He did was for my ultimate benefit. That very week, I met my new husband. I can't describe how special he is. Six weeks later, we were married; an outright miracle!

I want to add one more thing. Gratitude is not a ploy, to press a button in Heaven and to get a miracle, like getting a cup of coffee from a vending machine. Gratitude is getting to know Hashem and getting close to Him.

My story is real. Anyone who reads this should now that if they want to see salvation, they have to work. There are no shortcuts. The evil inclination will try to knock you down – don't let him do it. Keep thanking Hashem; He gives rewards for your suffering. Don't be afraid.

I must thank Rabbi Arush for the wonderful gift of gratitude. I said "Thank You" and I truly saw miracles.

-End of the letter –

Here is a young lady who didn't have it easy but she held on tight to her prayers of gratitude. She had her ups and downs. She had moments of impatience and near giving up. Yet, she always bounced back with gratitude, accepting Hashem's will no matter how difficult it was for her. No wonder she invoked such Divine compassion on herself.

But, when a person is dissatisfied, it means that he doesn't accept Hashem's will. Ultimately, when it's too late, he'll see that everything Hashem did was absolutely just, more than we deserve. How wonderful it is when we arrive at this understanding on our own.

People complain about their tribulations; I tell them that they are salvations, not tribulations. They bring a person to emuna. Is there any greater salvation than that? For sure, not!

55. The Stolen Motorcycle

A young man told me that when his motorcycle was stolen, the first thing he did was to thank Hashem. "Thanks Hashem for the few months that You let me enjoy the motorcycle. I know that You love me and that this is happening for my very best. You know what You're doing, Hashem. You know what miracles You do and only You know what kind of harsh decrees You're saving me from. I'm glad that my motorcycle was ripped off. Thank You, Hashem!"

Just as he was thanking Hashem, the police called and said that they found his motorcycle. Anyone who has any experience with stolen motorcycles knows what a miracle that is.

The young man's expressions of gratitude were the greatest thing he could possibly do for himself. This created a unfaltering bond with Hashem, for this was one of the finest and truest expressions of genuine emuna there could be. This was a sign that the young man accepted Hashem's Divine Providence wholeheartedly.

Expressions of gratitude must preface every prayer and request; they're even a prerequisite for teshuva. Gratitude brings us to the truth.

56. The Miraculous Test

Here's another story about motor vehicles. One of my students had to take his car in for its annual test. You could call his car a "deluxe jalopy". It's easier to check what works in the car, not what doesn't work. The car looks like it belongs on a junk heap. Before the test, my student thanked

Hashem for every part of the jalopy that worked. He thanked Hashem for the three tires that weren't yet completely bald. He thanked Hashem for the radiator that didn't leak and for the ignition that after a few "coughs" could still get the car started. When he went part-to-part from the front of the car to the tail lights that hadn't yet fallen off, he found that there was much more to be thankful for than he expected.

The jalopy passed the test on the first go-around. Meanwhile, relatively new cars were getting sent back for retests because of all types of little problems…

From this episode, my student learned to thank Hashem always, and for every detail too!

Human nature disregards outright miracles that one hears of; business as usual. But when miracles occur in one's own life, they can't be ignored. By paying attention to the miracles in our lives, we strengthen emuna.

Those who live their lives with emuna mitigate all stern judgments; they invoke abundance and salvations as well. Like we sing all the time, "It's either emuna or purgatory." With emuna, life is paradise. Without it, life is the opposite.

Here's a reminder to start your gratitude notebook and to list the miracles that happen to you every day so that you can thank Hashem for them. The miracles will become more and more frequent – so will the salvations!

Gratitude is really the only payback a person can give to Hashem in return for all of His loving kindness. Ingratitude is not tantamount to heresy – it *is* heresy, for the recipient doesn't believe that his gift has come from Hashem and therefore feels no need to express gratitude. Conversely, one's thanks to Hashem is a beautiful expression of emuna.

The full redemption of our people will come when we all learn to thank Hashem, especially for His limitless love for each of us. With gratitude, a person can lift himself from the deepest impurity and rise to a level where he merits miracles. Tell yourself how much Hashem loves you and how much He cares about your welfare – much more than you care about yourself.

57. Attaining Simple Emuna

A divorced woman came to me complaining about the difficulties of raising five children on her own. I told her, "I understand your difficulties. But, thank G-d, you have five healthy children. I can give you a long list of childless women who would be happy to switch with you. Decide with whom you would like to change places…"

I gave an emuna lesson in a prison. I told the inmates, "Come with me to the oncology ward of the nearest hospital; let's ask the patients where they'd rather be – sick in the hospital or healthy in jail. I promise you that they'd all be delighted to exchange "gifts" with you…"

With real emuna, you don't compare your fate to that of anyone else. However, when things are tough and darkness surrounds a person, he needs a reminder that many others have even greater difficulties.

A person who believes strongly in Hashem's individual precision Divine Providence never compares himself to anyone, for He believes that Hashem is directing his life in the very best manner imaginable.

58. Happiest in the World

A young man named Alon Paz was paralyzed from the neck down. He had a magnetic electrode on his forehead and he'd write by pointing at the letters on the visual keyboard on his computer screen in front of him. This electrode was a computer mouse that he'd move up or down, right or left by subtle movements of his forehead. Alon would write Torah commentaries and answer letters that people would send him. He wrote the following letter:

"Shalom! My name is Alon Paz and I'm 38. I was born in Hod Hasharon with handicapped legs, yet I grew up independent. I could walk a few steps, drive a car, write and do things on my own. Six years ago, driving my special car for handicapped people like myself, I was in a serious accident. Because of the accident, I became a paraplegic. My diaphragm was crushed so I'm now on a respirator. In effect, I have no use of my hands, legs or lungs. But, thank G-d, I'm alive.

"Today, I'm in a geriatric hospital, 'Beit Rivka' in Petah Tikva. The accident was instrumental in strengthening my emuna. Thanks to the rabbis and good people who visit me, I am able to learn Torah. I even have regular learning partners.

"I never leave my room which is a private one. Torah and prayer occupy all of my time. I'm sharing with you how I cope with my situation. Emuna gives me the will to keep on living. I hope you will derive encouragement from this letter. Usually, a person with the slightest difficulty or discomfort complains. He thinks that Hashem is not being fair to him. He cannot understand why he deserves anything outside his comfort zone. I don't remember ever asking why to Hashem. Indeed, I thank Him all day long for my ability to learn, to pray and to communicate with others. I know that the Creator is doing the very best in the world for me. There is no one but Him! Father in Heaven, I love You!

"Hashem is the Creator and I am His creation. He is the Father and I am His son. He is the King and I am the servant. There is no one but Him. Who am I to oppose His will? I trust Him no matter what He does or decides. He has His own considerations that I cannot begin to understand.

"No brains or emuna are required to say 'Thank You' for something obviously good that you're pleased with. We must thank Him, though, for the things that hurt and cause us to suffer. This purifies us and atones for sin, enabling us to walk right into paradise in the next world.

"You could compare me to a match living in a matchbox, alone most of the time in my tiny room. I don't see sun or stars, green grass or blue skies. I have four walls and a light bulb over my head. But I know that I'm not missing anything, for the material world is nothing more than a vanity fair of illusions and lusts. I spend all day long with Hashem in solitude and personal prayer when I'm not learning with my learning partners. I'm not missing out on anything. In the next world, I'll get a zillion times more than I got in this world. In that respect, my fate is better than almost everyone else's.

"Today, I understand what few others do – my body is of secondary importance. Life down here is oh so temporary. So is the body. But the soul is eternal and my soul is healthy. I'm happy – I have no complaints to the Creator. Thank You, Hashem!

"Did you ever appreciate your body and all the parts that function? Your eyes and your pinky finger – do you take them for granted? Do you appreciate the ability to scratch your nose when it itches? Why is that not a tremendous blessing? When was the last time that you thanked Hashem for your big toe? Do you know how many millions of brain impulses are required to lift a finger? Each is a gift!

"I can't lift a finger. If a fly lands on my nose and torments me, I can't scratch my nose or chase the fly away. Do you begin to realize all that you must be thankful for? Do yourself a favor and thank the Creator.

"Why complain that the elevator isn't working when you have legs that are healthy enough to climb the stairs? Don't be lazy. Don't whine. Use the staircase and thank Hashem on the way. Thank Him again when you reach your desired floor. Thank Him for the wonderful exercise that He chose for you to do, because He wants you – His beloved son and daughter – to be healthy. Say thank You when you shower and when you dress yourself because there are people like me who can't perform those functions.

"Appreciate everything the Creator gives you. Be happy – I am, because life is beautiful."

-        *This ends Alon's letter.*

Rabbi Kobi Levy, who wrote about Alon Paz in one of his books, said that not long ago, Alon was invited to speak in front of 1,800 volunteers of "Ezer Mitzion". He told them, "You look at me with no use of hands or legs. Don't pity me. I am very happy. If Hashem sent me a rich burly, healthy guy that would want to change places with me, I would not agree because I know that Hashem is doing what's best for Alon Paz. Anyone who has the emuna and closeness to

Hashem that I have is the really fortunate person."

Alon's story teaches us that the good life is a life of emuna, living the emuna that everything Hashem does is for the very best.

If you have a mouth and you can speak, you can talk to Hashem! What does a person need in this world? Prayer, Torah and closeness to Hashem is everything – nothing else matters. We should never stop saying thank You for what we have.

Any lack of joy a person has in this world is a lack of emuna. There is no bad in the world. Hashem does what's best for each of us. That is why we should never ever stop saying thank You.

59. True Emuna

A non-Jewish Spanish-speaking woman tried to have children for twenty years with no success. The doctors said that there was no way she could have children. As Hashem is the merciful Creator, He enabled her to hear a gratitude lesson of mine that was translated into Spanish by my student, Rabbi Yonatan Gal'ed shlit'a.

The above-mentioned woman had never read an emuna book or listened to an emuna CD in her life. Yet, she took the lesson to heart and started thanking Hashem for thirty minutes a day that she didn't have children. She didn't whine or complain – she was sincere. Within a month, she became pregnant! She wrote us, "The Jews have real emuna – I said thank You and I saw salvation."

Like Alon Paz in the previous story, this woman accepted the Creator's will with no reservations. She turned to Him with pure and innocent emuna and gratitude, truly happy with her lot in life. Hashem seemed to be saying, "If you're happy in this situation and still thanking Me, now I'll give you a really big reason to thank Me!" She saw the results.

Every one of us must take this to heart. Do we thank Hashem even though things aren't going the way we'd like them to? Are we discouraged by a little difficulty or disappointment?

Alon Paz had to cope with a ton of tribulations all at once. In most cases, Hashem gives people tribulations little by little. So whenever you encounter a painful setback or acute difficulty, remember that Hashem is giving you something that you are able to cope with that's entirely for your ultimate good. Does it still feel too painful? Remember Alon Paz's tribulations. Once you do, you can thank Hashem for your lot in life.

A person complained to me bitterly about his marital difficulties. I told him, "Sure – it's true what you are saying. But after all, you have healthy children. You too are healthy. You have the power to go out to the field and spend six hours in personal prayer. Why don't you?"

A person must express gratitude constantly, but especially at times of crises. The crisis is the best thing in the world for you because it will uplift you and bring you closer to Hashem.

The only trouble in the world is when a person lacks emuna. With emuna, there are no troubles.

Why are you crying? What are you complaining about? Rejoice! Be happy and never lay down your best weapon, emuna. Live the reality that Hashem is good and He knows what He's doing; and, everything He is doing for you is for your ultimate welfare!

60. A Ticket to Salvation

A man told me that he wanted to travel to Uman for Rosh Hashanah but that he lacked the funds. He figured that if he doesn't have the money for a plane ticket, then that's Hashem's will too. He began thanking Hashem, "Thank you, Hashem, that I don't have money to go to Uman."

At work, he asked his friend if he plans to go to Uman. The friend couldn't go that year but he said, "Here, take my credit card and go buy a ticket – you're going to Uman!"

This was the small miracle. The big miracle was that his army reserve unit called and told him that he had to stand trial for some offense and that he couldn't leave the country in the meanwhile. On the spot, he started thanking Hashem: "Master of the World, thank You for not letting me go to Uman, this time for a different reason, because You already gave me the money…" Suddenly, he received a phone call from his reserve duty unit that his commander decided to cancel the trial – the charges were dropped. We hear stories like this all the time. Gratitude leads from one salvation to another.

61. The Instant Ticket

A young man attended my lecture in Beitar. He heard about someone who didn't have money for a ticket to Uman who, after thanking Hashem for a mere half hour, received a gift from someone – a ticket to Uman! The young man then remembered that he didn't have a ticket yet either.

Meanwhile, the same young man heard another story about someone who suffered from terrible pains in his legs – he said thank You for a half hour and the pain disappeared. Encouraged by these stories, the young man started thanking Hashem that he didn't yet have a ticket. When he arrived home that evening, he met his neighbor. The neighbor asked, "So, are going to Uman this Rosh Hashanah?"

The young man answered, "May Hashem have mercy on me."

The neighbor said, "Of course Hashem has mercy! Here…" On the spot, the neighbor gave him a ticket voucher.

62. Painless Matchmaking

Someone told me about a 35-year-old bachelor in his neighborhood, a nice-looking fellow with a fantastic personality who everyone was fond of. Yet, he couldn't find a soul-mate. The whole neighborhood was praying for him, but nothing seemed to help. He finally listened to the CD, "Stop Crying."

The bachelor started to thank Hashem daily for the fact that he was not yet married. "Hashem, I know that whatever You do is the very best for me – thank You! I really mean it, with all my heart. I'm happy with whatever You give me, beloved Father!" Two weeks later, he found his soul-mate. Such is the power of gratitude.

Don't pray that your deficiency should disappear – pray for emuna. If you lack income, it's because you lack emuna. If you lack a soul-mate, that too is from a lack of emuna. Beg Hashem to give you real emuna!

When a person prays for income, there can be a complaint against him upstairs, that he doesn't believe that this too is for his ultimate good. The whole purpose of life's challenges is to bring us to emuna. If he believed in Hashem and believe that everything is for the very best, and if he sang, dance and thank Hashem, he'd truly be happy. Emuna is true happiness, being happy with one's lot in life. Since his challenge or deficiency triggered his emuna growth, it was surely the best thing in the world for him.

Are you having a hard time in life? Get to work on emuna. If a person has emuna, he doesn't need wake-up calls. Don't ever forget that gratitude is the greatest expression of emuna. With gratitude and emuna, one removes the root cause of any deficiency. So for any problem in life, thank Hashem with all your heart!

Realize that your deficiency is your perfection. There is no sorrow or no bad. Emuna teaches that the Creator in His omniscience knows that you can only fulfill your full inner potential if you have certain challenges in life. So as these challenges and difficulties have the potential of bringing you closer to emuna and to Hashem, they are truly and intrinsically good!

Hold on with emuna. Cast your logic aside. Logic says, "You're finished, pal! There's no hope…" Emuna says the opposite: "I'm just now beginning to get myself in gear; life is great! Thank You, Hashem!"

63. The Rescue Wedding

One of my students was at a wedding; everyone was dancing and having a great time except one man who was standing to the side with a look of melancholy on his face. My student went over to him and tried to cheer him up. The sad-looking man told him that a swindler had stolen hundreds of thousands of shekels from him in a fake business deal, leaving him penniless, depressed and severed from the Creator.

My student began to convince the man that this too was for his ultimate good. At first, the man didn't want to listen. Nevertheless, my student was insistent and persuasive. He succeeded in convincing the man to thank Hashem for one hour.

The man spent the hour thanking Hashem for losing his money. Four hours later, he received a telephone call that he had inherited a five-bedroom condominium that was worth more than double of the sum he lost. He also received enough cash to start a new business and get back on his feet. He called my student and thanked him: "You saved my life!"

Gratitude is one's personal redemption! Remember what Rebbe Natan of Breslev said: "If everyone listened to the tsaddikim who teach them that everything Hashem does is for the best; and if they believed that it's all for the best; and if they thanked Hashem for the seemingly bad as well as the good, all suffering and exile would end immediately and give way to the Geula, the full redemption of our people."

64. The Son who got Married

For fifteen years, a mother cried that her son had not yet married. She decided to change her approach and said to Hashem, "From now on, I won't cry anymore. I'll just thank You, both for Your loving-kindnesses and for my son who is not yet married. A short while later, her son met a wonderful girl and got married. The mother had merely decided to stop crying and to start thanking, and she received a salvation almost immediately…

This is what our esteemed teacher Rebbe Nachman of Breslev teaches us, namely, that **a person's only real suffering is from a lack of spiritual awareness. One who is spiritually aware knows that everything is a product of Hashem's precision Divine Providence; he therefore suffers no tribulations and he doesn't feel sorrow** (Likutei Moharan I:250)." One who clings to his emuna and knows that everything is from Hashem and all for the best lives a joy-filled life. He sees how everything always turns around for the very best.

65. Give me Burekas!

A heavy, bulletproof bus lost its brakes on the road to Beitar. Ultimately, it crashed into a car parked on the side of road and there it stopped. Only moments before the collision, a father and son got out of the car. People asked the father how he merited a miracle like that. He answered that he listens to Rabbi Shalom Arush's lectures and that he thanks Hashem all the time. By virtue of his daily prayers of gratitude, Hashem performed a miracle for him.

Grateful people see miracles that override nature – it's that simple! They know that Hashem can do whatever He wants whenever He wants.

I've explained repeatedly that a person sees salvations when he constantly expresses gratitude to Hashem. This is for several reasons:

1.   With gratitude, a person invokes Divine favor; his prayers assume a special charm to them and Hashem readily accepts them. The more a person expresses gratitude, the more Hashem is willing to help him in a beautifully upward spiral of thanks leading to salvations and more thanks leading to more salvations. Conversely, Hashem is not inclined to come to the aid of an ingrate. Indeed, one should not help an ingrate because he won't express thanks.

2.   Hashem leads a person down the path of that person's desires. When a person believes that Hashem does everything for the very best, Hashem makes everything turn out for the very best. Yet, when a person believes that there's bad in the world, Heaven forbid, things turn out bad according to his belief and his life goes askew.

3.   A person who expresses gratitude for everything fulfills the express purpose of creation, which is to reveal Hashem's mercy. He becomes firmly bound to the Creator and mitigates any stern judgments at their source.

4.   The Slonimer Rebbe osb"m says that when a person thanks Hashem and accepts the way He runs

his life, then measure-for-measure, Hashem accepts that person's actions with no stern judgments, only with love and mercy.

66. Thank You in Every Sense of the Word

An unmarried man came to me; over the years, he had done every fathomable spiritual ploy in order to get married. Meanwhile, all his brothers got married. At every wedding, family and friends would bless him, "May it be your turn soon." No prayers or blessings did any tangible good. He was still stuck. Finally, he learned about gratitude. For a while, he said "Thank You" to Hashem. He said to me, "I say nothing but thank You…and I'm still not married!"

In light of everything we've learned until now, is it feasible that a person expresses gratitude yet fails to see a salvation?

I told him, "You express gratitude as simply another ploy and not because you mean it. You still don't believe that everything is for the best and that's why you haven't yet seen salvation. Even if you say a thousand thank Yous, until you believe that everything is for the best and therefore be sincere in your thanks, forget about salvation. Sure, you'll mitigate stern judgments somewhat, because after all, you are saying thank You instead of whining. But, you won't hit the big jackpot unless you reinforce your emuna that everything is from Hashem and all for the best."

I told him to cast his logic aside and to thank Hashem in every sense of the word, with all his heart, and to accept whatever Hashem decides.

Not just this person, but many others as well complain to me that they said thank You but "it didn't work". That's because they aren't pleased with the way Hashem conducts their lives. True gratitude is not just when the sun is shining – it's when there are dark clouds overhead as well.

Gratitude isn't worth much when it is not sincere; when a person says a thank You that is not compatible with the way he feels. He still thinks that whatever is happening to him is bad. How can he see salvation when he's not telling the truth? Can dishonesty lead to salvation? No way! Only the truth can. Therefore, an expression of gratitude must be the outcome of a person's belief that everything Hashem is doing is truly for the best. No one is required to know that everything is for the best; only Hashem knows that. Yet, we are required to *believe* that it's all for the best.

An expression of gratitude that doesn't bring about a salvation is probably a request that was parading as a thank You. No wonder it failed to bring results. One's goal must be to get closer to Hashem and not to get rid of unwanted problems.

A person who desires to get close to Hashem is not looking for a solution to his problem per se. Since his goal is to get close to Hashem, he sees salvations on the way.

One whose goal is to effect a salvation is thinking about himself and not about his relationship with Hashem. It's just like those who try to get close to tsaddikim in order to merit salvations. If they thought that going to a doctor or a lawyer would bring them salvation, they'd do that instead. This is the result of a salvation-oriented motivation rather than a person's desire to get close to Hashem. Therefore, people who chase all types of solutions to problems never stop chasing – they solve nothing. But, those who use their problems as a catapult to get closer to Hashem succeed both in getting closer to Hashem and in seeing salvation to their problems.

In light of the above, my message to all those who tell me that they say "thank You" but their problems have yet to be solved: yes, you're right – you do say thank You, but it's because you heard that it's an effective ploy. If you look deeply at yourself, you'll see that your thank You has a whining tone to it. You're still complaining but you've changed your prayer strategy and have substituted the word "complaint" for the word "gratitude". This type of "gratitude", which comes from the lips of person whose heart still harbors complaints, will never be effective in solving anything. One must believe that Hashem is doing everything for the best in order to express gratitude with sincerity. Such expressions of gratitude bring salvations.

Strengthening our emuna that everything is for the best must therefore precede expressions of gratitude. Don't say thank You without thinking. Don't look at the clock like a factory worker about to punch out, as if all you care about is fulfilling your quota of thank You minutes. It's upsetting when people are looking at their watch when they're speaking to us; why should we do that to Hashem?

Don't turn gratitude into a rabbit's foot or some other good-luck charm. Believe that everything is from Hashem and all for the best, and then say thank You. It's not a ploy or a charm. Gratitude is the way to get close to Hashem. If that is a person's intention, he'll see every single salvation.

67. Saved by the Gravel

A certain business shark was super-successful in commerce and money-making, but his interpersonal relations were terrible. He was mean and unpleasant.

He was just about to purchase the entire seventeenth floor of Azrieli Towers in Tel Aviv. A shyster rip-off artist succeeded in tempting him to buy real estate in Romania instead, promising astronomical returns on his money. It was a scam for the land he purchased was zoned for agricultural use only and certainly not for real-estate development as the shyster had promised. The shark's loss was tremendous. Like dominoes, his fortune tumbled and the authorities issued a warrant against him for tax evasion.

He tried to borrow money but no one of his "friends" would lend him a dime. With no choice, he turned to a "gray-market" loan company that lent money to anyone, but at cut-throat interest rates. Their office was – you guessed it – in the prestigious Azrieli Towers building, on the seventeenth floor! All those spacious offices could have been his. Instead, he was here groveling for a loan…

He signed a whole stack of papers and then received the loan in cash. Before he left Azrieli Towers, he decided to tour the upper floors. He ascended floor by floor, surveying how the offices seemed to be thriving. Meanwhile, he was eating his heart out. Finally, he reached the roof. The door slammed behind him and he found himself locked out of the building. He tried to get back in but he couldn't.

He pounded on the door with his fists and yelled, but no one heard him. He looked down and saw people below on the sidewalks and tried yelling to them, but who can hear a voice calling from 49 floors up? No one looked up. He gesticulated wildly with his hands, but no one paid attention. He got the idea that maybe he should throw something down to catch someone's attention. What could interest people more than money from heaven? He'd throw money down, and then someone would have to look up to see where it's coming from, and then someone would rescue him from the locked roof.

And that's what he did. He started throwing down wads of 200-Shekel bills (about $50 each) to the people below. Sadly, no one lifted his gaze upwards. Rather, they just chased after the bills. He started to panic – now what would he do, die of hunger and exposure up on the locked roof? He decided in desperation to throw down the entire bag of money. Below, people went berserk chasing the "money from heaven" but still, no one looked up.

He reached the moment of truth that even the biggest skeptic and heretic reaches. With no one to turn to, he called out to G-d. "Master of the World, if You're around somewhere, save me! There's no one else to help me." Just then, a new idea flashed in his mind. He looked around on the roof, which was covered with all types of construction debris including gravel. He decided to throw gravel on the people's heads below – that would surely make them look up, to see who was tormenting them.

He threw down a handful of gravel, which reached its mark. People looked up - cursing, shouting and shaking their fists. Someone called the emergency police number and complained that some idiot was throwing down gravel from the roof of the Azrieli building endangering people below. The police rushed to the scene and wanted to arrest him on the spot, thinking he was intentionally malicious. He told them, "Come with me to the 17th floor and you'll see that a few hours ago, I borrowed money there. Then, I came up here and got locked in. I threw down all the money so that someone would notice me, but the pedestrians didn't even look up. Then, I got the idea that if I threw down a handful of gravel, someone would notice me. It worked, because you guys came right away!"

The police believed him and released him. He went home in a worse predicament than before. Not only did he have a warrant against him for tax evasion, but now he owed a huge sum of money to a gray-market loan shark. He pondered his situation: "When I threw down money, nobody looked at me. But, when I threw down gravel, everybody looked up. The Creator is conveying an important message to me. He's the One Who gave me the idea to throw down the gravel. That's what He does!"

The bankrupt businessman had a "eureka moment": he realized that when Hashem threw down riches from Heaven on him, he never looked up. Instead, he attributed all of his success to himself and to his own cunning in commerce. He never said "Thank You" a single time for his successes. But, when Hashem "threw gravel" on his head, he immediately looked up and turned to Him for help.

So many of us act like that, failing to look up when things are good but pleading to the Heavens when things seem otherwise…

At that point, the tough Israeli businessman broke down in deep sobs and apologized to Hashem for never thanking Him. He asked Hashem to accept his humble return to Him and he started thanking Him for every blessing in his life that he could ever remember. He thanked Hashem for the current difficulties and for waking him up the way He did.

A day or two later, the businessman received a phone call. An old longshot investment of agricultural land that he purchased outside of Bucharest, Romania had been rezoned for construction. Instantly, he became a billionaire! Now he really had a tremendous reason to thank Hashem!

This story has a deep moral to it. Hashem fills our lives with abundance and loving-kindness every moment of the day. People fail to look up and see where the abundance and loving-kindness are coming from. They only remember to lift their eyes in times of trouble. Therefore, we should profusely thank Hashem for everything we have before the gravel in life starts falling on our heads.

68. The Respectable Stipend

Our students were in Tzfat, distributing emuna books, pamphlets and CDs. They met someone who told them about a poor Torah student who gets a mere 900 shekel-per-month (about $225) stipend from his kollel. Despite all types of efforts, nothing helped the young man augment his meager income. He received a gratitude CD that explained the importance of daily personal prayer and expressions of gratitude. He began to incorporate the CD's advice into his life.

Several weeks later, a stranger approached the poor Torah student. The stranger was looking for a dependable Torah scholar who would learn in behalf of his deceased father's memory and credit, promising to attend to the needs of the scholar, his wife and children. From that day on, the Torah scholar received the respectable stipend of 7,000 shekels a month (about $1750).

A person must always be happy with his lot in life. But, even when he feels deficiency, he should thank Hashem for what He has. Such expressions of thanks generate Divine compassion. Also, when a person is happy all the time, no matter what, Hashem gives him more and more reasons to rejoice. At any rate, until the window of opportunity opens, a person should strengthen himself in emuna and trust, happily rejoicing in the blessings that he already has.

Rabbi Elimelech of Lizhensk writes (Noam Elimelech, parshat Beshalach): "If a person trusted in G-d with a believing heart, his income would arrive effortlessly". A little bit of gratitude goes a long way, so just imagine the power of profuse gratitude!

69. From Stroke to Simcha

A man in his sixties with no connection at all to Torah and mitzvah observance suffered a stroke that rendered him blind. While still very sick, he received a court order that threatened to confiscate all his possessions if he didn't urgently repay a long list of debts that he had.

The man fell into deep depression. Hashem had mercy on him and he received the CD "Stop Crying" from one of my students. He listened to it several times until he started humming the songs that we sing on that disc. He started thanking Hashem too and the cloud of depression began lifting to the extent that he was beginning to feel happy.

After a few hours of lying in bed, listening to the CD and thanking Hashem, he broke out in tears. He asked Hashem to forgive Him and to have mercy on him and come to his aid. Miraculously, his vision returned to him. Then, a person knocked on his door and gave him the gift of enough money to cover his debts – another unfathomable miracle. Remember, we're talking about a person with no connection to Torah observance. Yet, he contemplated teshuva while profusely and sincerely thanking Hashem for a few hours straight. This shows the immense power of gratitude.

People with difficulties make tremendous mistakes when they start doubting Hashem. Hashem isn't punishing them – they're punishing themselves! Rather than complaining and asking why, they should strengthen their emuna, for nothing else helps. Those who take advantage of challenging times to strengthen themselves climb the spiritual ladder and get so much closer to Hashem.

This is the song we've been singing for years: **I don't understand a thing; I only believe that it's all for the best.** We let our emuna override our logic. Hashem sees what we cannot. What might look bad to the human eye is nothing but Divine compassion and all for the very best. Therefore, anyone who clings to emuna ultimately sees big salvations.

70. Salvation in a Dream

A woman came up to me after my lecture in Ofrah and told me that her baby son was deathly sick and that he didn't have much longer to live. She cried her eyes out to Hashem, so much so that she fell asleep. In a dream, she saw the words, "Rabbi Shalom Arush" and "emuna". She saw a notice in the local newspaper about my upcoming lecture in her city. She came and began to learn about emuna. Her husband also attended the lecture. Since then, her baby began to eat and she sees salvations on top of salvations.

Oftentimes, the road to emuna is strewn with obstacles. As a test of our faith, things frequently get worse before they get better. That's exactly what happened to Moses when he first asked Pharaoh, "Let my people go!" Moses also suffered from internal strife, for Dothan, Aviram and Korach made life even more difficult for him.

Moses certainly believed that everything is for the best. He never put down his chief weapon – prayer. We must recall what we mentioned at the beginning of this book: Rebbe Natan of Breslev says that by believing that everything is for the best and by thanking Hashem for everything – for the seemingly bad as well as for the good – all exile and tribulations are nullified and we merit immediately the complete redemption of our people, the *Geula*.

Rebbe Natan also explains that there are Dothans and Avirams in every generation. These are the dark-side spiritual forces that challenge a person who is strengthening himself in emuna, on the way to his own personal redemption. They manifest themselves in all sorts of difficulties, which we have the power – with emuna and Hashem's assistance – to overcome.

The emuna-loyal individuals who heed the words of the generation's true righteous leader – the "Moses" of the generation – prevail in the challenges against them and their faith. By way of gratitude, they emerge from the deepest darkness. That darkness are the "Dothan and Aviram" of the generation - those who fall prey to the dark side and create dissension and opposition to the emuna-loyal individuals. That darkness perpetuates Diaspora and exile.

No matter how bleak the future might look, Hashem is with us. More and more people are following the path of emuna and gratitude, nullifying themselves to the Moses of the generation and thanking Hashem for everything. This will surely invoke Divine mercy and hasten the full and complete redemption, soon, amen.

71. Words of Consolation

On Lag B'Omer of 5769 (2009), a fatal road accident happened on the way home from Meron. Until 2:30 AM, I was at the funeral of the five martyrs, two adults and three children. The next morning, I woke up with a deep sorrow in my heart. I had to work hard to uplift myself from the abyss of sadness.

In the months before Lag B'Omer, Hashem had given me the privilege of teaching many lessons about gratitude. My heart always echoed that everything is for the best and that there is no bad in the world. I know nothing and understand nothing; I only believe that everything is for the best. By telling myself this repeatedly, my emuna and joy returned to me.

I then asked myself, "What does a person do without words of emuna to console himself? How does he live? How does he function? We see people break down all the time from tests of faith that are not as hard as this one. I resolved to spread and teach emuna and gratitude with even greater vigor.

We're humans; we must not deny the pain or our feelings, for they are real. Even if someone has perfect emuna, he still feels pain when he suffers an injury. Yet, emuna gives him the strength to continue in life.

I made a condolence call to a young widow. I came to console but I left consoled. The young widow told me that in her husband's final months, he discovered a treasure – the "Garden" series of emuna books. He learned them in depth and wrote notes on all the margins. They had dozens of emuna CDs in their home, which they listened to all day long. After several months of their learning together, her husband left her to go on his final journey…

The widow said, "I praise and thank Hashem for everything. If it were not improper, I'd sing and dance as well. My husband prepared for me for this. In his last will and testament, he ordered me to thank Hashem for everything. I am honoring my husband's words to the letter – yes, I am thanking Hashem all the time. He knows what He is doing and He does only good. Thank You, Hashem!"

If this courageous young widow cried and complained all the time, would she bring her husband back from the grave? Definitely not! She must continue in life and raise her orphans the best way possible. Crying would only destroy her emuna. Sure, tears of longing will trickle down her face - that's part of mourning. Yet, a mourner should never mourn more than what Jewish Law prescribes, for Hashem does only good. According to emuna, there's no bad in the world for Hashem does only good. Believing that something is bad is tantamount to heresy.

Jewish Law considers human nature. Even though emuna teaches that there is no bad in the world, Jewish Law has respective time periods for crying (the first three days after the loved one departs), for severe mourning (the *shiva* period, or first seven days), for moderate mourning (the first thirty days) and for lighter mourning (the first year). One should never be more stringent in mourning that what the Code of Jewish Law requires.

What about the good people who get plucked from the world at a young age? What about innocent babies and children who suffer terminal diseases? Hashem enabled me to understand that such incomprehensible scenarios are like a person who arrived late to the theater after the start of the play. The play is almost half over and he sees a male actor on stage yelling at a female actor. The late guy yells out, "Hey, you bully – what are you yelling at that poor defenseless woman for?"

Someone from the audience sneers at the late playgoer and snarls, "Will you please be quiet? If you had seen the beginning of the play, you would have understood that the woman is a wicked witch!"

That's the way things are with people. They make judgments without seeing the whole picture. There are so many details that they are not aware of. But, if a person had spiritual eyes, he'd know that Hashem is just and he wouldn't have any questions.

Since our sight is limited, we must believe that Hashem is doing everything for the very best. We frequently see how the seemingly bad turns out to be good. For example, a person who misses his flight and is sorely disappointed. Later, he hears that the plane crashed in midair. Now he realizes how the seemingly bad was a gift from Above.

Naturally, it's not easy to thank Hashem during times of disappointment when one can't yet see how everything is for the best. However, this is the time to thank Hashem, for this is emuna! Thank Him when you miss your bus, your train or your plane, immediately, on the spot in real time! Don't wait until later when you understand how it was all for the best, because that is simply normal gratitude without the added merit of emuna.

Missing the plane is just one small example. There are myriads in life. What's more, myriads of considerations go into one tiny decision that Hashem makes. One tiny Divine decision defy the greatest human brainpower. The concealed good in many things that Hashem does will not be apparent until Moshiach comes. Meanwhile, we must hold on with emuna that everything is for the best.

Hashem is the only One who sees and knows in depth the path that each person must pursue. Each person's path is full of hardships and obstacles; emuna is the only way to overcome them.

73. Guarding the Soul

There was another instance when I made a condolence call to a young widow and I went away consoled. Already by the fresh and yet uncovered grave, the widow departed from her husband by thanking Hashem. Those who attended the funeral shivered in awe of the young widow's emuna and inner strength.

Everyone would have understood her had she cried including the Heavenly Court. What could be more natural?

Yet, there's a thin line between crying and bitterness. People with emuna also cry when they feel pain. Yet without emuna, the tears of pain become tears of bitterness. Emuna eases the trauma.

What impressed me even more during the week of mourning were the children. They surrounded their mother with love, while they were smiling and joyful. If I hadn't seen it with my own eyes, I couldn't have believed it. Upon seeing this beautiful phenomenon, I said to myself, "Imagine how different the family would look if the mother was wailing and the children were sobbing, calling out for their father. Imagine how the family would function if the mother were casting questions and accusations at Hashem."

Children who hear accusing questions directed at Hashem become spiritually impaired for life. They are given legitimacy to pity themselves. Their chances of ever attaining emuna are close to nil.

How wonderful that the orphans have a mother with emuna, who thanks Hashem constantly! This is the superb role model that Hashem has granted them. They don't feel unfortunate or pitiful by virtue of the mother's emuna.

The widow's emuna strengthened all her family and friends. If she had broken down, they would have also. The deceased husband's brother, who was far from emuna, was so impressed with his sister-in-law's faith and courage that he too began learning about emuna. Had his sister-in-law wail in grief all day long, he would never want to hear anything about the Creator or about emuna. He would have asked belligerently, "Is this the reward that my sister-in-law got for becoming a *baalat teshuva*, a newly observant Jewess? Is this the reward that my dead brother got for doing teshuva and returning to Hashem – losing his wife, his life and his children?"

Living her life with the emuna that everything is truly for the best, the widow not only overcomes the evil inclination but serves as a shining example to everyone in her proximity. If she is happy and smiling, anyone can be happy and smiling.

There are few tests of faith that are more difficult than becoming a young widow and mother of orphans. She not only lost her friend for life, she lost the other half of her soul! Nevertheless, we see how learning emuna – especially by way of the emuna books and CDs – change the world for the better. When a widow can stand in front of her deceased husband's casket and thank Hashem, know full well that **the days of Moshiach are arriving**.

If emuna enables a young widow to cope so wonderfully and to continue on with her life, imagine what it does in much less severe cases. Anyone who encounters problems - even small ones – with whining and complaining will certainly live in darkness and depression. With emuna though, a person is vibrant, no matter what.

The way a person handles challenges affects his whole family. For example, two people can be in debt. Yet, one has emuna and the other doesn't. The emuna individual meets his challenges with lots of prayer and optimism. The other is full of stress and worry. Needless to say, the atmosphere of each of these two people's households is a direct result of the household-head's emuna. The one who meets his challenge with emuna creates an aura of positivity at home. The other one leaves his wife and children with worry and anxiety, and their home is a purgatory.

The emuna husband and father saves so much needless stress and worry from his wife and children. The worry doesn't pay off his debts, so who needs it? While he copes with emuna and seeks Hashem's assistance, his fortunate children don't even know that a problem exists.

With the above in mind, our lives are basically a choice between emuna and purgatory. Do we accept everything with joy and gratitude, or are we grouchy, worried and complaining? Anyone who therefore does his or her best to implement the lessons of this book will taste paradise in this world. Not only that, but they'll see miracles and salvations. Don't be discouraged, though. Gratitude is powerful, but so is the negative spiritual force that tries to keep a person from emuna and gratitude. Yet, our self-reinforcement in emuna and gratitude is the greatest investment we can make, for it stays with us in the next world as well as in this world. It's worth the effort!

We must be thankful for every little thing, taking nothing for granted! Nothing is too insignificant to thank Hashem for. If you take a good look, a thousand years of continuous thanks is not enough to pay for our life and livelihood, our health, our families and every tiny mitzvah and word of Torah that Hashem enables us to learn and perform. We must express gratitude for everything we can think of. Gratitude must be an integral part of our very being, like each breath and heartbeat.

73. The Boy Ran Away from School

One of my rabbinical students told me that his son came home crying from school in the middle of the morning. No parent enjoys such things, but like everything else, it's from Hashem and all for the best.

My student had heard quite a few lessons of mine on gratitude, so he began thanking Hashem. He did some soul-searching, asking himself what Hashem could possibly want from him. Only afterwards, he spoke to his son. His son told him that a bully was bothering him at school so he fled home. Patiently and calmly, his father told him how to deal with this problem through emuna:

"My son, who picked on you - the bully? You know that everything comes from Hashem, right? Hashem does everything for the best. It looks like Hashem loves your prayers and wants to hear more of them. So, from today on, pray to Hashem and ask that He protect you against bullies so that they won't bother you anymore. Ask Hashem to help you strengthen your emuna." He then sent his son back to school.

What do we learn from this story? The boy learned a lesson in emuna and learned to pray better. Even though his parents teach him to pray, it's not like experience teaching him to pray. The need to cope triggered a strengthening of emuna.

The father was faced with a painful situation that could have incited his anger or severe negative emotions such as a desire to retaliate against the bully, his parents and the school administration – the seemingly guilty parties. But, he first said "thank You" and he approached the crisis calmly and with emuna. When faced with such a challenge, it's difficult at the moment to see how it's for the best, but it surely is. With patience and in time, we see how such things turn out for the best. Therefore, where understanding kicks out, emuna kicks in. We must lean on our emuna always.

74. Thanking Hashem for the Little Things

Dear Rabbi Arush,

I'll be happy if you publicize my story – it will do much to help strengthen others.

I live in the town of Elad. Last year, I barely made a living doing all sorts of odd jobs. To make things worse, our ten-year-old washing machine broke down.

I didn't know what to do. At the time, I had no credit line at the bank and no money in my account to cover a check. I how no idea where salvation would come from.

Gathering my emuna, I decided to go window-shopping and search for a washing machine that suits our needs.

My husband tried to talk me out of it, saying that it's a waste of time. He wanted to try and give post-dated checks, but I refused to sign a check that we couldn't cover. I was just doing my effort, and I could afford to window-shop.

I went into store after store, checking models and prices. I asked about the advantages and disadvantages of various washing machines that were on the market. When I finished my window shopping, I phoned my dad and ask if he could help us purchase a washing machine. He was adamant that I must purchase the cheapest model, something that I can afford. I argued that with my many children, I need a large and durable machine. My father refused to help so I was back where I started.

As I walked out of the last store, and after my disappointing conversation with my father, I found a Torah newsletter on the sidewalk. There was an article there by Rabbi Arush speaking about the power of gratitude and how it turns severe judgments into merciful compassion, especially when a person thanks Hashem for his difficulties in life.

I arrived home and said to my husband, "Let's thank Hashem that our washing machine worked for ten years straight without giving us any problems. Let's also thank Him that we all have clothes and that there's something to throw in the washing machine. Now, let's thank Him that we don't have the money to purchase a washing machine now. That too is for the best."

Soon after we thanked Hashem, we received an ad brochure from a local appliance dealer in our mailbox. He had all types of machines on sale, cheaper than the ones I saw. I called my dad again and told him about the sale. This time, he softened up and said that he'd look for a suitable washing machine for us in a store near his house.

I got a call from the owner of the appliance store near my dad's house. He convinced my father not to buy the cheap machine and gave him a great deal with easy payments on the machine that I wanted. My dad agreed to purchase the machine!

I called my husband and told him to thank Hashem – this time, "Thank You, Hashem, for the privilege of saying 'Thank You'". Gratitude is living emuna!

We must pray for everything in life – big or small. Our sages teach us that when we pray for everything, every time our prayer is answered is another reinforcement of emuna.

Jewish law requires that we recite at least 100 benedictions every day. This was one of King David's statutes (see Midrash, Bamidbar Raba 18:21 and Tur, Orach Chaim 46). Rabbi Yehuda Halevi in his famed book "The Cuzari" (Essay 3) writes that one must thank Hashem for every tiny enjoyment in life and that the minimum thanks is 100 benedictions a day, not less. Yet, there is no amount of benedictions and thanks that can possibly and properly express Hashem's praise.

If a person is sick and becomes healed, he should certainly thank Hashem. But, if he isn't sick in the first place, shouldn't he thank Hashem tenfold? A person in debt who merits financial salvation must profusely thank Hashem. Isn't it proper when a person has food on the table and no debts to thank Hashem all the more? A person who has searched for his soul-mate for a dozen years finally finds her; he surely thanks Hashem! Yet, if he gets married relatively effortlessly having found his soul-mate at a young age, shouldn't he thank Hashem twenty times over? The same goes for children, for our home and for everything else big and small in life. Take nothing for granted and thank Hashem for everything, big and small!

We must remember that the most important thing to pray for is the spiritual aspect of our lives – emuna, character improvement and getting closer to Hashem. We must not forget on the way all the small spiritual favors that Hashem does for us and every tiny mitzvah that He enables us to perform. They may look small but they are big reasons to thank Hashem! Every prayer and every expression of gratitude revitalizes the soul.

Rebbe Natan once told his student, "I was once missing a button on my shirt. Rebbe Nachman told me, 'Pray to Hashem for a button.' I was shocked, thinking that I must pray for something so seemingly insignificant as a button in my shirt. Rebbe Nachman read my thoughts and asked, 'Is it beneath your dignity to pray for a button?' I learned my lesson…"

A person doesn't think that he must pray for the "small things" that he is capable of obtaining on his own. That's a mistaken and blemished notion! Such an attitude strengthens the heretical "might-of-my-right-hand" attitude. The spiritual reality of things is that we can do nothing, big or small, without Hashem's help.

The Ritb'a writes (commentary on Tractate Berachot 6) that the entire world was created for man's benefit and that man was created to thank and praise Hashem and to serve Him and fear Him. Those who do so sustain the world; the rest are like beasts who don't do the task that they were created to do. As such, those who thank Hashem fulfill their purpose in creation. They are worthy of miracles and great salvations.

75. The Smiling Parking Attendant

One of my students went into a parking lot. The attendant smiled at him. My student, accustomed to thanking Hashem for the big things as well as for the small, thanked Hashem that the parking attendant smiled at him. Then, he had doubts: "Maybe it's ridiculous for me to thank Hashem for something so insignificant?" This was only a fleeting thought and he quickly forgot all about it.

The next day, he had to park his car in the same lot. The parking attendant yelled at him this time and cursed him for parking the way he did. My student then understood that nothing should ever be taken for granted, for when Hashem wants, the same person or event can be pleasant or the total opposite. Therefore, we must thank Him for everything! We must educate ourselves to say thank You to Hashem, just like we educate our children to say thank you. Gratitude is a lofty form of Divine service, for it instills in a person he belief in and cognizance of Divine providence. It also brings a person closer to Hashem, for it uplifts a person from the heresy that conceals Hashem's light of loving-kindness.

76. Another Parking Story

Every day, a person must grow in spiritual awareness, in getting to know Hashem, in understanding the things that happen to him and in his ability to explain them better.

One Friday morning in the winter in Jerusalem, when Shabbat begins especially early, my student went shopping in the crowded Machane Yehuda market. He circled for twenty minutes but couldn't find a parking space. He prayed to Hashem for fifteen minutes more while circling and still didn't find a place to park. He remembered our teachings about gratitude, so as soon as he started thanking Hashem that he couldn't find a parking place, he saw a miracle – literally. Someone whom he didn't even know was sending other cars away and holding a perfect parking place for him right in front of the market. The guy called, "Hey, my brother – I've been holding this space for you!" My student had never seen that person before, and lo and behold, here he was calling him, "my brother" and holding a parking space for him. Weird, or what? No, with gratitude, you can work wonders.

Why doesn't prayer alone work the wonders that gratitude does?

Prayer is accepted according to a person's emuna – the more emuna he has, the more readily his prayers are accepted. A person's prayers for any deficiency he has indicate that he lacks emuna. Such a person prays, "Master of the World, I don't have a place to park. I need a parking space and only You can help me! Please have mercy on me, for I have no one else to turn to." It sounds like this person has emuna, right? Wrong – he lacks emuna. Why? He lacks the emuna that his current lack of a parking space is the best thing in the world for him. He perceives that his current situation is "bad" and he wants Hashem to make it good according to his wishes. But, Hashem does everything for the best. There is no bad in the world. If he thinks that his current lack of a parking space is bad, then he lacks emuna. This hinders his prayers from being accepted.

Gratitude, on the other hand, is an indication of complete emuna: everything is from Hashem and it's all great! The fact that I don't have a parking space is the best thing in the world for me. Thank You, Hashem. Once a person thanks Hashem, he can then ask for Hashem's help. That is prayer with emuna, the type of prayer that is answered.

77. Nobody Loses

Here's one more story about parking. My students live their gratitude, so they have many gratitude stories to tell me.

One of my students had a meeting in an office building in the Givat Shaul section of Jerusalem. He couldn't find a parking space and he was already late for the appointment. He circled around and around, but there wasn't even room to park a scooter. He was now fifteen minutes late so he began to pray, but his prayers didn't seem to be effective – there was still no place to park. Only then, he remembered one of the lessons he heard me deliver about gratitude.

My student told me, "Meanwhile, while thanking Hashem that I couldn't find a parking space and asking Hashem's forgiveness for not thanking Him for all the many blessings in my life, a car right behind me vacated its parking space, directly in front of the building where I needed to be. Before I knew it, another car came out of nowhere and grabbed the parking space that I was about to pull into. My first instinct was to fly out of the car and yell at the cheeky person who swiped my parking place. I caught myself and began thanking Hashem for losing this parking space. I told Hashem that I accept His will with no questions. I believe that everything He does is all for the best, no matter how far I have to walk to my appointment and no matter how late I'll be. That moment, a man from the car parked in front of where I was got out of his car and came up to my window. He told me that he was leaving his parking place to me; not only that, he gave me a paid parking coupon that was good for another whole hour."

"I learned two things," my student said. "First, with gratitude, you always benefit. Second, when you give in to someone to avoid an argument, you never lose."

78. A Fair Judgment Thanks to Gratitude

The next story shows how a person devoid of gratitude harbors negativity about himself, others and about the Creator, heaven forbid. On the other hand, grateful people are full of positivity and optimism. They see good in others and they avoid all sorts of stress and anxiety.

This story appeared on our Hebrew website at www. breslev.co.il:

"Last summer, I was involved in a road accident. Thank G-d, the elderly woman whom I was driving home and I escaped free of injury. At any rate, someone called an ambulance. The ambulance driver convinced the elderly woman to get into the ambulance and come to the hospital to undergo tests. She agreed.

"But, as soon as she got into the ambulance, the accident 'escalated' because now there was an officially 'injured' person. Now, there could be liability suits and I'd have to attend court cases. I could lose my license or even get time in jail…

"I'm familiar with Rav Arush's three principles of emuna, which he stresses throughout all of his books, especially "The Garden of Emuna": First, everything is from Hashem; second, everything is for the best; and third, everything is for a purpose – there must be a message for me in what is happening right now. I adjusted my thinking according to these three principles. It was a war fighting my evil inclination, which was telling me that I'm in big trouble. I was struggling to focus on Hashem and not on the evil inclination.

"In the midst of my inner struggle, I started blaming myself for what happened. Then, I shifted the blame to the Creator. After all, I was doing a favor – a mitzvah – by giving the old lady a free ride home; why would Hashem punish me for doing a mitzvah? Why do I have to go to court especially in these rough economic times when making even a minimal living is no joke?

"The recurrent thoughts of the accident and the prospects of a court case gave me no rest. I was full of bitterness and self-pity. I said to myself, "Rachel, it's just not fair that you're ending up as the victim of this accident…"

"A few months later, I received a letter from a lawyer saying that the old woman was suing me for damages that she incurred. My eyes couldn't believe what they saw. My blood boiled. The worst thoughts of revenge overcame me. I totally forgot about Hashem and the fact that He runs the world.

"Several weeks later, I began to feel physically ill. A few women in our community asked me to give a lesson about forgiveness. At the same time, I received a visit from a person who represented the elderly woman who was suing me. After giving me her name and contact information, he suggested that I call the woman and settle with her out of court.

"What's the common denominator of everything that I've told you till now?

"I decided to open one of Rav Shalom Arush's books. The page I "randomly" opened said, *'If a person doesn't see Hashem standing behind everything that's happening to him, he'll end up suffering even more…'*

"That's exactly what happened to me! Instead of thanking Hashem for the accident, I whined, complained and succumbed to a whole kaleidoscope of negativity. Because I didn't accept Hashem's verdict with love, I was now faced with a much worse verdict from flesh-and-blood. I should have thanked Hashem, but I didn't believe that everything was for the best. I failed to process Hashem's message. Then, I felt terrible.

"But, after reading one paragraph from a Rav Arush book, my mindset turned around. I understood that I must immediately stop feeling like a martyr. Although I still failed to understand how all this mess was for the best, I knew that I had to thank Hashem for all of it. It was time to cope with what Hashem put on my plate and to stop running away from it.

"Whatever the elderly woman sues me for is all from Hashem and I'll do His will.

"I tried calling the woman but it looked like the individual that was representing her gave me the wrong number. I decided to write her a letter but I didn't hear anything back from her. A thought occurred to me that it would be best to visit her in her home and to bring this whole affair to a mutually acceptable solution.

"Surprise #1: The accident was close to her home – I saw this as a clear sign of Hashem's Divine providence.

"Surprise #2: She wasn't suing me at all; she just wanted for someone to pay the ambulance bill, for she was an elderly woman who barely scraped by on Social Security. (She wanted National Health Insurance to pay for the ambulance, but they refused. Her son wrote a later to the lawyer and that's how the whole affair landed in my lap as a law suit.)

"Surprise #3: In the end, I didn't owe her anything, because just that week (when I decided to stop complaining and start thanking), the National Health Insurance decided to pay for the ambulance.

"We hugged each other and wished each other well. I returned home ashamed of myself. How could I have judged such a pleasant old woman so unfairly? She was simply a poor and righteous woman. How could I have judged Hashem so unfairly when He is the epitome of truth, justice and mercy? Wow, did I learn a lesson in life!

"I'm so sorry, Hashem. Please help me remember how much You love me, so I can thank You all the days of my life."

79. There's no Bad from Above

Here's another story that teaches us to say thank You for everything:

"I went to the ATM and withdrew 800 NIS in cash from my bank account. When I arrived at the store, I opened my wallet and there was only a 50-Shekel bill there. The money had disappeared. I retraced my steps to the ATM but I didn't find the money. I told myself that everything was for the very best. Sure, this was no easy test, especially when one of my girlfriends told me that if this happened to her, she would have cried. But, how could I cry after having read "The Garden of Gratitude"? I knew that I had to thank Hashem for the seemingly bad as well as for the good. It was hard to say thank You but I did, because this was really the first time that I ever thanked Hashem for something unpleasant that happened to me.

"A few days later, I went to my bank thinking that maybe some honest person found the money. The teller told me that a woman found 750 NIS near the ATM and returned it to the bank. They were holding the money until someone claimed it. You see, there is no bad from Above."

We are all obligated to thank Hashem even for the seemingly unpleasant things in life, when things don't go according the way we want them to. Hashem knows best.

80. The Famous Singer's Album

One of Israel's most popular singers came to see me and complained that his new album, which he expected to be a super-hit, was turning out to be a flop on the market. I told him that Hashem was doing him a favor. "What favor?" he asked, amazed at my response.

"Until now, did you ever thank Hashem for all your hit songs that made the Top Ten?

"No," he said.

I told him that Hashem was doing him a big favor. "When you succeeded, you thought that it was because of your talent. Fortunately, Hashem has decided to bring you closer to Him; He decided that in order to do so, He'd teach you how to pray and say thank You so that you'd understand that your success comes from Him."

The holy "Ohr Hachaim" writes that the Torah juxtaposes people's "might of my right hand" misconception with the commandment to remember that Hashem gives a person the power to succeed. This is to prod us to remember

Hashem always, lest we fall into the evil inclination's trap of self-deception that inflates one's ego and makes him forget Hashem, Heaven forbid.

The words in Hebrew for thanks (*hodaya*) and acknowledgment (*hoda'ah*) are almost identical. This teaches us that by thanking Hashem, we acknowledge that all of our successes come from Him. The Ba'al HaTanya writes that Hashem doesn't give tribulations or lack of success on a person for nothing; they are for the purpose of teaching a person humility and self-nullification to Hashem.

Gratitude enhances emuna. By way of gratitude, a person merits in seeing the Hand of Hashem. Therefore, we should try to observe everything in our lives through eyes of emuna and thank Hashem accordingly. That way, a person lives with Hashem; there is no greater happiness than knowing that Hashem is with you everywhere you go.

Every thank You we say to Hashem is tantamount to a gratitude offering in the Holy Temple. Whenever our forefathers would make a gratitude offering, Hashem would immediately reveal Himself to them. Even today, when a person thanks Hashem, he gets closer to Hashem and merits the revelation of Divine love and enhanced proximity to Hashem. What could be better?

Rebbe Nachman teaches that gratitude is an aspect of the world to come (see Likutei Moharan II:2). A person who thanks Hashem for everything discovers a paradise on earth, for he converts his life in this world to a life that resembles the sublime pleasure of the world to come.

81. Learning Gratitude

An expectant father told me that his wife's medical examinations revealed a complication in her pregnancy that would necessitate a Caesarian section. Because of this difficult news, she fell into deep depression, worry, loss of sleep and loss of appetite. She cried constantly. Hashem had pity on her and she learned that she must thank Him for everything; accordingly, she started to.

She said to Hashem, "Hashem, what am I worried about? A C-section? Anyway, whatever You do is all for the best, even if I do have the operation instead of giving birth naturally. I thank You – no matter what! There is no bad in the world…"

Her husband told me that she continued to thank Hashem like that. She even sang and danced. She had miracles. Not only did she have a natural birth, but an easy one at that!

Everyone should take advantage of the wonderful light of gratitude that Hashem sent down to this world and to begin learning gratitude. It's not enough to learn once – we must review all the time to internalize what our brain knows deep into our hearts. That way, we'll all see big miracles and salvations every day.

82. He Tried Everything

A 28-year-old rabbinical student from the prestigious Mirrer Yeshiva in Jerusalem attended my Wednesday night lecture. He hadn't succeeded in finding a soul-mate and he tried everything – all the known spiritual ploys such as praying at the Western Wall for forty days straight. He told me, "I'm willing to do anything that Rabbi Arush tells me to do." I told him to thank Hashem for 30 minutes a day that he hadn't yet found his soul-mate. Within two weeks, he found his match and they became engaged shortly thereafter.

A person who thanks Hashem is still happy in the meanwhile until his salvation comes. What's more, if he learns to be happy before his salvation, imagine how wonderful he feels after the salvation. The important thing is that he learns to live with Hashem in any situation. He also appreciates everything and doesn't act like a spoiled child with a sense of entitlement.

The underlying principle is that gratitude opens all the gates. Expressions of gratitude ascend directly to the Heavenly Throne with no obstructions. In fact, people's expressions of gratitude are loftier than the songs of praise that the angels sing to Hashem. The Midrash teaches that Hashem prefers our expressions of gratitude to the praises He receives from the many hundreds of thousands of angels.

83. You Can't, but Hashem Can

I attend many housewarmings, but this one was special. The owner of the house was a young man who when he first came to me, could not afford the rent of a tiny rental apartment.

I told him to do six hours of personal prayer, to thank Hashem and to ask Him to enable him to purchase an apartment in Jerusalem. For those who don't know, even if one has the half-million dollars needed to purchase a small apartment in Jerusalem, one still needs a miracle to find one, for the demand way exceeds the supply. Just imagine the miracles a person who can't even afford renting needs to purchase an apartment!

The young man did six hours as I told him, then shortly afterward came to tell me that he was evicted and now living in a hotel. I told him to do another six-hour personal prayer session. He did, and soon after got thrown out of the hotel, so he moved in with his wife's parents. He asked me what to do and I told him to do a third session of six hours. After four sessions of six hours, he had the money to buy an apartment, paying for it in cash! It doesn't matter how, but beforehand, he didn't have two shekels to rub together.

Expressing gratitude for all of Hashem's endless acts of loving-kindness from great to small is the heart of personal prayer. No day should go by without each of us devoting time to thanking Hashem.

Gratitude is an important part of one's daily personal prayer agenda. A person who fails to thank Hashem for his myriad of blessings every day both fails to recognize those blessings and takes them for granted. But, with daily thanks to Hashem, we observe the wonderful favors that Hashem does for us every day and we don't fall into the pitfalls of ingratitude.

No one likes an ingrate. Yet, if we're not perseverant about designating daily time for thanking Hashem, we either fail to recognize all the gifts that Hashem gave us that day (every heartbeat, every breath, shelter, clothing – think about it, the list is endless!) or we forget to thank Him altogether.

Gratitude mitigates stern judgments and strengthens emuna. It brings a person to the point of truth, where he sees the myriad of Hashem's blessings that he would otherwise have taken for granted or failed to acknowledge, had he failed to devote time to personal prayer and to giving thanks. Gratitude leads to happiness. Without happiness, a person can barely open his mouth. What's more, thanking Hashem for our blessings prevents a person from falling into the pitfalls of complaint, pessimism, grievances, the type of negativity that arouses and invokes harsh judgments, G-d forbid. Giving thanks has a marvelous effect on our souls, for it's like a sieve that sifts the good from the bad within us.

One might ask, "What's there to say for six hours?" The Gemara states, "One who prays at length, his prayer is not returned unfulfilled."

Prayer can achieve *anything*. Like the young man who couldn't pay his rent and ended up purchasing an apartment, you too can achieve your own salvation! It makes no sense wasting time running to free-loan funds or working 15-hour days. Instead, why not live a pleasant life? With prayer, and specifically a six-hour personal-prayer session when needed, you'll see miracles!

We all must plead with Hashem constantly, "Give me *emuna*! Give me *emuna* in the power of prayer, which is really emuna in You. Give me emuna that there is no power on earth but You, Hashem! You can do whatever You want whenever You want. Give me the emuna that everything is in Your hands, that You love me, and that You only want the best for me. Give me the emuna that I can turn to You for anything and for everything. Help me realize that any deficiency I have is merely a lack of prayer, so help me pray and sing Your praise more and more!"

84. Ticket to Paradise

A person told me that he does two hours of daily personal prayer. I asked him if he read "In Forest Fields". With a big smile, he nodded in the affirmative. This person had won his personal ticket to paradise.

An army commander came up to me after one of my lectures. "You saved my life," he said. I asked him what wonder drug he took. He answered, "In Forest Fields". That's the strongest wonder drug there is.

"In Forest Fields" is a guide to daily personal prayer. If a person believes in Hashem, he'll talk to Him. If he doesn't talk to Him, it's an indication that he doesn't believe.

Why is gratitude such an important part of personal prayer? As we showed in "In Forest Fields," gratitude is the truest and strongest connection that a person can have with Hashem. As long as a person lacks gratitude, his relationship with Hashem will be lacking. Gratitude is not only the result of intellectual honesty and personal integrity; it's the basis of emuna. A grateful person sees Hashem's many favors and acts of loving-kindness and is therefore on a higher level of spiritual awareness than other people, for he recognizes Hashem's Divine providence all around him. The grateful person more easily internalizes the principles of emuna, particularly that Hashem does everything for the best. People with gratitude are therefore happy and much better adjusted than those who lack gratitude.

The evil inclination tries to prod a person into being brief about gratitude but to rush right into seeking salvation and begging for what he needs. Yet, by way of gratitude, a person won't be yelling and whining for salvation because the gratitude helps him internalize that everything Hashem does is for the very best. Once a person believes that everything is for the very best, he see miraculous situations with his own two eyes.

Rebbe Nachman writes that by way of gratitude, a persona attains the truth. Without gratitude, a person is liable to fool himself and even his personal prayer will be full of lies. There is no bigger lie than ungratefulness. If a person doesn't say thank You to Hashem, in full belief that everything Hashem does is for the very best, he'll never escape the darkness that is liable to ensnare him in this world. What's more, gratitude brings a person to happiness.

Many times, a person comes to his daily personal prayer session with a pressing problem – something that's really disturbing. Sometimes, situations look bleak, even hopeless. He has difficulty in thanking Hashem for his troubles. He might use the strategy of thanking Hashem for his obvious blessings, like his eyesight or his lungs and then start asking Hashem for relief from his problems. He might even be planning to assess himself as to why he has been plagued with these problems and to do teshuva accordingly.

That's not the right way of doing things. Before a person prays for solutions and salvations, he must deal with the pressing problem that's disturbing him. He must use the negative spiritual momentum of the problem and turn it around to a positive spiritual momentum to the extent where happiness now replaces the feeling of being upset. Don't bury the disturbing feelings and don't deny them; use them to rejoice! How?

Jeremiah the Prophet said the times of trouble are a springboard to salvation (see Jeremiah 30:9). Now is the time to remind ourselves that everything is for the best, including the challenge at hand! It too comes from our loving Father in Heaven. When we think about how much He loves us and how much He wants us to have everything good, we can now thank Him sincerely for the troubles!

Without expressions of gratitude, a person can't possibly pray properly or assess himself. Why? With no gratitude, there's no emuna. Therefore, once we thank Hashem for everything, we solidify our emuna and prepare ourselves to move forward to the next stage of effective personal prayer. Everything starts with gratitude.

Rebbe Natan writes that a person should always remind himself of the favors that Hashem did for him in the past as well as the favors that Hashem did for his parents and ancestors. Without thanking for the past, one has difficulty in clinging to Hashem and calling out to Him, because his heart is preoccupied with the troubles of the present (see Likutei Halachot, Yora Dea, Klaei Behema 5:4-5).

85. They Did 6 Hours and Bought an Apartment

I was praying one evening at a synagogue in Bnei Brak after one of my lectures. When the service was over, I left and a young man was running behind me in the street, trying to catch up. He told me that he learns in a Lithuanian (not Breslev, by any means!) kollel and that he and many of the other students there have read "The Garden of Emuna." He told me that he and several others had purchased apartments after doing a six-hour personal prayer session.

The "Garden of Emuna" teaches that one can accomplish anything by way of prayer.

A young man in our rabbinical kollel did twenty six-hour personal prayer sessions until he saw the financial salvation that enabled him to purchase an apartment. There is no magic formula of cause-and-effect – what volume of prayer yields what results. Each case is individual. But as we cited previously, the Gemara in Tractate Berachot states, "One who prays at length, his prayer is not returned unfulfilled." I've seen apartment miracles with my own eyes. Through prayer and gratitude, I received my own apartment.

86. With Free Furniture Too!

Before I was married, when I was first introduced to my wife, may Hashem bless her with long life, I spoke with Hashem and said to Him: "Hashem, I'd like to continue learning Torah. You are the Master of the World. Give me an apartment, please. I need furniture, too. I have no one else to turn to – only You. I don't look to anyone. Once I aspired to receive something from a human, and I did teshuva on that act of folly, big-time!" I then thanked Hashem for everything.

A PhD in mathematics who learned in our yeshiva back then when I got engaged approached me and said, "I heard you're about to be married – mazal tov! Listen, I have an apartment that I rented for a year, but my wife can't stand it. Here, take the keys, and you can live there for a year, rent free." Meanwhile, someone else offered me an apartment that I can live in as long as I Like, rent-free! I said that I'd ask my fianceé, and whatever she wants, that's what I'll do. That's how I began married life, with a choice between two paid-for apartments. Someone else gave me free furniture too…

There are those who are locked up in the chains of heresy – they scoff at stories like these. But really, the only one that a person should scoff at is the one who doesn't believe in Hashem. Emuna – the simple and pure faith in the Creator – is no laughing matter. I believe in Him, so I talk to Him about everything. Why not be Hashem's pampered child and cuddle up to Him in our daily personal prayers? What could bring greater gratification to Him?

87. 82 Years Old with no Emuna

Some American Jews came to visit me in Jerusalem. One of them said that he came especially to say thank You. "I could have said thank You in a letter or by telephone, but I decided that it was more appropriate to thank you in person for the good life Hashem gave me by way of you."

This man was born into a religious home but he drifted away. He found his way to emuna and to the joy of Judaism by way of my books and today he does between two to three hours of personal prayer every day. For sure, he doesn't forget to thank Hashem for all of his blessings in life, and for the seemingly bad as well as for the good.

He told me about his 82 year-old father – a rabbi and author of scholarly works - who was born into a Haredi family but is devoid of emuna today, constantly angry and depressed. What good is Torah scholarship without emuna? It turns out that not every Torah scholar has emuna and not everyone who is Haredi from birth has emuna. Sometimes, it's the opposite.

Isaiah the prophet says (Isaiah 33:13): "Listen those afar to what I have done, and know, those who are close, My might." Rashi explains that "those afar" are those who were born into observant families while "those who are close" are the ones who have made teshuva and have renewed their closeness to Hashem.

Rebbe Nachman says that in the time of Moshiach, few will hold on in emuna. Sure, everyone believes in Hashem but few believe that everything He does is all for the best.

88. The Owner Did a "180"

Rabbi David Elkayam shlit'a tells this story:

A successful building contractor tasted the sweetness of emuna and personal prayer and enjoyed tremendous success for two years. Hashem decided to test him, for any big present in life comes only after a person passes a test of emuna. For the next six months, the contractor didn't make a dime; he wasn't even offered to give in a bid on any building project. His phone was idle – no one called.

Because he was so worried, he accepted a job at half the price of its real worth. He figured that this would give him the money to get back on his feet, but he ended up losing fifty thousand shekels.

The contractor's bad moods from his setbacks led to marital problems and complications with the property owner who he was building for. The contractor tried to convince the owner that he needed more money to remain afloat and to continue working, but the owner only thought that this was a crude effort to squeeze more money out of him. The owner refused to give him a cent and the contractor became broken, full of despair.

One afternoon, the contractor walked into Rabbi Elkayam's kollel in Netanya, for Rabbi Elkayam had been the one who introduced him to emuna and to observant Judaism. The Rabbi tried to encourage him, but the contractor broke down in tears of anger aimed at the property owner who was "sucking his blood." He told the rabbi about his anguish, financial problems and sleepless nights. His marriage was a wreck, too.

Rabbi Elkayam let the man finish his verbal outpour and said, "Where's the 'Garden of Emuna' that I taught you? Where are the words of faith and encouragement that you heard in Rabbi Arush's CDs? Where's your personal prayer? Where's Hashem in your life?"

Helplessly, the contractor looked at the rabbi, waiting for some magically instant solution. "What am I supposed to do?"

"Run quickly to the field and do an hour of personal prayer, " Rabbi Elkayam said. "Just thank Hashem – don't ask for a thing. Understand full well, it's not the property owner – Hashem hardened his heart, just like He hardened Pharaoh's heart. It's a mistake that you complain and don't say thank You; thank Hashem and you'll see miracles." The rabbi said these things with such confidence that the contractor was compelled to listen to him. His legs were soon carrying him to the field…

Shortly after he returned from the field, he told the rabbi, "You don't know what that hour did for me!" That was even before he knew that salvation was on the way.

The next day, the contractor came to Rabbi Elkayam's kollel with a sunshine-bright smile on his face. The property owner had turned completely around. The owner said that he made a few inquiries and he discovered that the contractor's work was on a level of quality much better than what he had thought. He had a few professionals assess the work and they told the property owner that he was virtually robbing the contractor. The property owner therefore agreed to pay the contractor the additional requested sum. The contractor couldn't believe the power of one hour's thanking Hashem.

Hashem's job is to show us salvations, but our job is to thank and praise Him always.

89. Healing the Post Traumatic Depression

Before he became observant, a young man had a problem and went to an evil psychologist in search of help. The psychologist hypnotized him and started to molest him. Before long, he felt something weird happening and woke up. Hashem saved him and eventually he became a *baal teshuva*. But, he remained traumatized from what happened to him at the psychologist's office. I told the young man, "By virtue of your terrible experience, you returned to Hashem. In that case, you should thank Hashem for this tribulation. Don't think about the psychologist; think about Hashem who had to do what He did to get you to become a baal teshuva."

Whenever we hear about something so painful as these types of experiences, we want to ask ourselves, "Why must a person undergo something so painful as molestation, Heaven forbid?" We don't always understand, but we believe that it's all for the best. In this case, it seems clear to me that were it not for the anguish this young man suffered, he would not have merited doing teshuva. By virtue of what I told him, he started to thank Hashem for a half an hour a day. His emuna that everything is for the best got much stronger and he became much happier. The daily gratitude healed him of his post-traumatic depression.

This is a big lesson for anyone who is walking around with PTSD or any other fears from the past. One person can't get the terrible car accident out of his mind. A soldier still has nightmares from the war, opening old emotional wounds again. Yet, back then, they didn't realize that everything is from Hashem and all for the best. There is no one but Him!

The solution is to begin to believe in Hashem. Now, one should say, "Master of the World, I thank You for all the suffering I went through over the years. Thank You for having me scared out of my wits. Thank You for the (war, the car accident, or whatever trauma you have experienced) that I can't get out of my mind. Thank You for not giving me the spiritual awareness at the time to realize that this was all for my good because You wanted me to experience this suffering. Thank You for having such mercy on me as to teach me emuna and gratitude, where I can now realize how this trauma was for the very best."

If a person strengthens his emuna in daily personal prayer while thanking Hashem for his traumas, he'll wipe all traumatic memories away.

People have negative emotions because they lack emuna. It's a pity that people suffer; if they only learned emuna, they'd find wonderful relief. Suffering comes from the lack of spiritual awareness that everything is from Hashem and all for the best. Without emuna, it's a miracle if a person maintains sanity.

If a person encounters a small problem, then a small amount of emuna will suffice for him to cope with it. But, when a person has a big problem or challenge, he accordingly needs a greater reserve of emuna to successfully weather it.

Major problems and troubles can distort a person's thinking and rob him of his joy in life. We can't judge people in such situations. On the other hand, I meet many people who think that minor problems justify their constant worry, anxiety and depression. They think that they are exempt from prayer and Torah learning, saying that "they can't".

Sadness and depression are terrible sins. People don't understand what these terrible emotions are. Rebbe Nachman says that the Creator departs from the sad and depressed individual. We must ask ourselves, why would He do that? Sadness and depression are a person's statement that he doesn't like the way that Hashem is running his life. Such an attitude is heresy. Once the Creator leaves a person, his predicament only worsens. Therefore, a person must do everything in his or her power to combat sadness and depression. Nothing defeats these negative emotions like emuna does. Consequently, the answer to overcoming sadness is to strengthen one's emuna.

The Heavenly Court looks at the sad individual and asks, "What does he have to lament about? According to our records, he has much more than what he deserves." With this in mind, when people come to me and complain about their troubles, I tell them to increase their expressions of gratitude, for their complaining will only invoke more troubles. Who needs more troubles?

Rebbe Yisroel of Ruzhin once heard his daughter sighing about a certain problem. He said, "My daughter, one sigh leads to another. Yet, one expression of gratitude leads to another as well. Try not to sigh about anything, but accept life's difficulties with love and joy, saying thank You to Hashem. By thanking Hashem, you'll invoke Divine compassion and abundance, and you'll get many more reasons to thank Him."

The Rebbe then told his daughter a story about a rich man who was never satisfied with his lot in life. Instead, he always complained about his bad luck. The Heavenly Court ruled that he should be "rewarded" with genuine bad luck so that he wouldn't be a liar. He therefore lost all his money and became destitute. Now, his complaining increased tenfold. He complained about his "unbearable" lot in life. Once more, the Heavenly Court decided to help him be a truthful person and thereby gave him something truly unbearable. The next morning, he woke up with leprosy all over his body. Now, he wasn't even able to knock on doors and plead for charity because everyone refused to have any contact with him. He continued to complain and his situation continued to worsen until he couldn't even swallow a morsel of food or stand up straight, for his spine became bent and crooked.

At the gate of oblivion, the former rich man decided that the only way to stay alive was to stop complaining. He was still alive and he was better off than those in a casket were. He decided to thank Hashem that he wasn't be hauled away in a wooden box. "He's thanking Hashem in his miserable predicament," the Heavenly Court noted, "so now we'll give him a reason to thank Hashem." Immediately, his spine straightened and he was once more able to stand erect. Once more, he thanked Hashem profusely. This time, his leprosy left him. He rejoiced in thanks and now was able to knock on doors and collect charity. He rejoiced again and thanked Hashem, for he was now able to purchase food and to swallow and enjoy it. What blessings – he couldn't stop saying thank You!

Hashem saw everything that was going on. He planted a thought in the mind of one of the former rich man's friends to loan him some money so that he could return to commerce and stand on his feet. The man never stopped saying thank You and subsequently saw tremendous miracles and salvations.

We see in this story what we've stressed this entire book – gratitude leads to miracles. We also see the opposite – ingratitude invokes all types of troubles.

True, people have troubles. But as they say in driving, "Be smart, not right!" The graveyard is full of people who said, "But I had the right of way."

Even when a person justifiably cries about his problems, the Heavenly Court says, "Yes, you're correct, but you're now living in purgatory. Try being a little less correct and you'll turn your life into a paradise. Say thank You, and your troubles will disappear."

There are only two options for living your life in this world, either paradise or purgatory. Gratitude not only leads to paradise but helps a person eradicate any trace of heresy that he might harbor in his heart or brain. Away go the negative emotions, the anger, worry and anxiety. Gratitude cleanses one's soul! Let's remember though that we must ask Hashem for the emuna that everything is from Him and for the best, the emuna that enables us to thank Him for everything. We must always pray, "Master of the World, give me emuna! Enable me to live the truth that everything is for the best." With this prayer on our lips, life begins to be paradise.

90. Expectant Parents

A young man ran after me in the street and asked me to bless his baby. The doctors had told him and his wife that they'd never have children. They decided to thank Hashem for half an hour every day that they couldn't become parents; within a month, they became expectant parents.

What are the spiritual dynamics of such stories, which we see and hear of repeatedly with our own eyes and ears? Gratitude nullifies all severe judgments. A person who truly believes that a difficult situation is good actually converts the situation to good. On a spiritual level, he turns stern judgments into absolute mercy. Such is the power of gratitude. One should therefore do his utmost to thank Hashem for everything, taking nothing for granted.

Hashem enabled me to advise people that if their prayers go unanswered, they should only praise and thank Hashem without asking for anything. Why? A person who begs for something, like a soul-mate or a job, can't help but falling into a mindset of a victim, as if Hashem is being unfair to him, Heaven forbid. As we've stressed repeatedly, such an attitude, especially when accompanied with whining, leads to stern judgments that only worsen things. Therefore, he should only say thank You, for expressions of gratitude silence stern judgments.

In addition to Hashem, one must also express gratitude to anyone who does a favor for him - spouse, parents, friends, children, neighbors, public servants – everyone! No one should ever take a single one of life's amenities for granted.

Prepare a gratitude notebook and jot down the many wonderful favors that Hashem does for you. You can't imagine how much joy this will bring you. It will also invoke more and more reasons to jot down thank Yous.

At our Shabbat Table, we thank Hashem for every little morsel of food on the table. We also thank Him for the table, the chairs, the plates and the cutlery. We profusely thank everyone who contributed to the cooking and the Shabbat preparations. A home of gratitude is paradise on earth!

91. The Gratitude Notebook

A well-known Yeshiva head was beleaguered with financial problems that threatened to bring the Yeshiva to closure. His worries affected his health so he decided to seek the counsel of Rabbi Shlomo Zalman Auerbach, of saintly and blessed memory.

"The psychotherapist says that I am incapable of handling such pressure and warned that I'm a candidate for a nervous breakdown," he told Rabbi Auerbach.

"How many years have you been head of the Yeshiva?" Rabbi Auerbach asked.

"Twenty five."

"Were there more difficult times than now?"

"Yes," answered the Rosh Yeshiva.

"And Hashem helped you?"

"Always, but the worries come back every month when I have to pay salaries."

"But you always pay them, true?"

Again, the Rosh Yeshiva answered in the affirmative.

"You see with your own eyes that Hashem always takes care of you and your Yeshiva. Why do you worry? Every single Rosh Kollel and Rosh Yeshiva is in the same predicament. So is every business proprietor and every person that marries off a child. The answer to all worries is trust – trust in Hashem! How do you build trust? Thank Him for everything, for with gratitude, a person takes nothing for granted. Keep a small notebook in your pocket and jot down every favor that Hashem does for you. Several times a day, read the entries in your notebook and your heart will fill with joy, more gratitude and trust. Express your gratitude vocally – don't let them become mere fleeting thoughts. If you do this, I promise that your worries will disappear."

Who can ignore a promise from the holy Rabbi Shlomo Zakman Auerbach, osb"m?

92. Return of the Missing Purse

A woman phoned in during my radio program and told that she went shopping then rested on a park bench on the way home. She gathered her shopping bags and continued home, only to discover that her purse was missing.

She had recently read one of our "Gems of Gratitude" pamphlets. She said, "I'll thank Hashem that my purse is missing. Whatever He does is certainly for the best."

Returning to the park bench, she didn't find her purse but continued to thank Hashem, sincerely and with joy: "If this is what You want, Master of the World, it's what I want too! Thank You!" She went home.

As soon as she walked in the front door, the phone rang. "I've been calling for a while now and no one has answered," said the voice on the other end of the line. "I found your purse; may I come to your home and bring it to you?" She received her purse, delivered to her home. The nice young man who brought it said, "Open the purse and check – nothing is missing."

"Why?" asked the woman. "I believe you."

The young man insisted that she open the purse. She did, finding everything just as she left it. Such is the power of gratitude!

Gratitude is such a wonderful way to live our lives. What's more, gratitude carries the promise of no more exile and diaspora and an end to one's problems. So why doesn't everyone adopt the way of gratitude?

The answer is that people fail to heed the spiritual leaders of the generation who call them to strengthen themselves in emuna. Where emuna is weak, so is gratitude.

The deficiency of emuna has been a problem that has plagued the generations ever since slavery in Egypt. People prefer to be slaves to hard labor rather than to smile and to thank Hashem. They prefer sadness to song. It's just not logical.

We see that no matter how many books a person reads or lectures he hears, he doesn't internalize the lessons. He doesn't seek emuna. The intransigent individual doesn't want to believe in a Creator Who is total compassion and mercy. Why? Emuna in the Creator behooves a person to acknowledge the Creator's infinite loving-kindnesses and express gratitude for them. The intransigents – the emuna refuseniks who generation after generation fail to heed the spiritual leaders – don't want to be obligated to anyone, even the Creator. Korach, Dothan and Aviram were not just revolting against Moses; they revolted against the Creator too. Such people are still around today. They don't realize how badly they need the righteous spiritual leaders of the generation to lead them on the path of emuna and gratitude.

In the future, when the gates of holiness open wide, everyone will realize that everything the Creator does is for the very best. The world will fill with the knowledge of the Creator and everyone will run to express gratitude. And, with the gratitude, comes more and more good and abundance.

93. Dentist on the Premises

Another woman called in during my radio program and said that she had a severe toothache. She thanked Hashem and was able to land an immediate appointment at the dentist, despite his tremendously busy schedule. She thanked Hashem all during her treatment and she experienced no pain at all…

During my lecture in Gan Yavne, a woman told me that her son was in trouble in the army. He said thank You and his troubles disappeared. She wasn't as excited about his miraculous rescue from his problems as she was about the strengthening in emuna that his expressions of gratitude brought him.

Even a person who is not Torah-observant will see big miracles if he only says thank You and realizes that everything is from the Creator and all for the best. Gratitude is a springboard that is capable of bringing a person to emuna and to proximity with the Creator and the world of Torah observance.

94. I Started to Shout Thank You

The way of gratitude is very effective in bringing people closer to the Creator. A well-known Israeli actor tells his story: "It was a day when everything went sour for me. I lost a role in a major film and received an unpleasant call from the bank. I was on the way to my agent, burning up with anger. When I stopped at a red light, there were some Breslevers giving out CDs and pamphlets. I gave them a few shekels and they gave me the CD, **Stop Crying**. I put the CD into my disc player and continued on to my agent's office. The CD filled me with joy. Instead of complaining, I started to shout in thanks to Hashem. That same day, I received a different role and an advance payment that went straight into my bank account."

"My life did a 180. Rebbe Nachman is awesome! He said things over 200 years ago that apply perfectly to our generation. He opens up your head and your heart. It's not always easy but it's effective – I'm learning new things all the time."

The actor has been strengthening his emuna ever since. Not only does he put on tefillin, but he and his family are now eating kosher and observing the Sabbath. His wife says that their marriage has never been better.

From the above story, we see the power of one CD and how it can make a monumental change for the better in a person's life. It doesn't matter who or what a person is – if he says thank You, he'll see miracles.

People have difficulty in changing their lifestyle from secular to Torah-observant. Yet, anyone can express gratitude, even a person who has been immersed in sin. By way of gratitude, one can find his way from the darkness of heresy to the bright light of emuna.

95. Clinging to the Light

Seeing miracles won't necessarily spiritually stimulate a person. Yet, gratitude for those miracles will. Gratitude opens the heart. A person who expresses gratitude for life's undesirable things will certainly express gratitude for life's desirable amenities, as we see in the following story.

Odelia Levy comes from the Sharon Valley area; she's a science teacher and the mother of three children. She tells, "One Saturday morning, my husband left early to go on a hike with some friends. I was still in bed and the kids were in their room. Suddenly, I felt excruciating pains. I was deathly afraid and I broke out in a cold sweat. I thought that in a matter of minutes, I'd die. I tried to call my children but my voice failed me. I phoned the emergency medical services and barely was able to tell them that I was in distress. With my luck, they sent an elderly Russian-speaking doctor who couldn't speak Hebrew. The doctor took out a pill and told me to swallow it. I did. I was so weak that it never occurred to me to resist."

"The pill, which was designed to widen the arteries, caused me to hemorrhage. I should have had a pill that did the opposite effect. The whole time, the doctor was on the phone with someone. They decided to summon an ambulance. My children, who were then teenagers, came into my room shocked. All of a sudden the room was filled with people and medical equipment. The paramedics hovered over me and the last thing I remember before losing consciousness was one of them yelling, 'There's no more pulse! She's not breathing! C'mon, we're losing her!' One of them yelled at the doctor, 'Why in the world did you call for a regular ambulance instead of an ICU vehicle? What the heck kind of doctor are you anyway?'"

My oldest son, who trained as a weightlifter, carried me to the ambulance. Later, he told me that carrying his mother was much more difficult than lifting weights. I saw everything from above, as if my soul hovered above my body. At one point, I felt someone slapping my face and calling my name. I saw the roof of the ambulance and I was disappointed, for the feeling of my soul leaving my body was wonderful. I saw this loving bright white light that engulfed me with love. I just wanted to cling to it, like a magnet."

"It's impossible to describe the loving white light that resembles nothing in the physical world. Thank Hashem, I have experienced love – the love of husband, children, parents and so forth; this light dwarfed everything else. I still yearn for that light. I wasn't afraid at all. The light was so loving and it seemed to understand me completely. I finally understood that this is death – going from one type of cognizance to another. It's not scary at all."

"Little by little, your soul ascends as if you're in a helium balloon, yearning for and seeking the loving white light. Suddenly, I heard a voice – not audibly, but telepathically. It said, 'Your time has not come yet.' An invisible hand blocked my continued ascent. Suddenly, my soul was shoved back into my body by way of my nostrils. That moment, I felt like I was put in a diver's suit that was too small for me and very restricting. I tried to resist but I couldn't. My body once again surrounded my soul and trapped it within."

"I returned to my non-spiritual routine existence. Like a good science teacher, I looked for all types of rational explanations for what happened to me. I treated the whole episode like a dream. For years afterwards, I continued to live a secular lifestyle."

"I was aroused when I saw a TV program about people who had experienced near-death experiences (NDE). Their descriptions were strikingly similar to what I saw. Yet, I was a hard nut to crack. I started to study the phenomena of NDEs yet I still refused to connect the dots and see the hand of Hashem. Rather than attributing my miraculous recovery to Him, I felt ego-inflated by my new-found 'powers'; the NDE left me with a heightened power of intuition. I could literally predict things. I figured that I'd use my power to make money."

"I quickly understood that I wasn't doing what Hashem wanted. As soon as I started marketing myself as a clairvoyant, I was hit with all kinds of troubles. My family and I had three car accidents and our household appliances were breaking down one by one. My husband was diagnosed with cancer, and that's not all…"

"One day, I visited a certain rabbi to ask him why I was suffering all these tribulations. His answer floored me – he told me that Hashem doesn't want me dealing in the clairvoyant. I was scared stiff and the next day, I closed shop. Meanwhile, my son was inducted into the army and he began to observe the Torah and its mitzvoth on his own, without me. When he informed us that he was becoming a *baal teshuva* – my husband and I told him to be religious in his own room but not to bother us. On Friday night, he'd say Kiddush in his bedroom and we'd watch TV in the living room. He would ask me many questions that I couldn't answer and tell me that all the science that I was teaching could be found in the Torah. Finally, I saw the truth."

"Due to unsuccessful surgery after one of my car accidents, I had to undergo a second surgery. For three months, I suffered severe pain. Eating and drinking were more than difficult for me. Then, someone gave me a copy of Rav Arush's **The Garden of Gratitude**. Instead of complaining, I started saying thank You."

"My teshuva process took time – so did my recovery. But, the more I said thank You, the less I suffered and the closer I came to Hashem. I promised Hashem that I'd tell the story, how He waited patiently for me until I had the spiritual sense to cast my intellect aside and to open up my heart and brain to emuna. Hashem never left me. By virtue of gratitude, I saw salvation; so will the entire world, if they only learn to thank Hashem."

96. Thanks for the Wounds

A woman complained to me about some ugly wounds on her face. I suggested that she devote six hours of consecutive personal prayer to this matter. I told her to begin by thanking Hashem for her wounds and consequent suffering, because they are intrinsically good in that they are bringing her closer to Hashem. Without them, she would have never spoken to Hashem for an hour, let alone six hours straight. Once she thanks Hashem and is in a good mindset, she can ask for relief and a cure.

Prayer that includes whining and complaining is worse than no prayer at all. Gratitude and the joyous attitude that characterizes emuna-filled prayers open the gates of salvation. Our sages teach that sadness and whining are worse than sin itself. On the other hand, joy and emuna bring a person to holiness. No wonder that the prayers said with joy and emuna are so readily answered. And, nothing brings a person to joy and emuna like gratitude does. With that in mind, prayers of gratitude are much more effective than tearful prayers. Even if a person prays with a sincerely broken heart – which is good – there's still a fine line between a broken heart and sadness. Prayer with gratitude is a much better choice.

The terrible punishment of Tisha B'Av and subsequent disasters was the result of the Sin of the Spies, when the Children of Israel cried needlessly. We must ask ourselves, what type of crying is the Gemara referring to when it says that the gates of tears are never locked? These are the tears of yearning, when one sees how merciful and compassionate the Creator is and how he longs to get closer to Him. These are the tears that unlock the Heavenly gates enabling the prayers to enter. Yet, with gratitude, there are no gates at all! Life becomes a Heaven on earth.

97. Two Hours of Gratitude and the Contract

Finding an apartment in the neighborhood of our Yeshiva in Jerusalem is virtually impossible. The demand far exceeds the supply, with prices rising accordingly. Many search for months without finding anything suitable.

One of my students searched for months but couldn't find an apartment. He ran a long marathon of obstacles in the process. On several occasions, he was about to sign a contract but at the last moment, something always went wrong.

Then, he decided to go the gratitude route. After my student heard one of my lessons on gratitude, he thanked Hashem for two hours that he hadn't found an apartment until now. Immediately afterward, he found an apartment that his wife liked, that he could afford, in a perfect location and near the Yeshiva! And, he signed the contract and successfully sealed the deal.

The great aspect of gratitude is that when a person says thank You to Hashem, without complaining or whining, and then sees salvation, he sees the hand of Divine Providence in his life. This makes the salvation even sweeter and it reinforces emuna.

Rebbe Elimelech of Lizhensk writes that expressions of gratitude are far more effective in evoking salvations than prayers of request. This is because nothing or no one can obstruct an expression of gratitude from ascending directly to the Heavenly Throne.

98. The Perfect Ploy

A woman who was childless for many years told that she tried everything – prayer, teshuva, charity, medical treatments, alternative medicine, diet and a host of spiritual ploys – nothing helped. She and her husband were exhausted emotionally and physically. Would they never have a child of their own?

I told the woman to stop everything, just to stand before Hashem for an hour a day and to thank Him for not giving her children. I showed her a few aspects of how this is truly for the best, because it brings her so much closer to Hashem, and so forth. I also told her not to be jealous of women who had children and to praise Hashem every time one of her girlfriends gives birth. I instructed her to add one sentence at the very end of her daily hour: "Master of the World, if You so desire, please give me children." I then promised her that she would become a mother.

She was skeptical and asked, "How is this advice any better from the tons of prayers and mitzvoth that I've already done to have a child? I've cried a river of tears…"

I answered, "Gratitude will lead you to emuna because gratitude is the expression of a person who believes that everything is for the best. If until now you haven't had children, this is Hashem's will. Believing in Him means accepting His will. Thanking Him shows that you accept his will wholeheartedly – that is the true emuna that invokes all types of blessings."

It's no coincidence that the Hebrew numerical value for "emuna" is 102, the same as the numerical value for the word "banim", children. If you have emuna, you'll have children.

Gratitude is not only a person's main task in this world; it's a principal function in the World to Come as well. Gratitude brings a person closer to the Creator and to genuine emuna. Nothing is as effective as gratitude in mitigating stern judgments. The full redemption of our people depends on gratitude, for gratitude brings *Geula*.

One must thank Hashem for the outright good things as well as for the seemingly bad. For example, a person must thank Hashem for being sick or for having a bodily pain. A person must thank Hashem for any deficiency in life, for any setback, failure or lack of success. All of life's tribulations are for a person's ultimate good, for if he looks at their purpose, he will rejoice in them. Rebbe Nachman writes (Likutei Moharan I:65): "The ultimate purpose is entirely good, for even all the trials, tribulations and troubles that befall a person, Heaven forbid, if he looks at the ultimate purpose, he will see that they are not bad at all, only big favors. They all come from Hashem, blessed be He, in order to remind him to rectify something, to atone for a sin or to help him make teshuva. Hashem's intent is entirely for the good. So, when a person looks at the ultimate purpose, in other words, Hashem's intent behind all of his suffering, he'll see that everything is truly for the ultimate best. He'll rejoice, for truly, there is no bad in the world, only good."

The mistake most people make is needless whining and complaining. Complaining is essentially a complaint against the Creator and doubting His absolute goodness. Such an attitude is heresy, which only triggers more troubles and stern judgments.

As I wrote in my book, **The Garden of Gratitude**, we learn these principles from the sin of the spies. They cried needlessly, and to this day, we're still paying the price. Why? Because many of us are still crying and complaining...

Who knows when the crying and complaining will end? May Hashem have mercy on us and bring Moshiach right now.

We learn from the sin of the spies that crying and complaining is even worse than idolatry, bloodshed and forbidden sex. Why? Crying and complaining is the total opposite of emuna.

Rashi teaches that a good measure is five hundred times better than a bad measure. With that in mind, as damaging as crying and complaining is, the good of gratitude is five hundred times stronger! No wonder that gratitude elicits miracles and salvations beyond anything we can imagine.

Do you realize what that means? The solution to any problem in the world is to say thank You to Hashem!

Thank Hashem for the deficiency itself, for this is the greatest expression of emuna that can be. The Creator knows that a particular deficiency is the best and sometimes only way to arouse a person out of his spiritual slumber and to bring him closer to Him. Therefore, the deficiency in its essence is actually a tremendous favor for posterity.

As long as a person cannot wholeheartedly thank Hashem for his deficiencies in life, he lacks emuna. As long as he lacks emuna, his prayers of request won't be effective. Instead, he should ask Hashem for enhanced emuna, especially the emuna that everything is for the best. One must be careful always to avoid the pitfalls of whining and complaining.

Back to the woman in our story: she filled nine whole notebooks full of thank Yous and within nine months, she gave birth to a healthy baby boy.

99. The Son that Veered from the Path

A father complained to me that his son had veered from the path of observant Judaism. I told him that until he starts thanking Hashem for this problem, looking for the good in it and realizing that it's all for the best, he shouldn't expect to see this problem resolved.

How can a person believe in Hashem yet doesn't believe that Hashem is good, merciful and just? And, if he does believe that Hashem is good, merciful and just, then why is he unhappy with his lot in life? Everything in life comes from Hashem, so discontent with life is discontent with Hashem, Heaven forbid.

To avoid the discontent ensnarement, a person must thank Hashem. Gratitude is highest priority in Divine service, even before teshuva and prayer. Gratitude not only connects us to emuna but connects us to truth, since emuna is synonymous to truth. With gratitude, a person merits every salvation.

Contrastingly, when a person is sad and suffering from an inflated sense of entitlement, the gates of salvation slam shut in his face. Even if he does ask something from Hashem, he thinks that Hashem owes him his request. The Heavenly Court looks into the matter and finds that Hashem owes him nothing. Indeed, he already has more than he deserves; now, he's in big trouble, for he's liable to forfeit what he already has.

There is not a single ray of truth in the supplications of a bitter individual. If he comes to Hashem with a shopping list before he said thank You for what he already has, he'll end up quarreling with Hashem. He thinks that he deserves something; if Hashem doesn't give him what he wants, he'll start a feud with Him…

A person can pray properly only after he lovingly accepts everything that Hashem does. He must understand that whatever is happening to him is part of his soul correction. He should turn to Hashem, saying, "Master of the World! What must I rectify? What transgression must I repent for? Help me pray and ask Your forgiveness."

By way of emuna and gratitude, a person submits himself to Divine will. Then, he can ask, "Master of the World! Have mercy on this child! Help him and heal his soul. Give him wisdom and understanding and help him succeed. Let him have self-confidence and a good life." Ask whatever you wish for your child, but do it with submissiveness.

If this matter depresses you or breaks you, you won't be able to pray properly. Even if you do pray, the prayer won't be genuine. The same goes for any other challenge in life.

Suppose a person has income difficulties. First of all, he should accept Hashem's judgments with love and express gratitude: "Master of the World, thank You! Everything I have until now is the product of Your infinite mercy. I deserve nothing. Until now, You have always provided for me in Your limitless compassion. There are no trials without prior tribulations, so I certainly must have sins that I haven't yet atoned for. I accept everything with love for this is part of my soul's rectification. Yet, now I beseech You, have mercy on me! Help me make teshuva and show me what to correct."

Our spiritual leaders from the beginning of our history have never harbored a sense of entitlement. They always prayed for a free gift. Rebbe Yitzchak Meir in his classic

"Chidushei Harim" writes that in the Heavens, the largest treasury is the "Treasury of Free Gifts." Its contents of treasures are bestowed only upon those people who realize that they deserve nothing and that everything is a free gift from Above. As we explained in our book, "The Gates of Gratitude", such a person's prayers are always answered. This is the humble person who resembles Moses and King David, who always considered themselves unworthy of everything the Almighty gave them. If *they* did, *we* should certainly view ourselves as recipients of free gifts that we don't deserve either.

100. Parents' Mirror

A father told me that without his knowledge, his son connected to unwholesome friends. Before the father knew about it, the son began doing the worst possible things. The father did six-hour personal prayer sessions on behalf of his son for three days straight, a total of eighteen (Hebrew equivalent of *Chai*, or life) hours of personal prayer. The lad soon left his friends and their evil ways and returned to himself.

Another broken-hearted parent came to me whose son roamed the streets and wouldn't come home to sleep. I gave him the advice of lengthy personal prayer sessions that he and his wife both agreed to do. Soon, their son was back of the upright path. Today, the lad is one of the best boys in his yeshiva. The power of prayer is prodigious – it succeeds where all other advice and ploys do not. Prayer – especially prayers of gratitude – works wonderfully even after damage has been done, Heaven forbid.

The above is testimony for those parents who ask how it's possible to spend six hours in prayer and gratitude on behalf of a child. Everything depends on desire; if a parent has a strong desire to save a child, he or she wouldn't look for an easy way out or an instant solution. Not only would they pray for six hours, they'd pray for hundreds of hours if they truly loved their child and wished for his or her very best.

Our sages teach us that children who fall of the path of righteousness render a person's home like the battlefield of Gog and Magog. Anyone who has a child that uses profane language and acts unruly will surely verify that this teaching is true. These are the worst type of tribulations for a parent, when children forsake the upright path for the fantasies of a world of lust and lies that's here today and gone tomorrow.

In such a situation, Heaven forbid, parents must realize that prayers of gratitude are their only hope! Other advice is like a Band-Aid for a broken arm. They don't solve the problem. Prayer –especially prayers of gratitude – penetrates to the root of the problem.

What's more difficult, to pray for six hours or to see a child going down the drain? Every parent must ask him/herself if the difficulty of praying for six hours is greater than the difficulty of a wayward child.

Do you love your son? Do you love your daughter? Then pray for them! Only Hashem can help you – He alone holds the steering wheel of the vehicle called life. Your kids won't listen to you anymore because they only hear the voices of their base desires and their peers. But don't forget – whereas you lack control, your children are in Hashem's hands. Hashem is the only One who can turn your child's heart around. For more details about the six-hour prayer session, see our book "In Forest Fields".

The greatest source of encouragement for a parent with a child-education crisis is the emuna that everything is for the best. Therefore, a parent must thank Hashem, no matter what. To those parents who ask me how it's humanly possible to thank Hashem when their children revolt against Him and they're walking around with a "sea of pain" as one parent put it, I say: of course you can't thank Him as long as you are miserable, whining and complaining as if Hashem has not been fair with you.

We already learned repeatedly in this book that we must thank Hashem for everything, for this is the truth! There are no tribulations without prior transgression. When parents lament that their children are off the path, they themselves must do teshuva! Why? Children are the mirrors of their parents. For example, if you want your child to pray, you must pray! In true child education, the approach of "Do as I say, and not as I do" is morally and ethically bankrupt! The root of a child's behavior is in the parent's actions and attitudes. Therefore, the only truly effective factors in educating children are parental example and tons of prayer.

I knew a young man whose father pleaded with him to devote his life to Torah study. The young man wasn't particularly interested; he preferred to invest his time in commerce, even though he was completely Torah-observant. The father had extreme sorrow that learning Torah was so low in his son's list of priorities.

After the father died, the young man had a son who grew up to be rebellious, failing to heed a word his father said. If the father had done teshuva for going against his father's will – which was Hashem's will – he would have never seen so much grief from his own son. But, he never did teshuva and therefore continued to suffer from his own son.

Make no mistakes – children are reliable mirrors of their parents' most innermost desires and traits. A parent may think that he or she has nothing to do with their children's straying off the path, but Hashem says otherwise. A child doesn't pray because the parent is far away from prayer! Does the parent invest in heartfelt, sincere prayer? Hashem says no; the parent needs to reinforce the very area where the child is weak. If he or she does, they'll see marvelous results with their very eyes!

Hashem shows each person according to his or her individual spiritual level what they need to rectify. Any person who tries his utmost to correct what he can will surely see salvation. Sometimes, he thinks he's trying his hardest, but in spite of his efforts, the problems are still far from solution. Apparently, the parent is capable of doing much more. This entails waking up and breaking the threshold of one's comfort zone.

For more on everything we've written here, be sure to see "The Garden of Emuna", "The Garden of Peace", "In Forest Fields", "Women's Wisdom" and of course "The Garden of Gratitude."

While the parent is working on himself, he must give the child love and support. The child is confused – he thinks he has found the best of life yet can't understand why his parents are against him. He doesn't realize that he has found the path to purgatory. This is not the time to give up on the child or wash one's hands of him. Instead, give the child unconditional love; that will leave him connected to his parents and family. This will also protect him, especially when he realizes that his peers and his skewed ways have betrayed him.

Emuna is the only way to handle such a crisis. Anyone who tries to muscle his tribulations will find that they only get worse. What are you fighting with, the stick in Hashem's hands? Who is making trouble for you, your child or Hashem? If you think that it's your child, then your suffering will get much worse.

On the other hand, when a person regards his tribulations with emuna and thanks Hashem for them together with introspection and teshuva, he'll see big salvations. It's as if Hashem is saying to him, "If you understand that your troubles are from Me, then I'll take control of them to your relief!"

Don't ever forget this solid fact: without believing in Hashem and that everything He does is for the best, one cannot pray properly. But when a person realizes that his problems are from Hashem to wake him up from his spiritual slumber or stagnation and thanks Hashem for them while looking for a message within them – he sees salvation and so does his errant child.

101. Instant Cure and Instant Riches

I knew a person who had to scrape pennies together to put food on his table. Yet, he was always optimistic and clinged to his emuna. He would say, "Master of the World, if it's Your will that I should be so poor, then I'm happy with what You are doing! Thank You!"

If his lack of finances weren't enough of a problem, he soon became inflicted with a terrible sickness that nearly paralyzed him. A rabbi who knows him told him to pray that Hashem should cure him. The poor man said, "Heck no! If the Creator wants me to be sick, I'll only thank Him. My job is to strengthen myself in emuna – everything else is up to Him. Whatever He wants to do is fine with me."

The poor and sick individual soon saw big miracles. His amazing recovery defied all medical textbooks and logic. In the past, he had dealt in international commerce. Suddenly, he received an offer from an African gold-mining company to be their representative in Israel and Europe. They had received a wonderful recommendation about him. Ultimately, he travelled to that African country and even met its president. He not only received a marvelous job but a lucrative franchise as well. Virtually overnight, he became wealthy on a grand scale.

He held on with emuna, and he saw huge miracles.

The once-poor-now-rich gold dealer told me that his emuna never wavered during the hard times. Even though he barely had a few coins in his pocket, he would always give charity to other poor people who came to him with an extended hand. His secret of success: "I held on with emuna and never stopped thanking the Creator for everything – the good and the seemingly otherwise. Hashem, this is what You want? It's not good, it's great! Thank You!"

What is a person's real test of faith? It's when logic works overtime to tell a person that there's no hope, only despair. A person must catch himself and say to the Creator: "I don't understand a thing. This is what You want? This is wonderful for me. Master of the World, whatever You want, I want too." A person must be happy with whatever his current lot in life is.

When logic works overtime, people in challenging situations tend to either beat themselves up or fall into hopelessness and despair. Neither is productive in the slightest. Rather, a person should cast his intellect aside and say, "Hashem, I don't understand a thing. But, if this is what You want, then it's certainly fine with me." That way, no matter what the pressure, a person can be happy in any situation. The only thing - and the best thing – to do is to ask Hashem to help us cling tightly to Him with emuna.

By holding on to emuna in this world, a person might not see instant salvation, but he'll undoubtedly see a dramatic improvement in his own mood, attitude and situation. In the next world though, Hashem "pays cash" for emuna.

As long as a person clings to the emuna that everything Hashem does is for the very best, everything will surely turn around for the very best. Therefore, the only punishment a person can have in this world is when his emuna is taken away from him.

Working on emuna is a lifelong endeavor. The emuna books and CDs are not something to read or listen to once or twice. We all must constantly refresh and reinforce our knowledge and internalization of emuna. Emuna should have a high priority in our daily learning and character-strengthening schedule.

102. I Don't Deserve a Thing

A father of many children who lacked an income came to me for guidance. I told him to thank Hashem for an hour a day for his lack of an income. Also, I said that if he did do so while realizing that everything Hashem does is for the very best, he'd surely see how everything turns around for the very best.

The father not only took my advice of the daily half hour of gratitude, he spent an entire day thanking Hashem for his financial difficulties. Soon, they were gone!

A sick woman came to me and asked me what to do to relieve her ills. I told her to thank Hashem for ten minutes a day for her healthy appendages – the eyes she sees with, the ears that hear, the fingers that function and so forth. After thanking Him, she can begin to pray, saying, "Master of the World, have mercy on me. Help me, for I don't deserve a thing. I appeal to Your infinite compassion to bestow on me the free gift of good health."

A person's feeling of dissatisfaction is essentially heresy, whether it has to do with material or spiritual matters. Such a feeling is tantamount to telling the Creator that He is not just and that He is treating the dissatisfied person unfairly.

One must know that Hashem owes nothing to a person and that we must thank Him for every tiny blessing in life, taking nothing for granted. Each of us must be pleased with his lot in life without comparing himself to a single other person on earth. One who is jealous of others and dissatisfied with his own lot ends up losing what he already has without gaining a morsel of whatever he covets. The Zohar tells us that the disgruntled person's loss is given to the person who is happy with his lot in life.

103. The Easy Way

A person fell into deep debt. His wife told him to fly to the USA and to try to raise the money to repay what he owed. He came to ask my advice in the matter.

I had no objection to his traveling abroad, but I had an easier, more time-efficient and economical suggestion where he wouldn't have to invest in plane tickets. My advice would solve his problem once and for all; I told him to do a six-hour personal prayer session regarding his debts.

The individual hesitated: "Rabbi, how can I talk to Hashem for six hours? I can barely talk to him for a few minutes…"

I told him that even if he spent a dozen or more hours in the air going, a dozen or more hours coming back, trapesing from town to town and door to door in the USA, and even if he miraculously raised all the money he needed, spending weeks away from his wife and children, he wouldn't solve the problem at the core. Eventually, he'd fall back into debt and repeat the cycle of leaving his family and traveling abroad. "Don't you think that six hours is a 'slightly' easier and less-complicated solution? Who would you rather appeal to, strangers who'll slam doors in your face or the Creator, your loving Father in Heaven?

He chose the Creator so I coached him what to do:

1.   First, thank Hashem for all the favors He has done for you until now, and how he has sustained you and your family in spite of your debts. Then, thank Him for the debts themselves, for as you see, they are the catalysts for your getting closer to Hashem and speaking to Him.

2.   Afterwards, say: "Master of the World, I don't have a livelihood because I don't deserve a livelihood. If I have debts – which are certainly great tribulations – it is because I have sinned. You are just in everything You do." Continue to acknowledge Hashem's justice and to thank Him for it.

3.   Now, ask Hashem to help you on the path of teshuva, like this: "Master of the World, everything is revealed to You; You know exactly what I must rectify on a spiritual level and what You are trying to communicate to me by way of my debts. Please help me and show me what You want me to rectify." Then, ask Hashem to illuminate your brain as to the sins you committed that brought about the debts. Try to understand what these sins are while doing intense self-assessment. Invest a long time on this matter.

4.   Ask Hashem to give you the emuna that He alone provides you with an income, without any effort on your part. Pray for trust in Hashem so that you should be free of worry. Trust in Hashem is the vessel of abundance, so pray for it profusely.

5.   Pray that you should merit in giving a tithe of any money you earn and that you should give charity with all your heart, knowing that you won't lack a thing because of the charity you give. Ask Hahem to have mercy on your wife and children. Tell Hashem that you are having difficulty focusing on Torah learning and mitzvah performance without having a steady income. Ask the Almighty for a source of income that will enable you to repay

your debts and set aside time to learn Torah and to serve Hashem.

6.	Ask the Almighty to give you the free gift of an adequate income and use Rebbe Natan's prayer: "Master of the World, I want to be an upright person but that takes time; in the meanwhile, please provide for me and give me the self-composure and time to work on myself and to rectify my soul.

7.	Make resolutions that will help you become an upright individual such as setting aside daily time for learning Torah and for personal prayer. Without such resolutions, your requests for an adequate income won't be convincing.

8.	Most importantly, make a strong commitment to speak to Hashem for an hour a day! One cannot be an upright individual without this.

When the Creator sees that you're making every effort to be a worthy and upright individual, He'll accept your prayers, rescue you from debt and give you an adequate income.

A person must act in the above manner to rid himself of debts. Debts are a message from Above that one needs to do teshuva. The difficulties in making a living are designed to wake a person up and give him the incentive to assess himself and to get closer to Hashem. Overseas travels and other ploys that will supposedly solve the debt problem will ultimately accomplish nothing, for a person can't outsmart or circumvent the Creator. If He wants a person to do teshuva – and that individual is trying alternate plans of action that have nothing to do with teshuva – he'll only perpetuate the debts.

A six-hour personal prayer session is adequate to cover the abovementioned eight points. Prayer in this manner will certainly invoke salvations. Remember, though, that after the six-hour session, one must continue to devote a daily hour to personal prayer. This hour can be split into three parts: gratitude, self-assessment and teshuva, and then prayers for trust in Hashem and income. In effect, the daily one-hour is an encapsulation of the six-hour session.

A person's thought process is like a magnet. If he harbors thoughts of doubt and fear, then the things that scare him will be drawn to him. Yet, if his mind focuses on his trust in Hashem and emuna, that Hashem will surely give him an adequate income, then his livelihood will be drawn to him in a pleasurable and adequate manner.

With the above in mind, one must always look for the "silver lining of the cloud" and find reasons to be optimistic and positive. The more we cling to emuna, the easier this task is. The evil inclination is called evil because all negative thoughts and emotions originate with the evil inclination. When a person clings to thoughts of Hashem and emuna, he or she subdues the dark-side forces of negativity.

The Gemara in Tractate Bava Metzia says that a person who fears poverty ends up poor. His negative thoughts and lack of trust in Hashem literally bring financial problems on him. The mind is so strong that it influences reality. This is apparent in every phase of life. Just as bad thoughts trigger the negative, the opposite is absolutely true. King David says in Psalm 32, "He who trusts in Hashem will be encompassed with loving-kindness"; that person's trust invokes Divine loving-kindness in measure-for-measure fashion.

A person should not worry about making a living. He shouldn't be elated when he has money and in despair when he lacks money. Either way, he should cling to his emuna and trust in Hashem. There's a folk-story about a poor man walking on the side of the road while carrying a heavy load on his shoulders. A rich man comes by in his fancy horse-drawn carriage and calls to the poor man to come aboard. The poor man sits down in the carriage but the heavy burlap sap is still on his shoulders.

The rich man says, "My friend, relax and enjoy the ride. Put the sack on the floor."

The poor man reacts, "Sir, the favor you are doing by giving me a ride in your carriage is more than enough. How can I be so insolent as to expect your carriage to shoulder my load?"

That describes a person who worries about making a living. Hashem is already giving you life, a working heart, brain and lungs. To sustain you, He'll give you a source of income as well. A person must do his job of strengthening emuna and rely on Hashem to do His job of providing an income.

Hashem sends salvation to those who trust in Him. The "Chafetz Chaim" writes in his elaboration on Psalm 31 that the measure of trust has nothing to do with the righteousness of a person. In other words, even if a person who is not upright trusts in Hashem, his measure of trust will invoke Divine protection on him.

King David says in Psalm 33 that the eye of Hashem is cast toward those who fear Him and yearn for His loving-kindness. Those who fear Him are the ones with emuna and those who look forward to His loving-kindness are the ones who trust in Him. Therefore, King David cites these two characteristics to show that such a person will never lack sufficient income.

104. I Said Thank You and I Heard

When I was in Meron at the holy gravesite of Rebbe Shimon bar Yochai, a young man from Tzfat told me the following story:

The young man suffered from ruptured eardrums and he could no longer hear. He paid a load of money to a private surgeon but the operation just made things worse. The surgeon felt bad about what happened and promised to perform corrective surgery.

The young man said, "I just finished reading 'The Gems of Gratitude' and I don't need your corrective surgery." He began thanking Hashem profusely for his hearing problem and for the fact that the surgery further ruptured his eardrums. He thanked Hashem for the money he lost on the doctors and their futile treatments. He would thank Hashem all day long. One day, he suddenly began to hear again.

The young man returned to the physician for a checkup. His eardrums were in perfect shape. The surgeon demanded to know the name of the physician who did the corrective surgery. The young man was hesitant to tell him that he just said thank You to Hashem, for he was afraid that he'd be sent to a mental hospital…

People hear such stories but they're still far away from thanking Hashem for their challenges in life. Why? They don't yet acknowledge that their whole purpose in life is to learn emuna. Since life's difficulties force us to learn emuna, they are intrinsically good! We should therefore thank Hashem profusely for them. That's why each of us must lovingly accept Hashem's amazing Divine Providence, realize that it's all for the best and thank Hashem accordingly. This is complete emuna.

The evil inclination knows that acquiring emuna is a person's ultimate purpose in life and therefore makes every effort to inject heresy in a person's heart and brain. He confuses people and pushes them into sadness and depression to the extent that they can't say thank You. Anyone who reads about the type of miracles we relate here knows that there are no natural remedies for tribulations. If a person needs miraculous salvation, he must turn to Hashem – there is no alternative.

The evil inclination attempts to harden a person's heart with bitterness so that he won't be able to express gratitude to Hashem. What's more, it tries to blind a person so that he won't be able to see Hashem's marvelous miracles. Therefore, one's spiritual first-aid is to stop whining and complaining immediately! A person who rejoices in his tribulations brings salvation to the world. What's more, he'll see miracles and salvations in his own life that completely defy nature.

105. I Said Thank You and I Breathed

Wherever I lecture, I ask people to write down their stories of "I said thank You and I saw miracles." After one of my lectures, a young man told me that he had terrible respiratory problems to the extent that he could barely breathe.

Lacking breath, he couldn't speak so he began thanking Hashem in his heart. "Thank You Hashem that it's so hard for me to breathe. Thank You for letting me breathe and stay alive until today. If You want to take away my breath, I'll thank You for that too." Two or three minutes later, his breathing difficulties passed as if nothing ever happened.

If a person can't find a reason to thank Hashem, then let him say thank You at least for his lungs that work and for the air he breathes. That's something we ought to thank Hashem for every single minute of our lives. Who is foolish enough to take a breath for granted?

Who can complain to Hashem? A person should be thankful for every minute of life, every hour and every day. Tosefot in the Gemara (tractate Kiddushin 80) tells a story about a woman with seven sons. One died and she cried all the time. When the prescribed mourning period was over, people warned her to stop crying and to rejoice in her six sons. She refused and kept on crying. A second son died. She continued crying and complaining until all seven died. Finally, she herself died because of all of her whining and complaining against the Almighty.

We see from the above that whining and complaining not only fail to bring about salvations but evoke stern judgments.

If a person chooses to cry, then he gets many more reasons to cry, Heaven forbid. Fortunately, if a person chooses to say thank You, he is given many more wonderful reasons to do so.

106. The Doctor Lacked an Explanation

A 26-year-old woman told that the gynecologist wanted to remove one of her vital inner organs, Heaven forbid. She thanked Hashem for her medical problem for a half hour every day. Six weeks later, she returned to the doctor for a checkup and her internal organ was completely healthy with no trace of lesions or any other problems. The doctor said, "I don't know how to explain what happened."

The young lady said, "You don't have to explain anything to me." Usually, the doctors in Israel say, "This is a medical miracle." That's the power of gratitude.

A person who lives with gratitude feels Divine compassion all the time. When seemingly bad things befall him, he focuses on Hashem's loving-kindness and all the wonderful things he has to say thank You for. He believes that everything is for the best and that only Hashem knows what's best for him.

Think about this: **if a person lives with "The Garden of Gratitude" and with the gratitude pamphlets and CDs, Moshiach won't teach him anything new**. Why? Moshiach will teach people emuna and gratitude; that everything is from Hashem and all for the best. Those who already know that and are already saying thank You are already living this wonderful truth.

107. The Problem Solved

Our Russian-speaking rabbi told the story of a young couple who had recently become observant. For a long time, they didn't have children. Yet, their prayers were answered and they had a baby girl but she was born sick. The doctors couldn't figure out what was wrong with her. The parents called their rabbi for advice; he told them to thank Hashem and that everything would work out.

The parents did what the rabbi told them to and the baby overcame her health challenges. Later, the baby began having respiratory problems. They were referred to a German doctor who treats such ailments with gas. The parents, offspring of Holocaust survivors, didn't like the idea of a German doctor and gas treatments. They called their rabbi once more and he advised them to say thank You again. They did. When the parents returned to the hospital, the local doctors were preparing the baby for treatment. They removed the respiratory apparatus that was inserted in the baby's throat but couldn't seem to put the apparatus back in place after the treatment. While they were trying, the baby expectorated a chunk of flesh by way of her esophagus. This was the obstruction that was preventing the baby from breathing normally! The baby needed no further treatment.

Why do we wait for troubles? Why aren't we thanking Hashem all the time? The reason is because we lack emuna, either in Hashem or in the power of our prayers and thanks. Every person must speak to Hashem all the time and in his own language. Talk about everything. Ask Hashem's advice and tell Him everything that's on your heart.

Another reason why people don't talk to Hashem and thank Him is because they don't believe that He loves them and wants to help them. They don't realize how infinite Hashem's mercy is, sufficient to help anyone in any predicament.

With the above in mind, a person should pray daily for more emuna, that Hashem should give him full emuna that He loves him unconditionally, wants to help him and listens to every word of his prayers. Hashem's mercy and goodness is limitless. Full emuna means that we know that He is a beloved Father in Heaven who only desires the very best for each of us. All we have to do is to turn to Him.

A person with full emuna never has enough of Hashem – he speaks to Him at every opportunity, all day long, and shares everything with Hashem.

108. Sweeter than Sugar

A person told that his father had diabetes and suffered terribly from pains in his feet. The father received our CD, "Stop Crying" and started thanking Hashem for his pains until they disappeared entirely.

The "Pele Yoetz" writes that it's only proper to thank the Creator for every tiny amenity in our lives. As soon as something good happens, his mouth should praise and thank Hashem on the spot. Even if he has tribulations, he should thank Hashem for He chastises those whom He loves (see Proverbs 3:12). We must also remember that Hashem is merciful in His judgments and even though we might experience suffering, we might have deserved much worse. This is also a reason to thank Him. We also see that we often enjoy blessings in life that even those who are more deserving than we are don't benefit.

Rabbenu Yona explains that a person must vocalize his thanks, for if Hashem gave that person the power of speech, he must use it to exalt Him. Throughout the day, our speech should sanctify Hashem's Name as much as possible. Conversely, one must make a concerted effort to avoid any forbidden speech. Forbidden speech constitutes a misuse of our mouth, teeth, tongue, vocal chords and all other bodily apparatus that contributes to the power of speech. Expressing one's praise of and gratitude to Hashem is a most lofty form of Divine service.

109. The Very Best for Us

Rabbi Shmuel Goldstein, who survived the deadly terrorist attack in the Har Nof synagogue, tells: "In the middle of the Amida prayer, I heard gunfire. My 12-year-old son Mordechai and I quickly hid under the table. I said "Shma Yisrael" under my breath and meanwhile the shooting continued. The terrorist with the butcher knife passed by me, hit me with the blade of the knife on my back and on the head, and continued on his way. While I was lying on the floor, I saw the second terrorist who was standing next to the cantor's podium. His gun was jammed and I called the police. I put my cellphone in my pocket and looked at the terrorist who was standing with his back to me. During those few seconds, Hashem empowered me. I grabbed the terrorist by the shoulders and pulled him down strongly. He started falling and he dropped the pistol. The second terrorist saw what was happening and came toward me. He yelled, "Get out of here!" and I fled outside. That moment, I realized what a tremendous miracle happened to me. Instead of grabbing the pistol on the floor, the terrorist chased me away. By then, the ambulances and the medics arrived, they put me in the ambulance and I lost consciousness."

Shmuel Goldstein's wife relates, "When my son Mordechai ran home that morning and said, 'Mommy, there are three Arab terrorists shooting in the synagogue,' the first thing that came into my mind is that everything Hashem does is for the very best. I hugged my son and thanked Hashem for saving him. He was a miracle packed into a 12-year-old's body. I then called the police and blurted out whatever information I could give them. I sat my other children down to recite Psalms. I told them briefly what I knew and promised that Hashem does everything for the best. My 2-year-old daughter woke up and my 4-year-old daughter reassured me that whatever Hashem does is the very best for us. We continued to say Psalms while the phone rang constantly. A social worker called and said that my husband had been hospitalized in Hadassah Hospital and that I should come quickly with someone to escort me. My mother, sister and brother-in-law picked me up."

"I told my children to remember that Hashem does everything for the very best. I always felt that our task as parents is to teach our children trust and simple emuna in Hashem. When we arrived at the hospital, the head physician explained that my husband condition was critical. They took us to the family room and we continued reciting Psalms. They explained to me that my husband was hacked by the butcher knife in his head and a piece of broken skull had penetrated the brain. The wound in his back was large, severe and deep. They let me see him briefly before he was wheeled into the operating room. When my husband heard my voice, he opened his eyes. The doctor couldn't believe it. I told my husband, 'Mordechai ran home – everything's OK'. I could see the joy in his eyes; that's how he entered the operating room, for an operation that lasted ten hours."

During the course of the operation, one of the surgeons came out and informed me that they had succeeded in removing the piece of broken bone that had penetrated the brain. He said that they would need to do a bone transplant where the skull had been broken. Then he paused and said, 'There's no connection between your husband's neurological condition and between what we're seeing. Your family has special protection from Above.' In the coming days, I saw more and more miracles. Ten days later, against all odds, we brought him home with Hashem's loving grace. When we entered the door, his first words were from Psalm 104, 'I'll sing to Hashem while I live…' Our mouths are full of praise to Hashem."

Rabbi Shmuel Goldstein adds, "When I woke up in the hospital the day after the operation, the first words that entered my mind were, , 'I'll sing to Hashem while I live.' Since then, I can't stop saying that passage. Death was right in my face and Hashem saved me. The terrorist attack gave me a new outlook on life. Everything is a miracle – I can't take a single breath for granted. People think that they only have to thank Hashem when they buy something new, but everything else is taken for granted. **We must thank Hashem for every heartbeat, for every step we take. We must never stop saying thank You!**"

110. Growing from Difficulties

Here's another story about the power of thanks that appeared on our website.

Galit Gilboa was a happy young woman about to be married.

A few months before the wedding, her fiancé was killed in Operation Protective Edge, the Gaza War of 2014.

Galit grew up in a well-to-do neighborhood in Petah Tikva. Overseas vacations and five-star hotel rooms were amenities that she was used to. She had a relatively unchallenging childhood, until…

When she was performing national service in the Judean settlement of Psagot, her brother arrived and said, "Galit, there's no home for you to come home to. Find a new place to live." Like thunder on a clear day, she discovered that her parents became divorced. For two difficult years, she literally had to find places to sleep on Shabbat. It was a most difficult time for her.

Despite the challenge, she strengthened herself in emuna and enrolled in a graphics course in "Emuna College" in Jerusalem. She lived in the dorm there. Galit tells, "Once, I came into the room and my roommates were whining about how difficult life is. I told them, 'Are you all crazy? You come from well-to-do homes and lack nothing!' I started lecturing them about how good they have it. No one knew what was going on in my house. One of my girlfriends said, 'Who are you to talk, Galit, with the silver spoon in your mouth.' I almost choked."

After much prodding, Galit agreed to meet Gad Ezra, of martyred and blessed memory, who soon became her fiancé. At the time, the Gaza War broke out. Gad, who served as a commander in a special ops unit, was rushed to Jenin.

"During the war, we spoke on the phone. Gad never told me what he did, but several of his friends had been killed. 'Galit, if something happens to me…' I wouldn't let him finish the sentence, but he was serious. I never knew him like that. He was insistent and he said there was something he had to tell me. I told him that he could write it down but right after to rip up what he wrote. The heavy conversation passed and everything returned to our happy mode of preparing for the wedding."

Galit was on the way home for marriage-preparation clothes shopping when her two brothers called her one after the other, each asking to meet her since they hadn't seen her for a long time. By the time she arrived home, both her brothers and her mother were waiting for her. Her birthday was still a few days away, so it couldn't be a surprise party. When she started to show them the clothes she bought, she sensed that something was wrong.

When her brother broke out in tears, she realized that something terrible had happened – her fiancé had been killed. "The realization suddenly hit me. I never believed that I could cry so many tears. A minute later, I got hold of myself. I started singing Psalm 23: 'Although I walk in the valley of death, I shall fear no evil for You are with me.' I then sang Psalm 92, 'It's good to thank Hashem'. My mother burst out crying – she thought I had lost my mind in grief. I told her, 'Mom, this is the most difficult test I've ever had in life; I'm completely disoriented now. I don't know what to do with myself or with my new clothes. Everything is foggy. But, one thing is clear to me – this is from Hashem and it's all for my very best.'"

When Galit arrived at Gadi's house, she remembered their conversation about the letter he wanted to write. "What a jerk I was; why didn't I let him write that letter. I don't know what happened to me. I entered his room and I opened his top drawer. He did write the letter and it was right there, addressed to me. I read its contents without interruption.

I debated whether to show it to his parents or to keep it to myself."

Gadi wrote, "…if this letter reaches your hands, it's a sign that something happened to me. I promise you, Galit, that everything is for the very best and that I am in a wonderful place – the best that can possibly be. I neither suffer nor do I have any sorrow. My only sorrow is the sorrow that you and my family feel. Please pass this message on – 'There is no despair in the world – be happy always." This is what I ask of you, even though it's not easy. I know that I can ask this of you, because I know the light of joy that you naturally reflect always…"

Because of the letter's tremendous value, Galit decided to let it be published.

"How do I continue living now? I said to myself, whatever I do, I must do it all the way. To live, live all the way! To die, die all the way! If Hashem wanted me to die, He'd take me. I decided to keep on living for there's a lot I have left to do in this world. I didn't know how I'd do it, but I decided to live all the way, to be happy and to appreciate everything. At the end of the *shiva*, the seven-day mourning period, I thought that I had swallowed an emuna pill."

A week later, Galit was invited to give a talk to girls doing their national service, the public service that religious girls perform instead of serving in the army. "There were a thousand girls at the assembly and I had no idea what to tell them. I had Gadi's letter in my blouse pocket." She started by singing Psalm 92 with the girls, *Tov lehodot L'Hashem* – it's good to thank Hashem. Half the girls in the auditorium were crying already. Then, she told her personal story; she spoke for four hours and not a single girl fidgeted in her chair. It was amazingly strengthening and uplifting.

"When I found out that Gadi got killed, I thought that I lost my life too. But Hashem makes no mistakes; it was no random bullet that struck Gadi in the neck. It was all from Hashem and all for the best. Meanwhile, I spread emuna everywhere. I am now married and a mother as well. I want to live in joy and in emuna and teach my children the joy of emuna. I want them to appreciate everything and to thank Hashem always."

"I can either cry and complain or say thank You – that's my free choice in life. But you know, as soon as a person realizes that he or she is in Hashem's hands, life is paradise. The feeling that a person is dependent on himself is really scary. Yet, when you know that everything is the product of the Creator's love for you – and that He personally is taking care of you – you attain such joy and inner peace that are simply unattainable without emuna. How fortunate we are!"

111. Zero on the Test

On one of my radio shows, a girl phoned in and said that although she was an excellent student in high school, she never succeeded in learning English. In her university entrance exams, she got a big fat zero in English. Her chances of being accepted were nil.

She began to thank Hashem. "Hashem, thank You for not letting me succeed in English. If You don't want me to be accepted to university, this is obviously the best-case scenario for me. I am pleased with whatever You do and decide." She had read all the Gems of Gratitude pamphlets and had listened to our gratitude CDs. A few days later, she received a letter from the university: "Although you failed the exam in English, in light of your other superior exam results, we've decided to accept you."

When you say thank You, all the laws change. It's impossible to understand how they change, but they do! With gratitude, a person flunks a key exam, but gets accepted. What's going on here?

Gratitude invokes every blessing while ingratitude does the opposite. A person who is grateful shows that he is happy with his lot in life; this is the indication of genuine emuna, the emuna that is the vessel for limitless abundance from Above. Emuna and gratitude open every blockage and bring about marvelous salvations. They open the gates of abundance.

If you'd like riches in material and spiritual abundance, go with gratitude and never stop saying thank You! Beware of ingratitude, for it is the escort of unspeakable troubles in life. Never stop saying thank You!

112. Looking at Riches

A couple came to me complaining about their limited income. I reminded them of their wealth. "You used to live outside of Israel and you were far away from observant Judaism. You were fortunate enough both to make teshuva and to move to Israel. You are able to learn Torah for half a day and to work as a scribe for the other half day. You guard your eyes and you care about your personal holiness. Do you know how far you've come?!?"

I told them that Haman was one of history's richest people. He was the viceroy of 127 countries and he had hundreds of sons. The whole world bowed down to him. But when he saw Mordechai the Jew, the one person who wouldn't bow down to him, Haman said that all his life with all his riches were worth nothing. That is the impure spiritual force of Haman-Amalek. As soon as the tiniest thing doesn't go the way you like, life is worthless. "Look, you have children – good ones – who are healthy and learning Torah. You live in Israel. Your family is together. Look at all these riches!" Suddenly, the couple was ashamed for feeling other than blessed.

That's how the *klipa*, the impure spiritual force of Haman-Amalek, works…

We all must learn that life is never perfect. But if we neutralize the *klipa* of Haman-Amalek, we can withstand the tests in life. This spiritual force of impurity is the source of sadness, depression and ingratitude, as well as self-persecution.

Every moment of life entails an ongoing battle against the force of Haman-Amalek, which blinds a person of his good fortune.

As soon as a person tastes the slightest taste of dissatisfaction, he should say, "Life is great. Look at all my blessings! I put on tefillin this morning! I prayed in a minyan! I wear tzitzit all day long. I said dozens of blessings today. I heard a Torah lesson. I went to Uman this year…"

The Zohar says that no good desire is ever lost. It's all recorded in a person's ledger of merits. Look for the diamonds in life and rejoice in them. Look at the riches you have.

A person who speaks the opposite of Haman's style and says, "It's all worth it", will pass life's tests with flying colors. He won't suffer from anxiety; he'll be strong and he'll constantly ascend. All year long, he's wiping out the klipa of Haman-Amalek.

The people who have started to keep gratitude notebooks and write down their daily blessings report that life has become paradise for them. Everyone of us has fantastic riches, if we only open our eyes to see all the blessings we have. If a person puts himself in the joy and gratitude mode, everything will work out for the very best.

The Holy Temple was destroyed because people failed to appreciate the indescribable riches in their midst. If everyone had lived with songs of praise and gratitude, the Holy Temple would not have been destroyed. When Moshiach will come, he'll tell everyone just to say thank You all day long!

113. The Tenth Apartment

A woman complained to me about her troubles and that she was about to move into her tenth apartment since she got married a few years ago. I told her to be happy, for this was an amazing atonement for her.

One of the students in our yeshiva suffered from difficult tribulations. He went to Rabbi Mordechai Eliahu osb"m and asked him for a blessing that the tribulations should cease. Rabbi Eliahu asked him, "Are you sure that you want to rid yourself of these tribulations?" Every person has an allotment of tribulations that save him from much more severe suffering. As I wrote in "The Garden of Peace", those who rid themselves of marital challenges by getting a divorce are merely substituting one set of tribulations for another set that is liable to be much worse.

The only way to gain relief from tribulations is to rejoice in them, to accept them lovingly. Remember – by accepting a few tribulations with love, a person won't need to suffer many additional tribulations. If a person doesn't accept a few day's tribulations willingly, he might end up suffering for forty years, as the Children of Israel did by wandering in the desert when they refused to weather three days of difficulties by entering the Land of Israel.

Back to the woman who moved to ten different apartments: perhaps, if she had lovingly accepted the disadvantages or whatever hardships she had in the first apartment, she might not have had to move ten times…

The question is, do you believe or don't you believe? If you believe that everything is for the very best, then start dancing and singing. Thank Hashem! For how long? Thank Him every day of your life for the rest of your life! That's what we're doing here in this world; we came here to learn emuna and to thank Hashem.

If you thank Hashem for all your blessings in life as well as for your deficiencies, your salvation has already arrived. You'll always be happy. It took Joseph 22 years to see salvation, but in the meanwhile, he was always happy, even in the worst of circumstances. Happiness invokes the Divine spirit of holiness.

Emuna will never change. Be strong in emuna and never fear. Tell Hashem, **"If this is what You want, Father in Heaven, I'm happy with it! I believe that You alone know what's best for me."**

Everyone's life resembles a magnificent landscape painting with a breathtaking view. But why don't we see the beauty in the painting of our own lives? If we don't look at life through our lenses of emuna, whatever tiny challenge we have turns into a foreboding, dark black cloud that obstructs our ability to see all the lovely scenery. The evil inclination masterfully and cynically takes that cloud and inflates it so much until a person sees nothing else but the menacing darkness. This cloud is also the cloud of ingratitude, where a person thinks that he deserves everything he wants but doesn't deserve and of the challenges that Hashem wants him to have. If life isn't exactly as he wants it, he becomes disgruntled and depressed.

It turns out that with the evil inclination's help, a person turns a relatively minor problem into a threatening storm cloud that obscures everything else. This is a lie.

Don't accept that lie! Don't let a small challenge overwrite a beautiful life. Put the small trouble aside for a moment and focus on all of your blessings in life. You have eyes, a beating heart, two healthy lungs, two kidneys of your own, clothes on your body and a roof over your head! If you haven't eaten today, it's because you decided to fast, not because there's no food in the house. Did you thank Hashem for all these blessings? For your spouse, your parents and your children? What right does anyone have to take this magnificent blessings for granted? What about all the fabulous mitzvoth that Hashem enables you to do every single day, including today? Start saying thank You and you'll see how beautiful life really is.

Here in Israel, we see Hashem's miracles every moment. Has anyone looked at the map and counted the tens of millions of hostile enemies who surround us, all armed to the hilt?

It's none other than Hashem's amazing loving-kindness that sustains us, protects us and vitalizes us every moment of the day.

A person must constantly take stock of the abundance, favors and blessings that Hashem bestows upon him every minute and every second. To ignore these priceless amenities is ingratitude at its worst. Therefore, we must never stop thanking Hashem!

114. The Cancelled Shidduchim

A young girl called in during one of my radio broadcasts and said that she was suffering much in the *shidduchim* (matchmaking) process. She had what she thought was a great match and proposal, but that was cancelled. A second time, she had something that she thought was even better, but that was cancelled too.

I said to her, "How lucky you are! You're accruing big rewards in the world to come and meanwhile you're suffering in this world. Hashem really loves you; we'll all be jealous of you in the next world. Thank Him!" These few words were sufficient to make her smile. Just by looking at things with emuna, we mitigate all stern judgments.

I explained to her that when a person doesn't accept a tribulation lovingly, he soon gets another tribulation. That's why she suffered the second cancelled shidduch, because she didn't accept the first cancellation with love. As with the Children of Israel and the sin of the spies, the failure to accept three days of tribulations carried a price tag of forty years of wandering in the desert. Why?

The Zohar explains that before the Jewish People sinned by their whining and complaining, they were on the required spiritual level to enter the Land of Israel. But, after they sinned, the Almighty had to wait until the generation of those who sided with the spies and slandered Hashem's magnificent gift of the Land of Israel died off. Then, the young generation who had not sinned by complaining and ingratitude, were worthy of entering the Land of Israel.

So what if someone backed down from a shidduch? It's all for the best! Accept it with love! Don't persecute yourself. This is what Hashem wants and it's all for your ultimate benefit. By accepting this tribulation with love, you'll atone for all your sins and soon find your real soul-mate.

We yearn to teach the wisdom of gratitude to all of humanity so that people will live beautiful lives and see miraculous salvations with their own eyes.

115. Rejoice in the Good, Grow from the Challenges

A person complained to me about his income problems. I told him, "Look how good life is to you: you've started to observe the Sabbath. You've started to engage in daily personal prayer. You are growing. Were it not for the income problems, you'd have never sought Hashem. Tell me the truth – without your income problems, would you have ever attended one of my emuna lectures? We both know the answer. Realize that your difficulties in life have brought you closer to Hashem."

A man from Netanya wanted to commit suicide. He heard one of my CDs and he came to speak to me. He overheard me asking my son if the travel agent had sent our tickets to Uman. He expressed his desire to go to Uman too. He ran home to pack a suitcase and met me at the airport that same evening. The next morning, we were in Uman. I gave him a rush course in emuna and gratitude.

When Hashem wants to rescue someone, in one day they can emerge from the deepest darkness to the brightest light. People must therefore rejoice in everything good and grow from life's challenges.

After he sinned, Adam had to leave the Garden of Eden. Why? Hashem knew that if Adam had remained in paradise, he'd never do teshuva. Personal and spiritual gain comes from the sweat of a person's brow. But, with a daily hour of personal prayer and the knowledge that everything is for the very best, this world returns to being a paradise.

By speaking to Hashem, a person builds emuna. By speaking to Hashem, he realizes that everything is for the best. Daily teshuva and self-assessment is the best spiritual hygiene there is. Without daily teshuva, a person can't attain emuna.

Teshuva is not a once-in-a-lifetime or annual affair – it's daily. A person must carefully assess everything he does, says and thinks. Confessing one's transgressions is one of the Torah's 613 mitzvoth. For a person who speaks to Hashem daily, every day is a Day of Atonement where he is cleansed of sin and forgiven for everything he ever did wrong. Furthermore, we must seek Hashem's assistance in fulfilling His commandments, for without Hashem's help, it's impossible. Guarding one's eyes is a prime example; as the Gemara says, if Hashem doesn't help him, he won't have the power on his own to overcome the evil inclination.

A person can learn the entire Torah and pray from a prayerbook for hours, but until he sets aside a daily hour to speak to Hashem, he'll never attain emuna. He certainly won't reach the level where he knows that everything Hashem does is for the very best. When you want to speak to your father, do you read from a book? No, you express yourself in your own words. Why? You believe that your father listens, loves you and understands you. Otherwise, you won't speak to him. The same goes for our Father in Heaven; if you believe that He is good, listening, understanding and loving, you'll speak to Him. That's why emuna begins with personal prayer. Those who believe, speak to Hashem; those who don't believe, don't speak. It's that simple.

Prayer should be with joy and gratitude, not with crying and complaining. If so, why did our sages praise crying and the shedding of tears in prayer? The tears and crying they refer to are the tears of yearning and not of melancholy. Even so, in most of our sages' references to prayer, they emphasize prayer with joy. And, the gates of tears that are never locked are the gates of tears that result from deepest love and yearning for Hashem that are also the products of joy.

116. Everyone is Following Emuna

Here's a parable that shows how gratitude unlocks all the gates and turns everything around for the very nest:

A righteous family lived in dire poverty in Odessa, Ukraine.

One day, the family heard knocking at their door. The head of the household opened the door and saw a group of people smiling from ear to ear. He asked them who they were. The first one said, "I'm Emuna"; the second said, "I'm Happiness"; the third said, "I'm Wealth"; the fourth said, "I'm Good Health"; the fifth said, "My name is Blessing."

"Welcome to my home," said the righteous poor man.

"No," they said in unison. "You must choose which one of us you want. We told you who we are, but only one of us can come inside your home."

"If that's the case," he said, "I must consult my wife and children." The poor man said to his family, "Look at the miracles at our doorstep! Look at their beautiful smiles! If we want, we can have happiness, good health, blessing, wealth or emuna. Which do you want?" The whole family agreed that Emuna was the guest they wanted to invite inside.

When Emuna entered their home, all the other guests came in as well. The poor man said, "I thought that only one of you was allowed to enter."

They replied happily, "True! If you had chosen anyone other than Emuna, then only one of us could come inside. But since you chose Emuna, we all follow, for we always follow her!"

This parable has a deep lesson to it: if you have emuna, you have everything.

Just as one mitzvah leads to another and one transgression leads to another, one expression of gratitude leads to another. The "Pele Yoetz" writes emphatically that expressions of gratitude lead to salvations, giving people more and more reasons to express their gratitude. That's why when we say thank You, we see miracles.

117. Nothing Goes Right

A young main complained to me, "Nothing goes right in my life." I told him that he should be happy that things don't come easy for him, that he must work hard to accomplish his goals. I also showed him a list of things that do go right for him: he became an observant Jew, he became close to tzaddikim and he knows that there's a Creator to the world. He also knows that there's a great gift in life called "personal prayer." He agreed with me.

As soon as people encounter the slightest obstacles, they lose heart and claim that nothing's going right. The truth is that they lack prayer and that they fail to thank Hashem for the many things that do "go right" in life, such as their heart, lungs, eyesight, and bodily functions, just to name an important few. If so, then their lack of success is a blessing, for any success that comes without prayer leads to arrogance. A lack of success is a tremendous blessing and a sign of Hashem's love – He wants to hear your voice and to bring you close to Him. Be happy and say, "Thank You, Hashem, for caring so much about me. You definitely know what's best for me. Thanking You for teaching me to invest more in prayer and gratitude. Thank You for bringing me closer to You!"

Why do people see life's setbacks as a license to be sad? Joseph's tribulations were unthinkably unbearable, yet he danced and sang while incarcerated in an Egyptian prison. Can you imagine how terrible the conditions were there? Yet, Joseph sang qand danced! No wonder everyone adored him and he rose to be viceroy of all of Egypt. It's our task to accept life's difficulties with joy, to strengthen ourselves in emuna and to believe that everything is for the very best!

If you feel alone, just imagine how a lone Jewish boy, cut off from his family, felt in an Egyptian dungeon! Yet with emuna, you're never alone. The pain of tribulations comes predominantly from a lack of emuna.

When the going is tough, a person must pray for the emuna that everything is for the best. These prayers are actually vessels of abundance, which are the wonderful vessels for receiving whatever that person is asking for. With no vessels, there's no abundance. Imagine that your prayers are shining crystal goblets, into which Hashem can pour "abundance", His finest wine. Where there are no goblets, Hashem won't waste the abundance by pouring it on the floor. As such, prayers and gratitude enable the abundance to flow – the more the prayers, the more the abundance.

There are those who want Hashem to run their lives exactly as they see fit. They refuse to do anything that's not to their liking. Their attitude is a statement to Hashem, saying: "OK, Hashem – I'll work for You, but you must meet my terms!" Can you imagine the chutzpa of talking to a flesh-and-blood employer like that? He'd say, "Go ahead and resign!" The moment a person isn't happy with serving Hashem the way Hashem wants, and according to the conditions that Hashem dictates, it's like the worker telling the employer how to run the firm. That certainly isn't acceptable. Emuna means serving Hashem with joy no matter what the circumstances that Hashem puts us in; that we learn humility and get close to Him.

From here, all our actions should be in Hashem's honor and not for our own personal convenience. A person shouldn't require a "spiritual arousal" or deep inspiration before serving Hashem. One should serve Hashem innocently, even and especially when the conditions are not ideal. By serving Hashem from a place of darkness, a person attains a much loftier spiritual accomplishment than by serving Him when the conditions are ideal.

Rebbe Nachman writes in his famous epistle (Likutei Moharan II:48): "One must be tenacious in the service of Hashem." Rebbe Nachman says that a person should hold on to whatever tiny spiritual gain he makes and not to relinquish it. In any event, he must persevere, even to the point of being obstinate. Good desires are something to be stubborn about. Furthermore, no one can ever take away your desire.

Rebbe Nachman emphasizes in the above teaching that one's unwillingness to let go of whatever tiny progress he made in serving Hashem is the exact solution to avoiding the pitfalls of self-persecution and despair during times of setbacks and challenges.

Even the greatest tsaddikim had to face excruciating tests of their faith as well as severe spiritual setbacks on their life's journey of getting close to Hashem. No one said that it's easy and no one promised that such a prized goal can be attained in a way that enables a person to remain within his comfort zone. Yet, the route of ups and downs tests a person's emuna and his desire. It lets us know how sincerely we really want to get close to Hashem.

Prepare yourself to run life's obstacle course of challenges with emuna and with the desire never to give up. No matter what, hold onto emuna! Say thank You to Hashem for everything He's doing, for it's surely for your ultimate benefit. Say to yourself, "I don't care what happens to me – I will be happy at all costs. I won't let anything rob me of my smile and of my emuna. I have Hashem! No one can take away my desire to get close to Him!"

Rebbe Nachman's advice of perseverance and tenacity is exactly what we all need to find the path of ultimate success. Just because things look dark and you don't feel like anyone Above is smiling at you, don't think for a moment that Hashem is unhappy with you! Just the opposite is true. Serving Hashem under a bombardment of difficulties brings the greatest gratification to Him. All the tsaddikim – Jacob, Joseph, Moses, King David and all subsequent greats – were faced with virtually unsurmountable difficulties. These are what made them tsaddikim!

Be strong and brave; accept whatever is happening in your life with emuna and with love, and never lay down your weapons of prayer and desire.

118. Born Anew

During one of my lessons, a person came up from the audience and told this story:

"I had a relative who rose to a lucrative position of authority in his company. His jealous peers plotted against him. Together with additional difficulties at work, he was unable to cope and consequently suffered a severe nervous breakdown. He was even hospitalized and put on psychiatric medications. Someone gave him a copy of 'The Garden of Emuna'; by reading and studying the book, he no longer needed hospitals, doctors and medications. He told me that he felt like he was 'born anew'".

Not a day goes by without my hearing such stories, how an emuna book or CD saved someone's life. People have arrived at the verge of suicide only to change their lives dramatically for the better thanks to one emuna book or CD.

A prestigious Rosh Kollel told his rabbinical students about the "importance of learning Rabbi Arush's books; they're the rescue squad of this generation."

Gratitude has the ability to revive the dead. I have seen so many people who were like zombies – walking dead. They had no will to live for nothing was going right in their lives. I tell them, "Don't ask for a thing; just say thank You all day long even if you are not yet sincere about it. You need the light of gratitude. Say thank You all day long. Say thank You for every breath you take and for every tooth in your mouth. Take nothing for granted. Just say thank You!" With gratitude, the walking dead come back to life because the light of gratitude is the light that is capable of reviving the dead, literally!

119. Thank You for the Fatigue

A Torah student told me that he was tired and he didn't have the power to learn Torah. He asked me what to do. I told him to thank Hashem for his fatigue and then Hashem would illuminate his brain as to why he is tired and as to what he needs to rectify.

Hashem enabled me to understand that after a person thanks Hashem, and asks Him what the benefit is from the fatigue (for everything Hashem does is for the best), then Hashem will illuminate his eyes and show him that he is tired because he doesn't sufficiently love the Torah! If he loved the Torah, he wouldn't feel any fatigue during learning.

I was travelling with tzaddikim and they didn't stop learning for a single moment. Even if they dozed off for a moment, they would awake immediately and dive right back into their learning. When you love something so much, you gladly and energetically involve yourself with it.

I explained the above concept to the Torah student. I suggested that he beg Hashem to instill the love of Torah within him. I gave him the example that if someone suddenly offered to take him to a place that he really loved, he'd jump at the opportunity and all his fatigue would disappear. Why? If you love something, there's no fatigue. But, if he had thanked Hashem for his fatigue, he would have understood all of this on his own.

Those who pursue the path of gratitude attain a deeper level of self-awareness. What's more, the evil inclination loses all control over them. A person who thanks Hashem for everything casts logic aside and clings to the emuna that everything is for the best. Such an individual becomes immune to despair and depression.

Don't think that anyone's life goes according to the way he or she desires, because only the Creator knows what's best for each individual, and not the individual himself. People devoid of emuna are therefore chronic sufferers of sorrow and negative emotions, for their lives are not progressing in the way they want. A person with emuna, on the other hand, accepts everything willingly because he knows that it's from Hashem and all for the best. He therefore thanks Hashem for everything. And, even if things don't go according to his will, he thanks Hashem for everything in his life that's askew. When he falls down, he sings immediately, "Thank You, Hashem, for my fall." The same goes for all his difficulties. If he gets insulted and embarrassed in public, he says, "Thank You, Hashem, for the insult and humiliation! You only want the best for me and I know that this is atonement for my sins. It beats a heart attack anytime! Thank You, thank You, thank You, Hashem!" Such a person ascends constantly and is always getting closer to Hashem.

An expression of gratitude in the face of difficulties shows that a person accepts Divine will and judgment with love. This humble individual has no sense of entitlement and he doesn't harbor the negative feelings that he deserves more from Hashem, or that he doesn't deserve the current difficulties. Since he is humble and happy, he will climb ever higher up the ladder of spirituality and spiritual awareness.

Consequently, gratitude brings a person to a stronger connection with Hashem. The closer he gets, the easier it is for him to ask for even more closeness. With gratitude, the same reason would have caused him to be depressed is now bringing him closer to Hashem.

Anything that looks negative – the type of things that cause people to be sad and depressed – become immediately positive as soon as a person understands that this is what Hashem wants. There is no longer reason to blame or persecute oneself, because whatever is happening is the outcome of Hashem's will and all for the best. The negative, once we take emuna into account, becomes positive and a good reason to rejoice and say thank You.

The way to be happy always is to cling to emuna always. Since the beginning of time, there has not been a human being whose life progressed along the lines of his desired scenario. This is the reality of creation. Therefore, **a person without emuna is sad**, for his life doesn't go the way he wants it to. He either persecutes himself or blames others, or both. Even if he smiles, deep down he's disgruntled for he harbors a long list of complaints in his heart.

With emuna, though, he's happy with whatever Hashem does and decides and he thanks Him accordingly. He doesn't concern himself with things that are outside the realm of his obligations at hand because he's happy with the way Hashem runs the world. He nullifies his desires to Hashem's desires and he's always happy.

A person who is happy in the face of setbacks, disappointments and difficulties should therefore realize that he is serving Hashem in the loftiest way. Even if he can't pick himself up emotionally, he pleads to Hashem and asks for His help in getting up and serving Hashem with joy, despite the challenges at hand. He reconciles himself lovingly to whatever way Hashem decides to handle his life even if he hasn't reached the stage where he can actually thank Hashem sincerely for his suffering.

Everyone wants to serve Hashem with joy, but sometimes Hashem takes our joy away in order to test us. Do we really want to serve Him and cling to Him no matter what? Such a person, who clings to his desire to be close to Hashem despite the pain and the setbacks, should know that he is serving Hashem in the loftiest way.

We don't serve Hashem because it uplifts and inspires us. We serve Him even in times of heavy fog and darkness when we don't feel inspired at all. Even in those dark places, the true servant of Hashem seeks to know what Hashem wants from him and he's happy with whatever lot in life Hashem gives him. He clings to his emuna and desire and thanks Hashem for them as well as for the darkness.

120. Advice for Being Happy

A person made an appointment with me and asked me how he could attain happiness. I told him to speak to the Creator for an hour a day and for most of the hour, simply to thank

Him for all his blessings in life. That way, he'd surely be happy.

He accepted my advice and began to implement both the daily personal prayer and the gratitude. Ever since, he no longer feels depressed and on the contrary, is actually happy. What's more, he has started to be Torah observant. That too added to his happiness for transgressions that go uncorrected are barriers that prevent Divine light from reaching a person.

Gratitude, and particularly gratitude in daily personal prayer, is a person's most important asset. Gratitude mitigates stern judgments, brings a person to emuna and helps him see the truth. With gratitude, he sees life in its proper perspective. He realizes that everything is the outcome of Divine will and providence. He attains the level of inner joy that enables him to pour his heart out to Hashem. Even when his heart aches and tears pour down his cheeks, he is truly happy for he knows that Hashem is with him and doing everything for the best. As such, Rebbe Nachman once said that only a joyous person can truly attain the level of a broken heart that is able to outpour its feelings to Hashem. Why? This sounds contradictory! It is not, because a person who lacks joy cannot open his mouth in sincere prayer. The sad person's prayers are full of whining and complaining. On the other hand, joy and gratitude erase the fantasies of entitlement and cleanse a person's soul, as Rebbe Nachman teaches (see Likutie Moharan I:54).

Even if a person feels that he's faking it by thanking Hashem for something that causes him pain and suffering, he should force himself to do it even though he would rather scream and cry. Why? The gratitude will illuminate the truth and enable him to yell out to Hashem in the proper way.

Even if this advice doesn't make sense, it's proven and time-tested. From my own experience, I've seen that I've often come to my personal prayer session bitter, confused and upset, as if the whole dark world was crashing down on me. As soon as I began to thank Hashem for the things that upset me, my emuna that everything's for the best became stronger. Gradually, I thanked Hashem with more sincerity until the sadness and bitterness left me altogether. I could then see the world in its proper, truthful perspective. I realized that everything is for the very best and that there is no bad in the world. There is no one but Hashem, and He in His infinite goodness and omniscience is running our lives. I stand before Him and can say whatever I like. I can request any and all assistance in the world. That way, I gain understanding what Hashem wants from me and in moving forward in my spiritual growth.

121. I'm Happy that I'm Sad

One of the married students in our yeshiva told me, "Rabbi, I'm tired all day long. Nothing goes right for me." I told him to thank Hashem for his fatigue and for his lack of success. Instead of being depressed, be grateful, for Hashem is doing everything for the best. I told him to avoid blaming himself or blaming his wife. Don't look for scapegoats or reasons. Hashem knows what He's doing, so say thank You. It's all good...

Even if you're down in the dumps, rejoice in your current circumstance. Thank Hashem for your sadness. "Hashem, if You want me to be sad, then that's the very best thing for me! Thank You, Hashem! I'm happy with whatever You do!"

Joy is the secret of Jewish survival. With joy, we merit Divine revelation. The worst curses in the Torah all stem from a lack of joy, as the Torah in Parshat Ki Tavo teaches us.

Over the years, I've presented the above ideas in a variety of ways to audiences around the globe. Many people have discovered that the advice of happiness and gratitude in the face of calamity literally strengthens their life force and gives then the will to live. The evil inclination is deathly afraid of joy and tries to rob a person of all joy, for that way, a person will never get close to Hashem or be satisfied with himself. The evil inclination says, "Be logical – look at all the pain and suffering in your life. How can you ignore them? Are you one of the great people of their world who can rejoice in pain? No – you're just a regular person; how can you be happy?"

People ask me this very question: "How can I be happy with all the pain in my life? I don't have the merits of the great tzaddikim to fall back on."

Here is the answer, based on Rebbe Nachman's teachings (see Likutei Moharan II:5):

1.   Every tiny mitzvah or compassionate deed that a person does has infinite worth, way beyond what any mortal can fathom. Don't think that you are "small" or "regular". Imagine that every time you give a coin to charity, a billion spiritual dollars are deposited in your Heavenly bank account. Any time you put on tefillin, light Shabbat candles or visit a sick person, another quadrillion merit dollars appear in your credit. The list is endless and mindboggling.

2.   Be happy that you consider yourself small, insignificant and undeserving. This even greater magnifies the value of every mitzvah you do. Despite your smallness, Hashem chose you to do a lofty deed. Thank Him accordingly!

3.   Hashem gives reward for a mitzvah in accordance with the way a person values that mitzvah. The more you rejoice in your mitzvoth, the greater their worth. One who fails to appreciate his mitzvoth actually depreciates them with his own two hands.

4.   Even if you consider yourself insignificant and unworthy, stop and think: do you want to move forward or to pity yourself and throw in the towel? Of course, you want to progress; that's wonderful, but you can't be great overnight. The great tzaddikim made slow and painful progress but they never gave up. Indeed, they were happy about every little bit they were able to do in the service of Hashem. If you don't value the little you do, you won't appreciate the greater measures either. Rejoice in what you have and in what you are able to do. This will give you the desire to achieve more and more, all of which adds up to a prodigious spiritual sum.

5.   Don't have a perfection-or-nothing mentality. Don't think that you haven't accomplished anything unless you recite the entire Book of Psalms in one reading. Be happy if you have five minutes that you set aside for reciting Psalms. Some people see that they only have five minutes, so they never

start. They end up doing nothing. Yet, the person who seizes every available minute, here on the bus and there waiting to checkout in the supermarket, ultimately accrues tremendous merit, whereas the all-or-nothing person is spiritually penniless. Remember, every tiny bit has great worth and is fuel for progress!

6.   A person rejoices in receiving something that he values. If he is not happy about the opportunity to perform a mitzva, it means that he doesn't value it. Such a lack of joy is an affront to the King and **therefore closes the gates to Divine abundance**. No one likes to give a gift that the recipient won't appreciate. As such, a person's lack of appreciation of whatever Hashem gives him, especially the opportunities of performing mitzvoth, blocks abundance of all sorts from reaching that person. He will find that progress slips through his fingers.

7.   Failure to appreciate Hashem's small gifts not only blocks progress and abundance, but invokes stern judgments against a person, including the 98 curses of Parshat Ki Tavo that we referred to above. Arrogance and a sense of entitlement especially invoke stern judgments and trigger troubles and tribulations.

8.   Be fully aware that the Creator doesn't own anyone a thing. Everything He gives a person is a free gift. A grateful person's prayers have charm and are readily answered. But, when the arrogant person prays with his inflated sense of entitlement, his prayers are actually complaints that he's lodging against what he considers Divine unfairness,

Heaven forbid. These prayers are disgusting and an insult to the King. Consequently, one's happiness and gratitude with his lot in life, great or small, is what makes his prayers appealing and leads to their being answered.

9.   Since joy in performing mitzvoth is a form of gratitude to Hashem, it is the basis for all good in life. Gratitude is the foundation of all good character traits. Ingratitude and sadness are the root of all evil.

10.   Hashem turns His countenance from the sad person. Without Hashem, the sad person goes from one setback to another. He brings upon himself tribulations, suffering, anger, fear, calamities and mental instability, often losing his income or even his family as well as his health. Even if he does feel justified in being sad, how will that help him? One should be wise, not right. Don't be a justified sufferer or else you'll suffer even more. Be wise and rejoice in every little good point that you can be thankful for.

11.   Sadness is a violation of Torah. Who has a license to violate Torah? This only perpetuates exile and Diaspora, as Rebbe Nachman and Rebbe Natan teach.

12.   Our sages teach that the Divine Presence dwells only in a place of joy (see Tractate Shabbat, 30). Hashem is with the joyous person. All blessings accompany joy, as well as miraculous salvations. Rebbe Nachman therefore said that it's a tremendous mitzvah to be happy always.

All of the above applies to a person who only has a few mitzvoth to his or her credit. Even so, they can rejoice! But in truth, as the Gemara says, most people are as full of mitzvoth as pomegranates have seeds. The feeling that a person's mitzvoth are small, insignificant and worthless stems from the evil inclination's lies. The evil inclination seeks to blind a person of his own worth in order to strip him of his joy in life and his power to serve Hashem.

Take time to evaluate yourself and the good you do every day. Count every good deed. Consider every moment that you wear tzitzit, cover your hair or go with emuna in your heart. Every moment is priceless! Consider every morsel of kosher food that you put in your mouth and every moment you refrain from eating something that is not kosher. All of this adds up to tremendous merit! What about all the Sabbaths that you observe? What about every word of prayer that you say and every benediction you recite? Each one is priceless. Even every good desire that you harbor in your heart is worth zillions…

Many people have had great results from keeping gratitude ledgers and writing down all the many reasons they have to be grateful for. Why? The evil inclination tries to make a person forget about the good and focus on the seemingly bad. **Writing strengthens memory against all the evil inclination's lies.**

Be careful about asking for spiritual growth without first thanking Hashem profusely for what you already have in your current spiritual rung. Requests without prior expressions of gratitude are liable to make a person forget the good he already has as well as inject him with a sense of entitlement. Therefore, gratitude should preface any personal prayer. A person should ponder all the good that Hashem does for him, from every little heartbeat to every tiny mitzvah, so that his thanks will be sincere and not mere lip service. This is the path of true progress in any endeavor, spiritual or otherwise.

Don't ever disregard your spiritual and material treasures. Just as there is no price tag for a single breath or heartbeat, there is no price tag for every time a person avoids looking at a forbidden sight or refrains from uttering a word of gossip or slander. Be happy with any tiny achievement, for it all adds up very quickly.

122. Waking up from Slumber

A young man complained to me that he had big problems in getting out of bed in the morning. No matter what he did or how many alarm clocks he set – or even if his wife poured buckets of water on his head – nothing helped and he couldn't get up. He'd wake up in the early afternoon and his day would naturally start on the left foot. He accomplished nothing and was in a lot of troubles.

One trouble leads to another. A wife can't stand to see a husband snoring in the middle of morning and failing to get to work. She's already threatening that if this continues… He doesn't know what to do. How can he be happy with this terrible problem? He suffers insults and humiliation from every direction. What's worse, he violates religious law because he doesn't say *Shema* or pray on time. Wouldn't this be gross negligence for him to rejoice in such a deficiency?

I told him that if this problem serves as a catalyst for him to seek Hashem with all his heart, then it too is something intrinsically good that he should thank Hashem for. I told him to thank Hashem for this problem for thirty minutes a day and to ask Hashem to help him get up in the morning and to strengthen his desire to pray and observe religious law. Therefore, thanking Hashem for this problem would certainly not be negligence, for this problem is now stimulating him to wake up from his spiritual and material slumber.

Even if the problem is not yet solved, by seeking Hashem and thanking Him for thirty minutes a day, a person is doing what he or she can. The rest is up to Hashem! Hashem doesn't expect you to do what you cannot, but He will fault a person for not turning to Him for help.

Understand full well that until a person is happy with his problems and deficiencies in life, he won't be able rid himself of them. Therefore, rejoice in your deficiencies and thank Hashem for them. What can be greater than something that arouses a person to prayer and teshuva? With gratitude, a person will ultimate rise above his troubles and deficiencies and he won't feel any pain or sorrow from them!

The above is a template for dealing with any problem or deficiency. We came to this world to rectify ourselves, not to persecute ourselves. In other words, to deal with your deficiency is the reason you came down to this world. Therefore, it is intrinsically good. By thanking Hashem for it, the problem will not only be solved but it will trigger tremendous abundance and personal growth as we have shown and stressed in previous pages.

When we think about it, we must thank Hashem for the evil inclination too. Thank You, Hashem for the chaos that the evil inclination causes in my life; thank You for its interference with everything of value that I do; thank You for all the damage it does to me. But remember, a person should never persecute himself, because he neither created himself nor did he create the evil inclination within him.

Why persecute ourselves about things that are beyond our control? Hashem has wonderful gratification from the fact that we serve Him despite the opposition and interference from the evil inclination! In this manner, Rebbe Natan of Breslev writes (Likutei Eitzot, Hitchazkut, 37):

"A person's evil inclination is actually a virtue, for a person can serve Hashem particularly with his evil inclination. One must overcome the evil inclination by way of enthusiasm in serving Hashem. Without the opposition of the evil inclination, one's Divine service is worthless. Hashem enables the evil inclination to obstruct a person who wants to serve Him, and especially those who desire to get close to Him. Even though the evil inclination incites a person to sin, even so, it's worth it to Hashem for one good deed that is the product of overcoming the evil inclination, more so than if a person served Hashem for a thousand years without an evil inclination. All of creation was created for man, because of his evil inclination that he must constantly fight to overcome. Hashem cherishes a person's struggle to overcome the evil inclination, and Hashem Himself will help a person overcome, as it is written: 'Hashem won't forsake him to the hand [of the evil inclination]'".

Do you realize what that means? Every tiny movement of one's pinky finger in overcoming the evil inclination is more valuable to Hashem than a thousand years of total Divine service without the evil inclination!

The evil inclination constantly bombards a person with messages of despair, that things are bad and that he or she will never overcome their bad habits and lusts. He wants to strip a person of his self-worth and of the value of his mitzvoth so that he'll give up on himself. But don't ever forget that one's service of Hashem is umpteen times greater with the evil inclination and its obstructions that it is without the evil inclination.

The evil inclination particularly attacks a person with the desire to be free of it and to think that he lacks the conditions to serve Hashem. It's Hashem Who wants us to have an evil inclination, for it forces us to strengthen ourselves constantly, just like a weightlifter who increases physical strength by lifting heavier and heavier weights. The more we yearn for Hashem, the more we have the desire to overcome the evil inclination and to do Hashem's will, the closer we get to Hashem. It is this desire that Hashem wants.

Rebbe Nachman stresses (see Sichot Haran, 51) that no one can be so presumptuous to think that he properly serves Hashem in accordance with His greatness, for not even an archangel can make such a claim. Yet, a person must rejoice in every tiny good point and every tiny movement of a finger that he or she does in the service of Hashem. If we believe that Hashem delights in every effort we make to serve Him, nothing can break us! The more a person feels vitality in every word of Torah that he learns and every tiny good deed that he does, he'll seek more and more, tasting constant spiritual and personal growth.

With the above in mind, the greatest expression of thanks that a person can make is to thank Hashem for his evil inclination. "Thank You, Father in Heaven, for giving me an evil inclination that I must constantly strengthen myself to overcome. To do so, I must seek Your help; thank You for the evil inclination, because it forces me to get close to You and to seek You all the time. What a gift, thank You!"

The Gemara, in elaborating the passage in Genesis that says that everything the Creator created was very good, says,

"Very good – this refers to the evil inclination." Since a person must thank Hashem for the seemingly bad as well as for the good, he must thank Him for his evil inclination. Our sages, in their elaboration of the *Shema* prayer, say that "with all your heart" refers to serving Hashem with both inclinations of the heart, the good one and the evil one. The evil inclination keeps a person's two feet firmly implanted on the ground; without it, the soul would simply want to fly away and cling to Hashem, shunning any physical endeavors such as eating, drinking and procreation.

Desire fuels a person and the evil inclination fuels desire. Rebbe Nachman says that obstacles in life are designed to fuel our desire to overcome them. Without the evil inclination and its obstacles, life would be a meaningless bore. Imagine, who would pay hundreds of dollars for a Super Bowl ticket if only one team were on the field? The tougher the opposition, the more interesting the game and the more valuable the victory is. For this reason, serving Hashem with the evil inclination "on the playing field" makes every tiny triumph so very valuable.

From this day on, if the evil inclination tells you that you can't serve Hashem because you have an evil inclination, tell it: "I can't serve Hashem *without* you – you are my best friend; thanks to you, I got where I am today." That's how to rid yourself of the evil inclination's worst nagging and of the myth that you can serve Hashem better without it.

If we remember that every little effort in getting close to Hashem is, now imagine the power of praying to overcome a certain bad habit or negative character trait for a half hour a day. It's ever so greater than the work of the loftiest angels, who couldn't bring such gratification to Hashem in a billion years of doing what they do.

A person who invests in daily personal prayer sees miracles. Each prayer is a valuable building block; eventually, a person sees these magnificent edifices arise before his eyes. And, he's the one who built them! None of this would have happened without the evil inclination that he had to overcome.

Don't spare any words – tell your beloved Father in Heaven everything. Tell Him your difficulties, how the evil inclination is always getting in your way and trying to trip you up with endless temptations that only seem to be getting stronger and stronger. Then, don't forget to thank Hashem for the evil inclination, for it motivates you to get stronger all the time. "Hashem, if this is the way You want me to serve You, then thank You! I accept this lovingly. If You have given me this evil inclination, You are undoubtedly confident that I can overcome it. Please help me!"

123. It's not Good to be Alone

A couple with marital problems came to consult with me. The husband convincingly explained that his wife was to blame for all their marital and child-rearing problems. His arguments were really persuasive…

Then, his wife's turn "at the microphone" came. She was even more persuasive…

I listened to them but I couldn't help them. My heart broke at their suffering. In my own personal prayer, I pleaded with Hashem to illuminate my eyes as to what was wrong with them. Why did the gate of marital peace lock them out? They were very wealthy, but they had nothing, for their money lacked blessings. Why weren't they living like kings with the opulence that Hashem gave them?

Then I realized. Rather than thanking Hashem, they only complained. They never heard the CD, "Stop Crying." They never learned about gratitude.

As an aside, it's not enough to listen to one gratitude CD or read one gratitude pamphlet. Gratitude affects every facet in life, so a person should read all the pamphlets and listen to all the CDs.

The gratitude booklets and CDs teach a person to be content with his lot in life. If the husband were content with his wife and she with him, all their problems would disappear.

He focused on all her shortcomings and she focused on all of his. According to the principles of emuna, each should have composed him/herself and say, "This is the spouse that Hashem gave me, shortcoming and all! I will rejoice in him/her and thank Hashem! This is my lot in life and I am happy with it." By lovingly accepting the spouse with all his/her drawbacks, a person fulfills his soul correction and performs the mission that he/she was sent down here to do.

Remember, there is no one but Hashem! Emuna means that everything is from Him and all for the best. It's not your spouse, it's Hashem doing everything in your life for the very best.

If the husband had emuna, he'd have rejoiced in his wife. He would thank Hashem for giving him the woman who is perfect for his soul correction. Hashem makes no mistakes…

A grateful husband would be able to see all of his wife's wonderful qualities and all the good she does for him. He would thank Hashem and appreciate her. He'd have no complaints and he'd even do teshuva for any deficiency he saw in her and for causing her the slightest anguish. He'd realize that she is his mirror and any shortcoming he sees in her is actually his own, as we elaborate in our book, "The Garden of Peace."

The wife is also obligated to have emuna. If she did, she'd be happy with her lot in life and thank Hashem too.

Know full well that if a person fails to respect his wife, he is slamming the door to Divine abundance. Abundance and marital bliss flow down the same spiritual conduit. Their strife wrecks their blessings in life. Peace, especially marital peace, is the finest goblet for the wine of abundance.

Here, we must emphasize that even justified arguments destroy the blessing of abundance. A couple who is apparently rich won't see any blessing to their money if they lack marital peace.

True abundance is not the physical money in the bank but Hashem's blessing. I have seen people with relatively limited means who live lives in bliss and don't owe a cent. How? They have Hashem's blessing. How do they manage? Only Hashem knows, but they do. On the other hand, there are bank managers, entrepreneurs and fabulously wealthy individuals who live miserable lives, because their money can't buy blessings.

In short, the couple that came to me agreed to read the Gems series of gratitude booklets and to listen to our gratitude CDs, and their lives turned completely around for the better.

124. Heaven at Home

Another person with a marital problem came to me thinking that his wife was to blame for all their troubles. He was sure that she had to change, etc. One of my students knocked on his door. He thought that here's another freeloader looking for money. He went to the door and asked, "What do you want – charity?"

"No," my student said. "I have a book to show you."

"What book?" asked the man.

"A book about marital peace," my student replied.

"I only read Spanish," the guy said.

"Fine," smiled my student. "I'll show you the book in Spanish."

My student ran out to his car and grabbed a copy of "The Garden of Peace" in Spanish.

When he came to me, the man told me that he devoured the book that same night and his life turned into a paradise on earth. In the recent months that transpired, his marriage improved a thousand percent and so has his income.

How did this individual merit marital peace so dramatically fast? He never knew me, but he came to thank me. The book taught him gratitude, especially in marriage. In a beautiful upward spiral, the gratitude has brought him every blessing, including emuna and a happy marriage. He now believes that everything is from Hashem and he's always thanking

Him, as well as thanking his wife and all those he feels indebted to.

With emuna and gratitude, a person has paradise – it's that simple.

125. I Began to Believe in Hashem

My neighbor was visiting the United States. A big burly man ran toward him but he wasn't afraid because the big guy had a smile on his face. He asked my neighbor, "You're from Israel, aren't you?" My neighbor nodded in the affirmative. "Are you from Jerusalem?" He said yes to that too. "Do you know Rabbi Shalom Arush?"

"Yes, he's my neighbor."

"Then tell him that Big Bob from the USA read the Garden of Emuna and that I started to believe in G-d. I also read the "Garden of Peace" and I finally have a happy marriage too!"

Here's another letter that we received from South America:

"Thanks to the advice of Rabbi Arush, Hashem heard my prayers and did a tremendous miracle for me. I was married for six years and was not yet blessed with children. My husband and I bickered all the time. He finally was fed up and after a terrible argument, left the house. This time, I didn't cry to my mother like I did after all the other quarrels we had. I understood that Hashem wanted to teach me something, so I waited patiently all alone at home to see what would unfold.

"To keep myself from falling into depression, I started surfing the web looking for something interesting. I came upon the Breslev Israel website in Spanish and I viewed two or three lectures. I learned the advice of thanking Hashem for my troubles for a half hour a day.

"I started thanking Hashem daily for a half hour that I had marital problems and that my husband doesn't want to be with me anymore. I thanked Hashem for my loneliness and for the fact that I didn't yet have children. I found many more reasons to thank Him too.

"At the same time, I started reading 'Women's Wisdom' in Spanish. I understood that I was at fault and not my husband. After a few more days of thanking Hashem for everything, I suddenly heard someone knocking at my door. My husband was standing there with tears in his eyes. He begged my forgiveness for leaving home and for all of his misbehavior and he said that he felt an inexplicable spiritual thirst that he didn't understand.

"Meanwhile, he had read a book that someone gave him by the name of "The Garden of Emuna" in Spanish; from this book, he understood that our lack of marital bliss was his fault.

"Even though I grew up in a non-observant home, my daily expressions of gratitude to Hashem gave me such a love and appreciation of Him that I began to observe more mitzvoth like family purity and kashruth.

"And then, surprise…

"A month after my husband returned home, I received good news – that I'm expecting a child. After six years of treatments and trying with no avail, here was the miracle!

"The first thing I said when I heard the good news was, 'Hashem, this is Your thank You baby.' My latent love for Hashem was kindled all the more.

"Thank you, Breslev Israel, for the lessons of Rabbi Yonatan Gal'ed in Spanish and thanks to Rabbi Shalom Arush for his wonderful teachings. May the Creator always be in our hearts!

"The world smiles to those who smile, M. A."

126. The Biggest Miracle

The next story is the biggest miracle I ever heard, a major supernatural occurrence. I would be less impressed even if someone told me that the moon was sliced into ten pieces. I went to the south of Israel to deliver a lecture, and a woman who always attends my lectures when I'm in her area would always complain to me after the lesson that she suffers unspeakable humiliation from her husband and that her life was a living death.

This time, she had a big smile on her face. She admitted that she'd always semi-doze through my lectures and just wait for the reception period afterwards when I would answer individual people's questions and give them blessings. All she wanted was the opportunity to tell me how miserable she was.

Meanwhile, though, she decided to try reading "The Garden of Emuna". She did, and she realized that everything was from Hashem and all for her own good. Her husband wasn't humiliating her – Hashem was, and for a good reason. She began to speak to Him daily in personal prayer and to thank

Him for all the insults and humiliations. She thanked Him for all the grief she received by way of her husband.

She also did teshuva every day and asked Hashem's forgiveness for all the years that she didn't believe in Him and didn't believe that everything was for the best. She apologized for all her whining and complaining. She asked forgiveness for not appreciating all her blessings in life – her husband, her children and her home. She accepted Hashem's judgments with love because she had sinned in her early years and she knew that she deserved whatever tribulations she had.

Ever since reading the Garden of Emuna, she is happier than she ever was! This was without even hearing the gratitude CDs or reading the Gems; imagine what they would do for her!

She also asked Hashem to show her what she must rectify. Eventually, her enthusiasm spread to others and she began teaching "The Garden of Emuna" to a small group of women.

Her husband couldn't ignore the change in her. "What happened to you? You don't scream or complain anymore. You smile instead of cry. What's going on?"

"I'm happy," she said, "that I don't have bliss in my marriage."

Her husband was dumbstruck: "What?! You're happy that our marriage is terrible?!"

"Yes," she said. "This has brought me much closer to Hashem. All of your insults and humiliation have been gifts from Above for me; you are merely Hashem's messenger to give me what I deserve. If I don't get the suffering from you, then I'll get it from someone else. Meanwhile, I'm doing teshuva every day because Hashem is showing me what I need to correct. I don't care if there's no peace between us, just as long as I get closer to Hashem. That's my purpose in life; what do I care about anything else?"

That fact that a woman should so lovingly reconcile herself with humiliation and a bitter marriage is a supernatural occurrence – nothing less. A woman naturally yearns for love and respect. Insult her and she feels like dying. Yet, this woman overturned nature! Not only had she not received love and respect, not only was she systematically verbally abused in the worst way, but she said thank You for this? Phenomenal!

This woman's submission to Hashem and to His will caused her husband to change. He was ashamed at himself and he told her, "With a wonderful woman like you, I don't want to be Hashem's disciplinary rod; instead, let me be a staff that you can lean on." He too made complete teshuva.

So long as the woman viewed her husband as a tormentor, that's the way he was! As soon as she started looking at Hashem and at His loving-kindness, he started seeing Hashem too. This is the amazing power of emuna.

127. Anyone Can Do Miracles

From all the above stories, we see how anyone can invoke miracles. Rebbe Nachman of Breslev says that pray overrides nature. We see over and over what seemingly ordinary people can accomplish with their prayers.

Someone once asked Rabbi Nachman of Tulchin to tell a miracle story about Rebbe Nachman of Breslev. He said, "I'm the miracle! I was a beast on two legs and Rebbe Nachman made a human being out of me. That's the biggest miracle."

Whenever he needed to perform a miracle, Rebbe Nachman prayed that people would forget about it; that's why we don't tell miracle stories about him. But, there was once a paralyzed person who couldn't move his arm; he attended one of Rebbe Nachman's lessons. Rebbe Nachman asked him three times if he had emuna. The man answered yes. Rebbe Nachman told him to move his arm, which he did in front of everyone that was there.

Rebbe Nachman wanted people to remember his teachings about serving Hashem and not the miracles he did, so he prayed that they would forget them. Rebbe Nachman's teaching illustrates why we need our righteous spiritual leaders who show us how to properly observe Torah and serve Hashem.

Yet, anyone can perform miracles. Many of my students have told me how they've seen miraculous salvations from their prayers. Every individual must believe in himself and in his power of prayer, that he too can invoke miracles.

Hashem listens to our prayers. If a person lacks emuna in himself, he lacks emuna in Hashem!

Why? If a person believes that Hashem can do anything, then why shouldn't he believe that Hashem can bring miracles and salvations for him?

Rebbe Nachman told the story of two friends who loved each other very much. One of them was deathly ill, Heaven forbid. The other one began to pray for him. After several intensive hours of praying, he asked his friend's family how his friend was doing. They told him that the sick young man had not yet recovered. He returned to praying several times and alternately inquired about his friend's wellbeing. Finally, the family told him that his friend had come out of a coma, broke into a cold sweat and was on the way to recovery.

Rebbe Nachman told us this story to show us the power of prayer and so that each of us would believe in ourselves and our ability to work wonders with our prayers. If a person really believed that Hashem hears and answers prayers, he'd pray with much more enthusiasm and fervor.

With my own eyes, I've seen how my own rabbinical students who could barely afford groceries bought apartments in Jerusalem after devoting hours to prayer and gratitude. These are the same students who couldn't afford a bus ticket to the realtor's office.

Such is the power of prayer and gratitude. This affects every area of life. Believe in your power of prayer! Speak to Hashem in your own words: "Father in Heaven, I have no other address to turn to! Please have mercy on me!" Say thank You to Hashem, the more the better!

128. Five Minutes of Gratitude

A guest in my home from Rishon Letzion said that he had a neighbor who had nothing to do with the Chassidic movement, who was not yet blessed with children. He phoned Rabbi Eliahu Godlevsky and told him that he tried everything but to no avail. Rabbi Godlevsky suggested that he follow my advice and thank Hashem for five minutes a day that he doesn't have children. He and his wife should do so for forty days straight.

Forty days later, his wife was expecting.

The man later told that every evening at eight PM, he and his wife would each go to their respective corners in the living room and thank Hashem for five minutes that they didn't yet have children, expressing their belief that everything was for the very best. And it worked!

From every aspect, gratitude is obligatory, and not just for those who have a problem. It's only basic decency to express appreciation to someone who does a favor for you. In that case, shouldn't we be thanking Hashem every moment, for every breath and every heartbeat? Aren't they priceless favors? That's what the *Nishmat* prayer is all about, when we tell Hashem that if our mouths were as wide as the sea, if our tongues were as full of joy as the waves in the sea and our lips as wide as the horizon, we couldn't capably thank Hashem for a single one of the millions and billions of favors He does for us every moment of the day. Yet, we must do what we can in expressing our gratitude to Him.

Gratitude opens all of the Heavenly gates. It nullifies all stern judgments. It enables a person's prayers to ascend all the way to the Heavenly Throne. Were it not for gratitude, writes Nachmanides, the Creator wouldn't have desire for His universe.

Rebbe Avraham of Slonim learned from his teacher Rebbe Moshe of Kobrin that a person who willingly accepts Divine will and judgment doesn't need all kinds of fast and self-flagellation. Why? By accepting Hashem's will with joy, one atones for all his sins and spares himself from all types of grief and tribulations.

Rabbi Alexander Ziskind of Grodno wrote to his sons in his will: "I was careful to thank Hashem for everything that happened in my life, for better or for otherwise...I would gladly justify whatever Hashem did, and I would give Him great thanks for my painful toothaches...I would certainly praise Him for every tiny favor He did for me."

129. Nullifying Traumas

Someone told me that several years ago, a person threatened to kill him. Hashem did a miracle for him and saved him for that aggressor. Yet since then, he suffers trauma and anxiety every time he thinks about the aggressor.

I told him that his anguish was because then, and still now, he doesn't fully believe in Hashem, that there is no one but Him. I also told him that there are no tribulations without prior transgression and suggested that he pray for more emuna and do teshuva for the past.

Many people have traumatic emotional scars from the past. By way of gratitude, a person can cure himself. Trauma simple means that a person did not accept a trying situation with emuna. He feels that he experienced something bad and tragic. "Bad" only exists in a context of a lack of emuna.

Clearly, if a person accepted the past with emuna, he wouldn't feel trauma.

Rebbe Nachman writes that the life of a person who lacks emuna is not a life. A person with emuna feels no sorrow because he sees everything that Hashem does as the very best. The notion of "bad" comes from a person's disbelief.

I therefore told the person who told me about the threat against his life that if he wanted to clean his past of sorrow and anxiety, he should thank Hashem for a half hour a day for the ordeal he went through. He should do a double atonement: first, for the sin that led to this tribulation and second, for not having done teshuva previously. If he didn't thank Hashem back then, then he should start now.

I told him to say, "Master of the World, thank You for all the anguish I suffered, which was the result of my lack of belief in You. I attributed power to the aggressor rather than realizing that there is no one but You. I thank You for using him to arouse me from my spiritual slumber. Please illuminate my eyes as to what I need to rectify, for I understand that this was none other than a message from You for my own benefit."

"I'm sorrow to say, Father in Heaven, that I still feel sorrow from this. I still suffer. I realize that I still lack emuna. Therefore, I first of all thank You for enabling me to thank You. Second, I ask You for a free gift – please give me full and complete emuna, so that I can thank You with utmost sincerity for the painful thing that happened to me." I told him to express himself in this manner for a half hour a day, until he no longer felt any sorrow or trauma, for this really works.

130. Make His Will Your Will

One of my students holds regular emuna workshops where he teaches people to say thank You. He calls me all the time to tell me of the miracles that he hears about. One woman with a daughter who suffered from epilepsy and fell down several times a day was constantly feeling fear and anxiety.

Once the mother started tahnking Hashem for twenty minutes a day (she couldn't do thirty), the daughter stopped collapsing. Not only that, but the mother's anxiety had disappeared and she started living with emuna.

The advice of gratitude is the answer to all fear and anxiety. Once a person internalizes that everything is from Hashem and that it's all for the best, he or she no longer fears anything.

This is the foundational idea that we write about in the "Garden of Gratitude", in the Gems series of gratitude booklets and in the gratitude CDs. What's the intrinsic aspect of thanking Hashem for everything? It means that you accept Hashem's will with love and that you are happy with whatever He does in your life. "Thank You, Hashem, for the pain and the tribulations! Everything You do is all for the best!" The elixir for any suffering is emuna! That's why Rebbe Nachman says that the main reason of exile and Diaspora is the lack of emuna (Likutei Moharan I:7); a person who doesn't believe that everything Hashem does is for the very best is in emotional exile.

If a person is happy in spite of exile, his personal Moshiach has already arrived. Exile is not a geographical place – it is a state of mind. Even today's exile is the result of a lack of emuna. We must all attain the emuna where we can say to Hashem, "If this is what You want from me, then it's surely the very best."

Gratitude means that a person accepts Divine will and that he doesn't kick in the face of tribulations. Know full well that tribulations are a sign of Divine love for you. Therefore, a person should never protest his tribulations. Elijah the Prophet says that if a person does protest them, they become multiplied. But, if a person accepts them lovingly, he is rewarded.

Imagine that a person made a small traffic violation and received a small monetary penalty. But, the violator began cursing and shouting at the policeman who was writing the ticket. Instead, the policeman ripped up the small ticket and wrote him a much more severe ticket with four times the penalty.

On the other hand, if he had readily and politely received the small ticket, the policeman might have been inclined to turn it into a warning only. Rabbenu Yona writes in Shaarei Teshuva (4:12), that accepting tribulations with love lead to their ultimate disappearance altogether.

As we wrote in the "Garden of Gratitude", the Creator runs the world measure-for-measure. Those who don't accept small tribulations lovingly will be faced with much larger tribulations. As we mentioned in the name of the "Sfat Emet" of Gur, by thanking Hashem for the small tribulations, one spares himself of calamities 5,000 times worse!

By knowing that everything is from Hashem and all for the best, a person nullifies Divine concealment. Rebbe Nachman stresses (Likutei Moharan I:250): "A person with spiritual awareness who knows that everything results from Divine Providence, feels no tribulations and so suffering." Not only does he feel no suffering, but he invokes protection for the whole world.

131. Sadness and Melancholy

During one of my radio programs, I explained that emuna means that a person must thank Hashem for everything. A woman phoned in and said that her son had forsaken the path of observant Judaism and now, among other things, he was violating the Sabbath. She asked if she was obligated to thank Hashem for that too.

By the answer I gave her, you'll understand the inner dimension of gratitude. Prefacing my in-depth answer, I told her the simple reason for thanking Hashem: "If you think that you and your husband's sadness and melancholy will bring your son back to observing Hashem's commandments, then I'm willing to grant you a rabbinical dispensation to be sad." I say this to everyone: if you think that sadness, depression and melancholy will solve your problem, I'm willing to permit you to be sad. But, we all know that sadness, depression and melancholy will solve nothing, only make things worse.

Now, I'll explain from several angles:

First of all, when a child sees a sad, angry, worried or complaining parent, he doesn't want to be like them. He subconsciously says to himself that if his parents' way of life leads to such gloom, he wants no part of it. Why should he buy their damaged goods? If their Torah doesn't bring joy in life, who needs it? Not him…

On the other hand, when a child sees his parents singing, dancing and cheerful, accepting everything with emuna, he wants to be like them! Their joy will bring him back to the fold. A child loves, respects and admires happy parents. Like them, he begins to see things in the light of emuna.

Parents must therefore live in joy and emuna. They must thank Hashem for thirty minutes a day for a wayward child. When they are happy, their prayers are readily accepted. So, in answering our question at hand, should parents thank Hashem for an off-the-path child? The answer is yes, because such a child was never really on the path of Torah observance. Otherwise, he'd have never forsaken it. Anyone who once tastes the true taste of Torah and emuna would never leave them for a moment, not even for all the money in Switzerland's banks!

It turns out that the boy's heart was always off the path; only recently, he stopped masquerading. Therefore, the parents must surely thank Hashem for revealing the truth to them and for triggering a needed change in their own attitude and outlook. Now that they know where they and their son really stand, they can begin to rectify all the way around. If they too acknowledged the truth that their sadness and melancholy indicated that they too lacked the true light of Torah and emuna, they'd make a giant stride to correcting themselves and to getting closer to Hashem. They'd be illuminated with a new light that would surely have influence on their son, especially if they did everything in their power to be happy all the time no matter what. It turns out that their son's manifest departure from the path of Torah was a wonderful Divine favor that they should thank Hashem for.

Such an attitude is called spiritual awareness, understanding that everything is from the Creator and all for the best! Hashem is only good; there truly is no bad in the world! That's what we mean when we recite in the Kaddish prayer, "Glorified and sanctified be God's great Name throughout the world that He has created according to His will…May His great name be blessed forever and to all eternity."

A person with spiritual awareness is saddened only by the world's lack of spiritual awareness, where they don't yet know that, "Glorified and sanctified be God's great Name," because everything in the world comes from Him and it's all for the best. We're saddened by the people who suffer needlessly because they lack emuna.

The rebuilding of our Holy Temple in essence means the return of spiritual awareness on earth. This was the power of the High Priest, the tzaddik of the generation, who would instill emuna in people. Without emuna, we truly lack the tools to rebuild the Holy Temple. To do so, we all must begin searching for spiritual awareness and full emuna.

One's private exile, like witnessing a child leave the fold, is for the purpose of his feeling the general exile and our lack of Moshiach and the Holy Temple. Problems like this are geared to stimulate teshuva and our wholehearted return to Hashem.

There's a happy ending: the woman who phoned in took my advice – she and her husband made teshuva and started living their Torah observance with joy while profusely thanking Hashem for their wayward son. They gained emuna, spiritual awareness and joy in life. Soon, their son joined them.

132. He Said Thank You and Was Freed from Prison

A prison inmate obtained a copy of "The Garden of Gratitude." He was held in custody pending his trial. He thanked Hashem for a half hour a day that he was imprisoned and promised Hashem that if he got an innocent verdict in the trial, he'd continue thanking Hashem for a half hour a day after his release from prison.

Hashem believed his promise and granted him a verdict of "not guilty". What a salvation!

The book "Me'orot Hagedolim" (page 118) tells about the Chafetz Chaim osb"m, who would profusely thank Hashem for all His favors and loving-kindnesses every day. Rabbi Yechezkel Avramsky osb"m was a guest in a hotel as a young man; through the thin wall he could hear someone reciting the *Nishmat* prayer with the sweetness of an archangel, translating word by word of each praise and expression of gratitude into Yiddish. The next day, he found out that the individual in the room next door was the Chafetz Chaim.

133. Personal Prayer Instead of Suicide

A 60-year old woman from South Africa who didn't know that she was Jewish wanted to commit suicide. Someone gave her a copy of "The Garden of Emuna"; she started to talk to the Creator and to believe in Him. She began to thank Him for everything and before long, she rose above her depression. Afterwards, she discovered that she was Jewish, the daughter of a mother who survived the Holocaust, and she became observant.

The Gem pamphlets are truly gems. They're a bright light – each one is a 1000-carat diamond. So are the gratitude CDs, especially "Stop Crying" and "Learn to Say Thank You." Each emuna book is a priceless life guide.

When I hold private meetings with people, I hear of indescribable troubles, almost every day. How can I help them? Even if I pray for them, it won't help much unless they decide to help themselves. Nothing is more powerful than a person's prayers for himself.

134. Gratitude against Missiles

Here's a story from the Gaza War of 2014. A woman was on a long drive home in her car, listening to one of my emuna broadcasts on the radio. I spoke about the importance of gratitude, that everything is from Hashem and that it's all good. I said that gratitude triggers miraculous salvations.

Later at home during dinner, the woman told her family what she heard from my broadcast. She explained how thanking Hashem for life's trying difficulties shows that a person believes that Hashem loves him with no bounds and that gratitude nullifies all stern judgments.

Her daughters then said to each other, "If that's the case, we should start thanking Hashem every time the bomb siren goes off." They lived close to the Gaza border. "Every time we hear a missile exploding, we should say thank You again." A few days later, there was a ceasefire. The family hadn't been out of the house for three weeks, so they decided to have an outing at the park and breathe some fresh air. The park was empty. The family spread a blanket on the ground and unpacked their picnic lunch. Meanwhile, they discussed emuna and gratitude. Suddenly, they saw that their little daughter was missing. They all ran in different directions to look for her. The husband, who was near his wife, heard her mumble, "Thank You, Hashem, that my daughter is missing."

Her husband snorted, "Dear, in all due respect, what the heck are you saying thank You for, that our daughter is missing, and in these tense times?"

The bomb siren started wailing. Each member of the family scurried to cover. The mother once more said, "Thank

You Hashem for the siren, thank You that my daughter is missing." She did a great job in internalizing my lesson.

Her husband scolded her, saying, "This time, you've gone too far. I've seen exaggerated spirituality, but this takes the cake…"

VAROOOOOM!!!

A missile landed and exploded exactly where their picnic lunch was. Instead of the blanket and the food, there was a scorched crater in the ground. They found the little daughter, frightened and whimpering behind their parked car. Had she not strayed away and forced the whole family to spread out looking for her, the missile would have exploded right on them…

How magnificent is Hashem, praised be His Name!

No one in the family argued with the mother anymore. They all started saying thank You even when they didn't understand how something is for the best.

The above story of the Gaza-belt family shows us how everything Hashem does is truly for the best. But, even when we don't see how things are for the best like they ultimately did, we must nevertheless believe that they are and thank Hashem accordingly.

Look at the influence that a brief radio show had on an entire family! That behooves us to spread the light of emuna far and wide. Even if a person is not observant, he or she can still speak to Hashem and thank Him, for this is a reboot for a better life. Gratitude and emuna invoke every blessing and bring a person closer to Hashem.

135. Saying "Thank You" in English

Rabbi Yosef Shalom Elyashiv osb"m asked to be taught how to say thank You in English. His students asked him why. He explained that his dentist was an American who only knew English and he wanted to express his appreciation to him. The elderly rabbi had to practice hard to say the English "th" consonant, which is nonexistent in Hebrew or Yiddish, his native languages.

The students couldn't understand why the rabbi was trying so hard. He explained, "In the cantor's repetition of the *Amida* prayer, his benedictions fulfill the obligations of the entire congregation, except for the *Modim* prayer, the prayer of gratitude. Each person must say this benediction on his own. We learn from here that no one else can say thank You for you – you must do it yourself! That's why I must learn to say thank You properly in English."

We also learn here that a person must say thank you for the thank you, as Rashi explains in his elaboration of the *Modim* prayer in the Gemara (Tractate Sota, 40). Our sages explain further that thanking Hashem for all His loving-kindness in giving us life is the ultimate purpose of life (see Malbim on Psalm 63:4).

In light of the above, we must thank Hashem for every moment of life, and thank Him for the privilege of being able to thank Him.

Gratitude is no spiritual ploy or a matter of piety. It is a basic commandment of Torah. Rabbi Elazar Azkari in his classic "Sefer Charedim" writes that the Torah commands us to remember the compassionate acts that the Creator did for our forefathers, such as taking them out of bondage in Egypt. He adds, "each person is obligated to thank Hashem for each act of loving-kindness that He does for them daily, and for everything since the day he was born."

Rabbenu Yona in "Shaarei Teshuva" agrees. So does Rabbenu Bachiya in "Duties of the Heart". Nachmanides says that the reason the Almighty took our people out of Egypt was to teach us gratitude, that we are beholden to thank Him every day of our lives.

The following is an assortment of letters from around the world, from Jews and non-Jews, observant and non-observant. Many of the people who wrote them never met me or saw me, but their lives underwent dramatic changes. They said thank You and they saw miracles.

136. Open Miracle

Shalom and blessings!

I wanted to tell you about the miracles I've seen since reading "The Garden of Gratitude."

Nobody ever believed that I'd remarry with four kids, a pile of debts and not a penny in my pocket. They thought I was crazy in wishing to find a Torah scholar who'd want to marry me. I told everyone that Hashem can do whatever He wants whenever He wants. The rabbi said to ask for whatever I want and to thank Hashem for everything. Over and over, I thanked him for being a single mother with a scant income and five mouths to feed. Thank You, Hashem!

After the smoke has cleared from eighteen months of thanking Hashem, I'm now remarried to a Torah scholar who is a dream of a human being. We had a lavish wedding and I've covered the 71,000 NIS that I owed. Life has been better than winning the lottery! Even my daughters are praying and expressing gratitude daily, all of this thanks to prayers and gratitude.

137. My Defense Attorney

Shalom and blessings!

I became connected to Rabbi Arush through his books. I've read them all. The most powerful one is "The Garden of Gratitude." It transformed me into a new person. My wife and children have also started thanking Hashem. Our home has become paradise. My life can be divided into two time periods – before I read "The Garden of Gratitude" and after. It's a spiritual revival of the dead.

Anyway, I had a court case because I signed as a guarantor to a person who defaulted on a loan. They were demanding a lot of money from me. I thanked Hashem for this predicament and for the court case, for they were bringing me closer to Hashem. I came to the hearing without any legal representation, only with Hashem and with "The Garden of Gratitude" in my heart. I saw an open miracle. The presiding judge started to scold the prosecuting attorney, "What are you suing him for? He didn't borrow the money!"

The astonished attorney gulped and responded, "But he cosigned as a guarantor for the loan."

The judge said, "I don't care – case dismissed!"

I told the judge that I was willing to accept responsibility and to pay for a portion of the debt, but without the inflated interest, court costs and lawyer's fees that the prosecution was suing for, which amounted to more than double of the original loan.

Again, the judge yelled at the plaintiff's lawyer: "What more do you want from this man? He's willing to repay a portion of the loan! Why in the world are you suing him?"

The judge then ruled that I would repay the principle with no other costs and that I could spread it out in as many payments as I pleased. A miracle, before everyone's eyes! After the hearing, the lawyer came up to me and said, "When I asked for a lien on your bank account, I discovered that you have an old savings plan that you even forget about; it's the exact sum that the court ordered you to pay. So, if you want, I'll extract the money from there and you won't have to pay anything more." I couldn't stop the tears of gratitude from dripping down my cheeks. I said thank You and I saw miracles!

138. The German Court

Shalom and blessings!

I was accused of tax evasions and money laundering in Germany and was about to stand trial. I was looking down the throat of a probable five-year prison sentence.

I discovered the Breslev Israel website at www.breslev.co.il and I ordered "The Garden of Emuna". As a result, I began daily conversations with Hashem and thanked Him.

Yesterday, my trial was supposed to take place. I stood at the entrance to the courtroom, but my lawyer didn't arrive. I called him and he told me to come urgently to his office. I was shocked because the trial was about to begin. I asked, "What happened?" He wouldn't answer but insisted that I come right away.

I arrived at the lawyer's office. Thanks to "The Garden of Emuna", I saw my own private miracle. The dossier that the Income Tax authorities gathered against me was in chaotic disarray. Unlike the Germans, it was disorganized and not chronological – a big mess. An argument broke out among the government prosecutors, who scoffed at the inane method of filing a claim that would turn them into a laughing stock.

A senior counsel for the German Income Tax Bureau wanted to avoid the bickering and blaming that was tearing his staff apart. He called my lawyer and offered him a deal – he'd forego the five-year prison sentence if I paid a penalty of 10,000 Eurodollars. A miracle from Heaven!

Today, I talk to Hashem for an hour every day.

(From the Breslev Israel German-language website)

139. Thank You for the Thank You

The following story arrived in the "Letters to the Editor" of Breslev Israel from a woman in Europe:

I came home and found a package that the Breslev Israel office sent me, including a book that I ordered from their website. With a cynical attitude, I was awaiting a book: could Rabbi Arush outdo his previous books that had already influenced me so profoundly? Can he write a book solely about gratitude?

By reading "The Garden of Gratitude", I realized this was a beautiful complement to "The Garden of Emuna", "In Forest Fields", "The Garden of Yearning" and "The Garden of Wisdom." Each book added a beautiful addition to the previous one with words that touch you exactly where you need them.

As a newly observant person (I don't like labels) and as someone who has been active in outreach, I hesitate talking too heavily about emuna, and especially about personal prayer. Many consider these to be eccentricities.

A few years ago while sitting in the lobby of a Jerusalem hotel, I overheard a discussion between two non-Jewish tourists. One woman complained about a problem and her girlfriend suggested that she pray – right then and there in the lobby. I had two opposite feelings: a feeling of skepticism, and on the other hand, a feeling of envy for those who had the creator to turn to, anytime and anywhere, even there in the lobby.

Then why don't I do it?

Now, a few years later, after I learned and relearned "In Forest Fields", I too speak to Hashem. You have no idea how sublime this is. Sometimes I feel like a prisoner that has been released from an iron ball and chain that he had been carrying for years.

The great aspect about the book "In Forest Fields" is that Rabbi Shalom Arush offers the spiritual searcher a refreshing path that will gratify his soul, a path that we've forgotten about in two thousand years of exile.

As to gratitude...

After reading "The Garden of Gratitude" again and again, I have a few thoughts that I want to share with you:

I never understood that as a nation, we have a past with too much whining and complaining that surprisingly enough is easy to rectify. We think we have gratitude but we're fooling ourselves. In times of tribulations, we tend to forget about all the things we have to be thankful for and focus on the difficulties, blowing them out of proportion.

I love Rabbi Arush's definition of "exile" – he says it's the situation where people don't want to hear the truth; it's living without an ultimate goal. That is so true.

People are depressed and full of despair – they see no hope. If they only learn to thank Hashem, their lives would be different. Every moment is a new opportunity to serve Hashem and to thank Him. Little things do big wonders, like smiling at the supermarket cashier or doing a tiny thoughtful favor for your spouse or child. Thank Hashem for the bus that arrived on time and for all the conveniences you have, like a supermarket near your home so that you don't have to make long journeys in search of food. Thank Hashem for everything, taking nothing for granted. The list is so long, but I'll leave it at that.

Read Rabbi Arush's books and set yourself free.

140. From Prison to Uman

Hello, my name is Jonathan, and I'm still a soldier in mandatory military service. A year ago, I was on a maneuver near the Syrian border. I tried to convince my commander to grant me a furlough but he didn't agree. I said thank You to Hashem that I couldn't go home. That same evening, the commander came to me and said, "You can go home for Shabbat…" I didn't tarry a second and I left the base but I forgot to ask for a pass (written permission for furlough, proving that I wasn't AWOL - Absent Without Official Leave). I was way up on Mount Hermon and there was no longer bus service – it was Friday afternoon already. I started thanking Hashem that I was stuck way up in the Northern Golan with Shabbat only a few hours away. All of a sudden, a car picked me up and took me all the way to the Golani crossroads, west of Tiberias on the way to Afula and all points south.

I grabbed another hitch at Golani crossroads but I didn't know that these were two military cops in plainclothes. Instead of taking me to Jerusalem, they took me to a nearby base and put me in detention, accusing me of being AWOL. They released me and ordered me to appear before a military court a week before Rosh Hashana. Meanwhile, I bought a ticket to Uman.

Two weeks before Rosh Hashana, I received a reminder summons to my military trial where I was charged with being AWOL. The expected punishment was two months in a military prison. I went out to the field, sang and danced and thanked Hashem over and over. I had Rabbi Arush's gratitude "Gems" booklet in my pocket.

The morning of the trial, the army messed up. They sent a jeep very early to pick me up from my base and take me to Tzfat, where the military court was, but there was a long time until the trial. Meanwhile, I had a jeep, a driver and an escort all day long. I took them to the ancient cemetery in Tzfat and we went to the Arizal's mikva. All day long, I was reading them segments of "The Garden of Gratitude." I played them a CD of Rabbi Arush's lessons in the jeep and I was laughing and dancing all day long. The two other soldiers – the driver and my escort – thought I was crazy. They said to each other, "This lunatic is about to get eight weeks in the slammer and he's singing and dancing?" They phoned the base psychiatrist and said, "This soldier is bona fide insane!" I didn't pay any attention to them; I just kept on singing songs of thanks to Hashem. It soon rubbed off on them. They weren't religious but they started thanking Hashem too.

That afternoon, there was a line of soldiers in the military court headquarters waiting to be tried. I kept on singing and dancing there too. When my turn came to stand trial, the military judge look confused. He asked me, "Were you off base without official leave?"

"Yessir!" I answered with a big smile.

"Did the military police have to use force to get you in the car when they arrested you?"

"No sir!"

The judge started telling me jokes about hitchhikers. The military prosecutors looked at each other in bewilderment. No one in the courtroom understood what was happening.

The judge became serious again. "Well, I can't let you off without punishment – eight days in military prison!"

Despite the fact that I was scheduled to go to Uman in a few days, I thanked Hashem on the spot. A military paddy wagon took me directly to jail.

The next day, in prison, I presented the trial protocol to a female officer who was in charge. She looked at it and said, "This is counterfeit – get out of here!" They released me from prison and I went home. Unbelievable!

Now, I had another challenge. I needed a permission paper from the army to leave the country so that I could fly to Uman. If returned to my unit, they wouldn't believe that I was released and they might have returned me to prison. I said thank You to Hashem and I danced some more. I had three days to go until Uman. Anyway, I wasn't afraid and I returned to my unit. They thought I escaped prison and they tried me again. I just thanked Hashem and danced. The base commander tried me and found me innocent. What's more, my unit gave me a written OK to fly to Uman. I know who the real Judge is and nobody can overturn His decisions!

141. Open Miracles

To Rabbi Shalom Arush shlit'a, may Hashem bless you and protect you,

The book "The Garden of Gratitude" changed my life dramatically and saved my home, thank G-d. My husband would be very cruel to me, but since I've been thanking Hashem, he frequently acts like an angel, as if he read "The Garden of Peace" (but I read "Women's Wisdom"). Our financial situation was disastrous but recently it has improved. My husband's family has means, but they give him and don't give me and the weight of making a living falls on my shoulders. Since I started thanking Hashem for everything, almost magically, I've been able to cover all the family expenses.

Our kids have had difficult educational issues. The school authorities recommended that they get psychiatric help and take pills. Their situation is difficult, because they are mine from a previous marriage. I was at loss how to deal with this.

Since I've been thanking Hashem, I've seen open miracles. The children settled down and are now in good yeshivas and cheders. The teachers in Beit Yaacov love my daughter and say that she's something special.

Rabbi Arush, you know that our sages say that saving a life is like saving a whole world. You saved an entire family of nine souls. Thank you so much.

142. The Matchmaker Offered Her Daughter

Shalom and blessings!

Several years ago, when I was dating, I met a girl that I really wanted but the day after the first date, I was informed that she wasn't interested. I was so sorry. I went to the local synagogue and stood in front of the ark and just said thank

You to Hashem, over and over, assuring myself that it's all for the best. As soon as I left the synagogue, I looked at my cellphone and there was an unanswered call. I dialed the number – it was a well-known matchmaker who offered me her own daughter! Today, she is my wife and the mother to my two daughters.

Thank You, Hashem! Thank you, Rabbi Arush!

143. A Match from Heaven

One of my students teaches a study-group about gratitude. One of the group's participants was a sad and depressed mother who had a handicapped son in his twenties. The mother lost hope of ever seeing him get married. My student told her to thank Hashem for a half hour a day that her son was handicapped and not yet married. She did so for four months. Her son met a completely healthy girl and they got engaged – a match straight from Heaven. When people say thank You, they see that everything turns out good.

Hashem doesn't demand so much from us. He just wants us to learn how to say thank You and to realize that there's no bad in the world. That's what we say in Psalm 136:1, "Give thanks to Hashem for He is good; His kindness endures forever." After hearing so many miracle stories, there's nothing to add…

We simply must review constantly until we internalize in our hearts, "Give thanks to Hashem for He is good". This is the truth that we must live by.

It's easy to say, but how do we do it? It's not easy to live the truth that everything is good when logic shows us so many difficulties in life. The world is full of evil, cruelty and brutality – people who aren't willing to accept Hashem's will. Logic asks, "So what's there to thank Hashem for?" To do so, we must cast logic aside and cling to emuna. Human logic can't understand Hashem and His way of running the world. But, emuna tells us that everything is from Hashem and it's all good, whether or not we understand how or why.

The great tzaddikim endured unspeakable hardships. How? They held on tightly to simple emuna, knowing that whatever happened in their lives was Hashem's will and all for the very best. My esteemed teacher, Rabbi Yehuda Zev Leibowitz osb"m, who himself suffered so much as a young boy in the Auschwitz concentration camp during the Holocaust, would say that whoever says that everything is good, despite his tribulations, the Creator will surely do good for him and for his offspring.

Let's explain further: the tribulations of our sages seem terrible. Look at all the suffering our forefather Abraham, Joseph, King David, Rebbe Akiva and Nachum Ish Gamzu had. Their emuna kept them strong. Our goal should be to strive for such emuna. Their emuna enabled them to defy logic. Who would think that Joseph had any future in a filthy Egyptian dungeon prison? He clung to emuna and thanked Hashem constantly. Everyone loved his cheeriness. He was given a position of responsibility, for the warden put him in charge of all the other prisoners. Eventually, he attained his miraculous release; not only that, he became the viceroy of all of Egypt.

Logic said that Joseph's life was over at age seventeen when he was sold into slavery and thrown into prison. Emuna said otherwise: this descent would lead to one of history greatest ascents to greatness. Logic told Joseph to despair. Emuna told him to sing, dance and thank Hashem. This is the emuna template that gave all the great tzaddikim the power to endure what they had to endure. They didn't become great from eating chocolate ice-cream.

Who had more troubles in life than King David? His father thought that he was an illegitimate child. His father-in-law tried to kill him. His sons revolted against him as well as his closest ministers. He lived from one conflict to another. Yet he says, "In my distress, You have relieved me, comforted me and heard my prayers" (Psalm 4). Even in his distress, he feels Hashem comforting him. No wonder King David became the King of Israel and the forefather of Moshiach. King David would thank Hashem constantly – his Book of Psalms is his testimony that he never stopped talking to Hashem, praising Him and thanking Him.

King David says, "I thank You Hashem for You have answered/tormented me and have become my salvation" (Psalm 118:21). The Chattam Sofer points out that the Hebrew word *anitani* has a double meaning: You have answered me and You have tormented me. King David, the master poet and Psalmist, is purposely using this play on words to tell us that thanking Hashem for his tribulations, Hashem has not only answered him but has become his salvation. King David teaches us unequivocally that by saying thank You for our suffering, Hashem answers our prayers and becomes our miraculous source of salvation.

144. The Voice of Joy and Salvation

A childless couple who had tried everything came to seek my advice. I told them to thank Hashem for a half hour a day that they didn't have children.

The woman was shocked. "What?! Thank Hashem?! I'm miserable – I cry constantly, and you want me to say thank You?" I empathized with her. Apparently, she was right. This was a painful tribulation for her. How would gratitude help her?

When she calmed down, I continued: "The Gaon of Vilna asks why King David said, 'the voice of joy and salvation'. Shouldn't Hashem first send the salvation and then we'll joyously thank Him? But no – the Gaon teaches that if a person first sings joyous songs of gratitude, then he will surely see salvation.

Why does gratitude trigger salvation? Accepting life's many challenges with gratitude is the loftiest manifestation of true emuna. This is the emuna that elicits salvations. In order to accept our challenges with emuna, we must remind ourselves that this is Hashem's will. As such, our sages instructed us to "make His will our will" (see Pikei Avot, ch. 2).

A person who thanks Hashem for his tribulations makes the following statement: "Master of the World, You want me to endure this hardship. If that's the case, I want to as well. Heaven forbid, I don't disagree with anything You decide and I certainly don't oppose it. Thank You!" This emuna-filled person has nullified his own will to Hashem's will.

The result is, as our sages promise (ibid.) that He bends other people's will to your will.

Where do all a person's problems stem from? They don't accept Hashem's will and they want Him to accept their will. That's why so many sick, childless and unmarried people pray for years but their prayers remain unanswered. But, as many testify, the moment they listen to our CDs. "Stop Crying" and "Kisses to the Creator" and they read "The Garden of Gratitude", they see salvation! They begin to accept Hashem's will because they realize that everything He does is for the very best.

It's not always easy to nullify our will to the Creator's will, but that's our lifelong task. We must pray to Hashem to help us attain the level where we truly nullify our will to His will. These are not mere flowery words for the Shabbat table or the coffee table. These are guidelines to live by. Before people run to rabbis and so-called miracle workers in search of salvation, they should go to Hashem and nullify their will to His will; then, they'll truly see salvation. Once they do, they should share their success stories with others, so that more and more people can begin thanking Hashem and seeing salvations. We were created to praise and thank Hashem. That's why King David ends the Book of Psalms with, "All the souls shall praise G-d, Halleluya!"

145. I Received 30,000 NIS

Shalom and blessing,

I wanted to share my gratitude miracle with you. For two years now, I've been devoting a daily hour to personal prayer and I've started to read the works of Rebbe Nachman of Breslev and to read the books and listen to the CD lessons of Rabbi Shalom Arush. This has brought me from darkness to light.

My wife called me one day and said frantically, "We must scrape up money from the free loan societies because we're terribly overdrawn at the bank. What's more, our apartment needs urgent repairs." Meanwhile, my daughter was telling my wife that she heard about a spiritual ploy from Rabbi Yehuda the Chassid that if a person says the *Nishmat* prayer in a quorum of ten men, he merits salvation.

I asked my wife, "How much money do you need?"

She stuttered…

"Tell me how much you need," I pressed. "Don't be shy – Hashem can flash you a million shekels this minute if He feels like it."

Then she said, "Twenty or so thousand shekels."

I said, "Let's round it out to thirty thousand. I pledge to thank Hashem for everything, and with His help, I'll round up another nine people to say *Nishmat*. Hashem will surely send us the thirty grand." I did what I pledged, and then…

You won't believe it. The next morning, an old employer of mine called me and said, "I need you urgently for a brief project."

I told him, "I'm not doing that line of work anymore."

He said, "I know that you can deliver." I sent him an estimate and he approved it.

Later that day, my wife asked me if I want to go to the Kotel

(Western Wall) in Jerusalem with her. I said, "Gladly!" She asked how much profit I was likely to make from the project with my former employer. I said that I didn't make the final calculation yet.

My wife said, "Maybe you should calculate it?" I agreed.

I sat down with a pencil and paper, calculated time and materials, and discovered that my net profit was – 30,000 Shekels!

I was in shock.

At the Kotel, we prayed *Maariv*, the evening prayer; I wanted to gather another ten men to say *Nishmat*, but they all scurried away. I resigned to thank Hashem by myself. All of a sudden, I heard a voice call out: " *Nishmat! Nishmat!* Come say *Nishmat* – we need a tenth man. With tears rolling down my cheeks, I smiled at that miracle too thanking Hashem for the privilege of saying thank You to him for my salvation. I sang out with a combination of laughing and crying with joy at the top of my voice, "If our mouths were as wide as the sea, if our tongues were as full of joy as the waves in the sea and our lips as wide as the horizon, we couldn't capably thank You Hashem for a single one of the millions and billions of favor You do for us every moment of the day…"

146. The Return to Yeshiva and Subsequent Ascent

Here are a few more stories where we see the power of Rabbi Yehuda the Chassid's spiritual ploy of saying the *Nishmat* prayer in a quorum of ten men.

The *Nishmat* prayer is mentioned in the Mishna and in the Gemara as well as in the writings of the Rambam. It is effective in saving a person from peril, as is brought down in the book, "Derech Yeshara". If a person is in danger while traveling, he should say, "I hereby commit to say the *Nishmat* prayer when I safely arrive at my destination."

Rabbi Eliezer Papo of Bulgaria, author of the classic "Pele Yoetz", says that the *Nishmat* prayer is capable of rescuing a person from any calamity, especially when that individual commits to saying it in front of ten people. Many were rescued in this manner. The holy Steipler, Rabbi Yaakov Yisroel Kanievsky osb"m, would advise people in trouble, Heaven forbid, to do the following:

1.   Give charity;

2.   When the trouble passes, say the *Nishmat* prayer until the end of *Yishtabach*, making the final blessing.

Here are a few more stories from Rabbi Aaron Gamliel's book, "Mateh Aaron", about people who saw salvation by saying the *Nishmat* prayer. Rabbi Gamliel tells:

A young man left the yeshiva and went to work, changing his appearance as well. I met him at a gathering where ten people were saying the *Nishmat* prayer. I asked him why he left the yeshiva and went to work. He was still single and he didn't have to earn a living for his family. He answered that he lost his desire for learning, so he went to work.

I told him, "Stop and think about what you're doing. You didn't like your yeshiva or your teachers; that's OK, for our sages said that a person can only learn Torah in a place that he desires. Find a different yeshiva. You're single and you don't have a family to support. The quality girls in our community are looking for a guy whose head is in Torah all day long. Besides, in the yeshiva, your room and board is taken care of. Out working, you'll have to rent an apartment and buy your own food. That's big bucks. How much will you possibly be able to save in a year?"

I added the other advantages of regular prayers, wholesome atmosphere and the mind and character development that a young man attains in the yeshiva framework. Yet, a young man on the outside, especially without a wife, can go haywire in every crazy direction. Most guys who leave their learning before marriage for a working environment fall into negative influences. They're not the same quality boys as they used to be. Their appearance, their manner and their speech changes. They end up marrying girls on their level.

The young man answered, "Rabbi Gamliel, I know that you're right, but it's hard for me."

I told him that this was a dangerous situation for him. In dangerous situations, a person must commit to saying the *Nishmat* prayer. "Once Hashem finds you a yeshiva you like, commit to saying it with ten men, give a coin to charity, and I'm sure that you'll see success." The young man wrote down his commitment in a little pocket notebook he carried around.

A few months later, the young man contacted me and told me that he was now successfully learning in an outstanding yeshiva with a gtreat reputation. He loved his friends and teachers. And, he fulfilled his commitment of saying the *Nishmat* prayer in a public quorum of ten.

A year after he entered his new yeshiva, the young man felt that he was ready for marriage. This time, he decided to use

Rebbe Zusha of Annipoli's ploy not only saying the *Nishmat* prayer with ten men, but hosting them for a festive meal as well. In the middle of the meal, he received a phone call from a local matchmaker, who offered him a lovely match – the young lady who shortly afterwards became his wife.

147. Married 21 Years, and then a Child

Rabbi Gamliel continues telling:

"In that same *Nishmat* prayer gathering and meal that the young man in the previous story hosted in the center of Israel, participated a man who had been married for 21 years but had never been blessed with children. This person had a sullen mood because he and his wife had tried everything – medical and spiritual – with no success. I encouraged him to commit on hosting his own *Nishmat* prayer and gratitude meal for ten men if he was blessed with a child. This person, in front of the other ten men, made a solemn commitment to do so if he was so blessed.

"The childless man made an additional commitment on his own initiative. He said that he'd make one *Nishmat* prayer and gratitude meal for ten men as soon as he'd find out that his wife became pregnant, and a second one as soon as she gave birth. Three months later, he hosted his first *Nishmat* prayer and gratitude meal for ten men, and as soon as she gave birth, he hosted the second. What's more, at the baby's bris, he and all his guests said the *Nishmat* prayer once more to thank Hashem for their miraculous salvation."

148. The Policeman's Salvation

A policeman with a gloomy face knocked on Rabbi Gamliel's door. He had been married for five years but had not yet been blessed with children. The policeman had heard about the power of the *Nishmat* prayer and gratitude meal for ten men and asked the rabbi to explain the details to him.

The rabbi told him exactly what to do and the policemen committed to fulfilling the rabbi's advice and host such a gratitude meal for ten men as soon as he'd hear that his wife was expecting.

Two years transpired and once again, Rabbi Gamliel heard knocking at his door. A happy young man with a bearded face and dressed in a dark suit said, "Rabbi don't you recognize me?" The rabbi didn't know who he was. "I'm the sour-faced cop that knocked on your door two years ago. Six months ago, my wife gave birth to twins. Not only did I make the *Nishmat* prayer and gratitude meal for ten men, but I decided to become a baal teshuva and observe all of Hashem's mitzvoth." Such is the power of the *Nishmat* prayer and gratitude meal, which elicits salvations for everything a person needs.

149. Salvation by Virtue of "Nishmat"

Another young man heard about the power of the *Nishmat* prayer and gratitude meal for ten men from Rabbi Gamliel. He also saw that Rabbi Chaim Fallagi had referred to this in his book "Chaim L'Rosh."

The young man went to Rabbi Ovadiah Yosef osb"m and asked him if he should commit to saying the *Nishmat* prayer with ten men. Rabbi Ovadiah said that the sources are certainly solid sources that one can depend on. The man then made a tearful commitment that if he saw salvation in making a living and freeing himself from debt, he would say the *Nishmat* prayer with ten men.

Several days later, his friend took him to a righteous and wealthy benefactor for advice. The benefactor told him to remain in the Kollel framework and arranged for him to consolidate his debts while making a no-interest monthly payment that he could afford. As an outright gift, the benefactor gave him rent money for a year, paid for his children's nursery school expenses and gave him another 5000 NIS in coupons for groceries. The young man was now able to learn for a year with no worries, so he happily mead a meal for 200 people where they all said the the *Nishmat* prayer. But at the end of the year, the young man began to worry about what will be for the following year. The benefactor, without any prompting, extended the arrangement for another year. Thrilled with Hashem's loving-kindness, he and his wife committed to saying the the *Nishmat* prayer at every opportunity.

150. One Salvation Leads to Another

Rabbi Gamliel participated in a memorial gathering at a moshav near Jerusalem in memory of one of the holy tzaddikim, Rabbi Yochanan ben Serach, osb"m. He explained to the participants the power of saying the *Nishmat* prayer with ten men in having any of their heart's wishes being answered.

The participants of the gathering were traditional and secular people but they seemed eager to hear all about this.

Many of the people that attended the memorial lesson that night committed in their hearts to saying the *Nishmat* prayer with ten men once they saw a salvation that they were deeply hoping for. One man, a building contractor who didn't yet have children, was blessed within the year. During the "Brit Yitzchak" (the Sefardi counterpart of the Ashkenazi *Vacht Nacht*, an evening of praise to Hashem the night before the bris), the contractor stood up and tearfully and joyfully recited the the *Nishmat* prayer with all the participants, more than ten men.

The contractor's brother attended the "Brit Yitzchak" and agreed to say the the *Nishmat* prayer with ten men as soon as he found a soul-mate. The brother's friend jumped on the bandwagon, for he needed a soul-mate too. The brother of the contractor was the moshavnik who hosted the memorial lesson. Both he and his friend made the *Nishmat* prayer gatherings with festive meals during the coming months.

At the same memorial lesson, participated the contractor's sister, who was totally secular. She thought that the the *Nishmat* prayer would only work for religious people. We told her that even when Ishmael cried out to Hashem, He answered the lad's prayers. All the more so when a person praises and thanks Hashem! The sister had an eight-year-old son, but since then, she didn't have any more children. She committed to saying the the *Nishmat* prayer with ten people present if she was blessed with another child. A few months later, we heard that she was expecting.

This ends the collection of Rabbi Gamliel's stories, of which there are many more.

The Following letters are not connected directly to "I Said Thank You and Saw Miracles", but they teach the power of the emuna that everything Hashem does is for the very best. With this level of emuna, a person's life changes for the better. Once he begins to live this emuna, he lives with gratitude as well.

151. Amazing Message

We received the following letter from a university student in Egypt who learns Hebrew. She writes in Hebrew and says:

Shalom!

I am a 23-year-old student at Azhar University in Cairo. I learn Hebrew in my spare time. I have three Hebrew books by Rabbi Shalom Arush. When I read the wonderful book, "The Garden of Emuna", I felt that this book is significant for me even though I'm not a Jew. I found wonderful ideas in the book that we also believe in. But, it's easy to forget that there's no one but G-d when we encounter situations that anger and upset us. I learned that if someone's thoughts are always with the Creator – that everything is from Him and all for the best so that we thank Him always – this can bring humanity to genuine peace.

I too have a problem I've been suffering from for many years. I prayed and repented but I didn't see relief. Finally, I read the chapter, "Say Thank You and be Healed". I tried the advice there of thanking the Creator for my health issue, and praise to Him, my problem has since been solved.

I want to express my gratitude to Rabbi Arush. I am happy that there are people in Israel like him – even his name means "peace". Even though our situation in the Middle East is not an easy one, I believe that emuna in the Creator can bring us peace. I will pray that peace overcomes war, terror and strife and that everyone should be subservient to the Creator.

All the best and many blessings.

What's left to say about a letter like this? It certainly behooves every one of us to get to work on emuna and to pray that the entire world should get to know the Creator and to accept the yoke of His kingship.

152. Strengthening Connection to Hashem

The following letter arrived from one of the Gulf States to Rabbi Lazer Brody, editor of our English-language website:

"My name is Abu Jalad. The book "The Garden of Emuna" that appeared on your website in serial form caught my attention. Its ideas are brilliant. The book strengthens one's personal connection with the Creator. As a news editor on a well-known news website from the Gulf States and as a Sunni Moslem, I'm walking a tightrope. It doesn't scare me, though. A G-d fearing journalist must take responsibility for molding world opinion and must be courageous. Many want to destroy the world, so we must build the world.

Few seek truth. Your message is universal; I doubt whether you properly recognize your own potential. It's not easy for me, but I hope that we will be able to continue this correspondence and even expand on it."

153. I Became Full of Emuna and Hope

Here's a letter from South Africa:

I'm 41, and I was raised as a Catholic. I am a university graduate who majored in Christian Theology. I am also an ordained minister who gives lessons in religion in the local school system. One clear day, I started feeling like a two-faced person. I hated myself and I couldn't go on teaching material that I myself failed to believe in. I started living a life of lust and I became even more depressed. I lost my money, my health and nearly all of my sanity. The only thing left for me was to scream out to the Creator for help.

The Creator heard my call and led me to your English-language website. The first thing I did was to devour the "Garden of Emuna" serial lessons. No words can describe the amazing combination of brilliance and simplicity that characterizes Rabbi Arush's writings, something I've never encountered anywhere else. I became full of emuna and hope, for today, I know that everything is for the best. Thanks to the book, a man whose life was at risk in South Africa received a new life. I am so thankful to you.

154. The Facial Hole Disappeared

Dear Rabbi Shalom Arush,

My name is Anna Benvides and I'm from Peru in South America. I want to tell you about a true story that happened to me on the first day of your Chanuka holiday. This is not the product of my imagination or of substance influence – it's real. I tell it in honor of the King of the Universe.

A few hours before the Jewish Chanuka holiday, I was involved in a terrible automobile accident. My face was cut and bruised to the extent that the most ridiculous clown face looked better than mine. I thought that I'd have to live with such an ugly face forever and I was deeply upset.

Helpless and despairing, I realized that until then, I had never been sick. How merciful the Creator has been to me always! So now, the new predicament shocked me. I couldn't stand to see myself in the mirror – it was disgusting.

During that time, I received a book that was later to become my guide to life – "The Garden of Emuna" in Spanish. The book encouraged me that I wasn't dependent on physicians or on anyone else – only the Creator. Why do I say this? The books message came to me right on time. My attending physician was heartless and told me that if I was lucky, my face might begin healing in six months or a year, if at all. He gave me a prescription for a drug named "Seridasa" that relieves pain and reduces swelling.

I looked for the drug in three different pharmacies but couldn't find it. When I got home, I did a computer search on the drug, trying to find out what's so special about it.

I discovered that this drug is produced from silk-worm bacteria, a substance that the Jews do not regard as kosher. Even though I'm not Jewish, I decided against taking the drug. Now, I realized why the Creator of the Universe wouldn't let me find it anywhere.

"The Garden of Emuna" that was now lifting me out of depression was written according to the wisdom of the Jews. How could I take medicine that according to Jewish law was unfit for consumption?

I followed the advice of the book. What did the Creator want from me? Why did the accident happen to me? I started saying personal prayers every day, sure that He would open my eyes in understanding. Anyway, only He really knows me. I started to realize how narcissistic I was and vain too, looking at myself in the mirror all the time. I had been nothing but superficial. The Creator now wanted me to connect to my inner dimension. Thanks to "The Garden of Emuna" and my daily personal prayer, I was now developing an intimate personal relationship with Him.

I began apologizing to the Creator for my vanity and superficiality all these years. I thanked Him for His patience with me and I realized that my fate was in His hands only, for He is the only true physician Who cares about me. Without the "Garden of Emuna", my prior feeling of dependence on the doctors would have made me insane.

I can't tell you that I was singing and dancing with joy like a person of true emuna should. No, not yet. I was spilling rivers of tears in my private prayer sessions; rivers that could make our own Amazon River here in South America look small. But, between tears, I was thanking the Creator. I wasn't asking for healing – I was praying for humility, so that I could remember the lesson of my car accident forever.

I not only said thank You to the Creator but I prayed for all the Jewish People. Then, the miracle happened. Within the course of five days, my distorted face returned to normal. It was so astonishing and even hard for me to believe that it was really happening. I could feel a new life force in my face. I remember yelling with glee, "Is this really happening to me?!" I can't begin to describe how elated I felt. A rehab process of no less than five or six months in five days?! Who ever heard of such a thing? When the doctor saw me, he couldn't believe it. He was angry because he couldn't explain it. The Creator showed me that I was in His hands only – I felt like the most fortunate young lady in the world.

I'm writing this letter because your Chanuka holiday teaches that a person must publicize his miracles. So here I am, praising and thanking the Creator! May the entire world know that the G-d of Israel is truth!

I want to add that I am now in the process of becoming a convert to Judaism and my Jewish learning is in high gear. I wait for the wonderful moment when I can receive my Jewish name.

With limitless gratitude,

Anna

155. I Merited a Happy Marriage

Dear Breslev Israel,

I was born a Muslim and I lived in Europe. I suffered from depression and chronic anxiety. I had fits of anger and would even throw things. My wife tried everything and took me to a number of counselors. Once, I met a person who gave me "The Garden of Emuna". I devoured the book in one sitting and it has changed my life. Everything I had previously tried had no influence on me the way this book influenced me. This book has enabled me to have a happy marriage – its very presence in our home brings an aura of peace and calm.

156. The Book that Prevented Suicide

Rabbi David Kraus, our German-language translator, told the following story that he heard from a man who lives in Vienna, Austria:

In the beginning of November, 2009, Robert Enke, the goalkeeper of the German national soccer team and captain of the Hanover 96 team in the German national league, drove his car over train tracks just as the train was coming and committed suicide. This tragedy jolted all of Germany.

The Austrian guy who came to me was a friend of the new goalee on Enke's team who was deeply shaken by the suicide. He decided that he too would commit suicide in the same place that Enke did. In an inexplicable way, the Austrian got hold of a copy of "The Garden of Emuna" in German. He read the book and was profoundly influenced by it. He decided to send it to his friend the soccer player in Hannover.

Several weeks later, the Austrian received a phone call from his German friend the soccer player, who said: "If I hadn't received that book from you that same night, you'd have found me in pieces on the same railroad track where Robert Enke was."

He continued to say that he had already planned his suicide for that night; he didn't even want to look at the book when it arrived earlier in the day. But, he didn't want to be an ingrate to his Austrian friend who took the trouble of sending the book to him, so he opened it. That day, he just wanted to be alone. He didn't even want to talk to his wife.

The German soccer player said, "I took the book and I got into my car. I drove out to the train tracks where my dear friend ended his life. I waited for nightfall and total darkness. Meanwhile, I started to read. Instead of committing suicide, I was glued to the book until I finished it, 24 hours later. I just read – didn't drink, eat or sleep. When I finished the last page I said to myself, 'That's it – there's no one but Him.' The book gave me a new lease on life and I realized how terribly dumb I was. For soccer I'd give up my life? There's a Creator to the world. I came home, apologized to my wife and began a new life.

All thanks to one book…

157. I Found the Answers

Shalom, Rabbi Arush,

I wanted to tell you how much I love your teachings. During my vacation, I visited Israel and I bought a copy of "The Garden of Emuna" at the central bus station. The book is amazing.

Everyone who saw me holding the book came up to me and said how wonderful it is. I came to Israel to find answers; without "The Garden of Emuna", I wouldn't have succeeded.

I ordered all the CDs from the Breslev Israel English website and I've almost finished listening to them all. I thirst for the Divine wisdom in those CDs. They are so soothing and encouraging and a pleasure to listen to. Thanks to them, I'm at peace with myself.

I am now stationed in Iraq and next month I hope to be going home to El Paso, Texas.

I asked the Creator to run my life for me and to lead me on the right path. Thanks for helping me connect to Him.

Sergeant April Tesmer, US Army, Iraq

158. The Gift of Peace of Mind

Shalom!

I discovered your wonderful website and your emuna books and CDs. After I heard a CD narrated by Rabbi Brody (Rabbi Arush's English-language translator), I was hooked. I bought another thirty CDs as well as many of the books, including "The Garden of Emuna"and "The Garden of Yearning". I listen to Rabbi Brody's weekly emuna broadcasts in English on the Breslev Israel website – these lessons touch my heart.

Here's the deal – I'm not Jewish. I'm a retired Methodist minister who holds a number of degrees in theology and ordinations. I never heard such wonderful things before in my entire life!

You have given me the gift of peace of mind. Thank you so much.

Jeff Foster, Lawrenceburg, Tennessee, USA

159. A Giant Smile from Above

I want to express my gratitude for all your books, CDs and the articles on your website.

My husband was raised Reform and he decided to leave Judaism altogether. We were living in a religious neighborhood and he moved us to a rural area where there wasn't a single Jew. I had to leave a wonderful job as a writer for a Jewish newspaper. My husband's spiritual dive was so deep that he was arrested and released on bail. My children's and my Judaism went down the drain.

I hit a rock-bottom of hopelessness. My two sons were in the American Army, one of whom was stationed in Iraq. I decide to visit our old neighborhood. I saw that everyone was talking about "The Garden of Emuna" and a book for men called "The Garden of Peace."

I came home and ordered both books as well as a stack of CDs. I started reading the Breslev Israel website every day. I signed up for the mailing list to receive all the updates. What vitamins!!! My joy of life returned to me. I was born anew, connected to my spiritual soul.

I realized that the Creator gave me a gift of being out here in a rural setting with plenty of lakes and forests to speak to Him from. I became a new, improved and happy version of myself. To add my joy, my sons came home safely from the army.

One day, my husband complained that he's fed up with his emptiness in life. He agreed to read "The Garden of Emuna" and "The Garden of Peace." I almost had a cardiac seizure then and there! Again, I felt that Hashem was smiling at me from above. Tears of joy trickled down my face.

Several weeks ago, we started having Sabbath dinner. The tefillin and tzitzit are back too. He walks around with an MP3 and listens to emuna CDs all day long.

This world is starving for genuine spirituality. Hashem is using you to spread His truth. You are light in the darkness.

Thank you from the bottom of my heart!

160. Hallel Prayers

Here's another letter from our German website that Mahmoud D. wrote from Germany:

Hello to my rabbi,

My family is originally from Jerusalem. Although I was born and raised in Germany, my family fled to Amman, Jordan in 1948. Today I'm 38 and for the past three months, I've felt a strong connection to Judaism. Your book "The Garden of Emuna" has touched me – I read it daily. I also watch the vids of the Hallel prayers in your yeshiva. Whenever I view them on your website, I feel tremendous joy. (*Every month on Rosh Chodesh and during Chol Hamoed, lengthy Hallel prayers with musical accompaniment and dancing are recited at our Chut Shel Chesed Yeshiva in Jerusalem and are broadcast around the world on our Breslev Israel multi-language website – the publisher*).

I don't know how to explain this, but Judaism captures my interest. I love its true joy and love of the Creator.

Dear Rabbi Arush, thank you. You give me much power that I never had.

It's mindboggling how my life has changed for the better.

161. The Successful Transaction

After my army service in the IDF, I went to a Judaism seminar sponsored by Tsohar where I first discovered Judaism. Afterwards, my enthusiasm waned. I flew to work in the USA and I took a copy of "The Garden of Emuna" with me. After working in a mall for six months, my visa expired. I had to return to Israel to renew it. I planned to return to the USA after a month. Meanwhile, I was working as a waitress. Meanwhile, my sister in the USA sealed for me a great contract for selling from a kiosk in a mall, something that would enable me to make a chunk of money in a short time.

Three months had passed and I was still in Israel, getting closer to Judaism. The lessons from "The Garden of Emuna" were always echoing in my mind. I learned that income was from Hashem; why should I cheapen myself in the atmosphere of a mall all day long, just for the lust of money?

So, I made a deal with Hashem. I'll stay in Israel and continue getting closer to Him, and He should take away my lust for money. I kept my word and relinquished my dream of becoming rich in America. Meanwhile, I've married a wonderful Torah scholar, have a new baby and work in Jewish outreach. How's that for a successful transaction?

162. The Book with the Hat

Rabbi Meir Mazouz's son told me that when he was in France, he visited the Israeli Foreign Ministry and he saw one of my books. He said that it was "the book with the hat" and I told him that this was "The Garden of Wisdom".

An Arab came there with his wife who is an Arab-language writer. She saw the book and during the time that her husband was in his meeting, she sat down and started to read it. She read for about half an hour until her husband's meeting was over.

She wanted the book. The clerks there said that they have several copies so she is welcome to take that one. She sent them a subsequent email that said, "Now that I have read the book, I understand why the Jews are wise and cultured. Now I know."

Rabbi Mazouz told me, "You sit in Jerusalem and you don't realize how you are sanctifying Hashem's Name the world over."

163. The Vice President of the Ukraine

I was at the wedding of a millionaire who recently moved to Israel. The Vice President of the Ukraine was there. When he met me, he was as excited as a little boy. "I read your books," he exclaimed. "I quote them; I even give them out to others!" He was truly excited. He spoke Russian and someone was translating for me.

The light of emuna is spreading all over. **You have no idea what the light of emuna is. Anyone who merely touches this light starts to live a new life. He learns what paradise on earth is. This is the light of Rebbe Nachman of Breslev and his student Rebbe Natan that has descended to the world in simple language for this generation by way of us**. As Rebbe Nachman promises, with the mindset of emuna, there is no suffering. With spiritual awareness, there are no troubles. What do we lack – only spiritual awareness!

164. Engaging in Personal Prayer

My multi-lingual students receive questions from around the world. A non-Jew from France received the book, "The Garden of Peace" in French. He started getting close to Judaism and he bought all my books. He writes, "Are you sure that a mortal wrote this book?" This is the reaction of a non-Jew! You don't have to be Jewish to realize what a treasure the emuna books are.

A Christian Minister from South Africa came to me with his wife, sons and daughters in law. I hosted them, fourteen people in all, and gave them a private emuna lesson.

They asked me to take them to a field for a personal prayer session. They went in their rented minibus and I drove my car. I told their Israeli driver when we arrived at a secluded field, "They'll probably do 10 or 15 minutes of personal prayer. Take them to their hotel afterwards, because I'm staying here for a while."

I walked from one end of the field to another. Every one of them had found a private niche to speak to Hashem from; even their little eight-year old boy was speaking to Hashem form behind a tree. Oh, my goodness! Look how non-Jews are hungrily talking to Hashem! Where are all the Jews?

That's why every one of us must strengthen himself and learn "In Forest Fields' – how to speak to Hashem. **A person cannot rectify himself without personal prayer**. A person can't change without working on himself, even if he learns

Torah. If he learns Torah but doesn't work on himself, he'll never improve!

165. He Travelled to Uman

A person who wanted to travel to Uman came to me and complained that he was penniless. What's more, because of his debts, the court wouldn't allow him to leave the country. I told him to do a six-hour session of personal prayer, and then he'd be able to go. He was in disbelief; I assured him that I wasn't joking.

He stood for six hours and begged Hashem to enable him to travel to Uman for Rosh Hashana. "Hashem, Rebbe Nachman himself commanded that no one should be missing from the Rosh Hashana gathering in Uman." For six hours, he yearned. Shortly afterward, he received a windfall and repaid his debts. The court lifted the ban against his leaving the country and he was able to travel to Uman for Rosh Hashana.

This is real! All the obstacles fell aside! By virtue of his six-hour personal prayer session, he also merited a much greater rectification of the soul in this trip than he would have without the six hours.

The ticket to Uman is mostly yearning and tons of prayer. We used to pray for hours to reach Uman. The Ukraine was still part of the USSR, which was closed to Israelis. We prayed for hours and we made it.

A great rabbi once said, "With Hashem, you can cross the Red Sea on foot. Without Him, you can't get past the doorway."

Everyone must understand that with emuna, true emuna, you can attain whatever your heart wishes simply by speaking with Hashem in your own words. The salvations you need are available with no natural limitations. Prayer alters nature. Hashem can do whatever he wants whenever he wants. As soon as one of His creations turns to Him simply and sincerely, he can accomplish virtually anything.

Rebeb Natan of breslev said that wherever he sees deficiency, he sees a lack of prayer or insufficient prayer. This is a spiritual law that is just as valid as natural laws are. Everything has its price-tag of required prayers.

166. An Escape from Depression

A person grabbed me and asked to speak to me. I was in a hurry because I had to be in three more places that day. He told me that his father was in deep depression so he gave him a copy of "The Garden of Emuna" but he refused to read it.

The same father was acquainted with another person who also used to be depressed but recently had started smiling. "Hey," he inquired, "you used to be down in the dumps like me; what makes you so smiley lately?" The acquaintance said that he has a book that he doesn't budge from - "The Garden of Emuna". The father figured that if from Above, he's being shown this book for a second time, he had better read it. He did, and he too has escaped from depression.

167. The CDs that Save Lives

Yosef Dan, may Hashem bless him, one of my students who traverse the world spreading emuna, came to Canada. A person approached him and asked, "Weren't you here last year? Do you remember that you gave me a book and four CDs? You saved four people from death!"

The Canadian man told him that he had a lucrative business with a partner. The partner died suddenly and the inheritors wanted to kick him out of the business. They said that the business was totally theirs and that he had no share in it. The thoughts of hate and revenge against the inheritors who were trying to disenfranchise him ate him up. He decided to put out a contract on the four inheritors. He didn't care what it would cost him…

He said to Yosef Dan, "I heard those four CDs in my car. I heard the words of emuna and realized that everything is from Hashem and all for the best. I pursued the path of gratitude rather than violence. In the end, I came to a compromise with them. I lost a lot of money but I'm happy about it. Know that you saved four lives by way of these CDs."

168. Beyond Death

Since I've written "The Garden of Gratitude" and the Gems series of gratitude pamphlets as well as producing the emuna and gratitude CDS, many people who used to complain to me all the time no longer chase after me. Frequently, I hear: "I started to say thank You and my life has become good."

I was giving a lecture in Afula when a young man jumped up from the audience and said, "Rabbi, I was beyond death before I heard your CD 'Stop Crying'. Since then, I came back to life." I hear such expressions constantly from people: "You've saved my life!" I have even learned this expression in several languages, for I hear this repeatedly from around the globe.

169. You Changed My Life!

Recently, I made a trip to five countries. Everywhere we were, the auditoriums were packed. Every day, I lectured in a different place. After the lectures, when people sought my blessings or book signatures, I heard the expression "You changed my life" repeatedly in English, French and Spanish. People I never met were telling me that they now spend a daily hour in personal prayer. Some even told me that they had done six-hour personal prayer sessions. What's behind all this?

For thousands of years, the Jewish People have been yearning for Hashem and saying in the Aleinu prayer three times a day, "Therefore we put our hope in You, Hashem our God, to soon see the glory of Your strength, to remove all idols from the Earth, and to completely cut off all false gods; to repair the world, Your holy empire. And for all living flesh to call Your name, and for all the wicked of the earth to turn to You. May all the world's inhabitants recognize and know that to You every knee must bend…" Two thousand years of yearning for Hashem.

Bringing people close to Hashem is easy. Thousands of years of prayer come to our assistance. Thousands of years of the Jewish People yearning for Hashem is helping emuna to be revealed in the world, so that all of humanity will believe in the Almighty. That's why so many non-Jews attend our lectures and read our books.

Moshiach, who we all eagerly await, will come to the world to teach all of mankind the power of prayer, especially personal prayer.

Anyone who truly wants to bring others close to Hashem is bound to succeed. Thousands of years of prayer have been begging that emuna be spread in the world.

We should all pray for ten minutes a day that the whole world learn the "Universal Garden of Emuna," "The Garden of Gratitude" and listen to the emuna CDs.

From around the world, I've seen how tens of thousands of non-Jews are already engaged in daily personal prayer.

170. Kidnapped in Mexico

One of the stories we heard in Mexico dealt with the terrible phenomenon of kidnappings there for ransom. Any child or spouse of a rich person is a prime target, not to be released until the ransom is paid in full. The kidnapped person suffers unspeakable brutality, both physical and mental. One such kidnapped person came to one of our lectures. In total despair, he had decided to commit suicide. He had crawled under the bed and he saw Hashem's Name written there, so he received a new will to live. Hashem's Name there was probably written by another Jew who had been previously kidnapped.

Ultimately, the ransom was paid and the young man was freed. He searched the internet for our Spanish website and he saw the "Garden of Emuna" in serial form there, which he began to read. He soon began to believe in Hashem, to speak to Him and to thank Him. He understood that everything that happened to him was for the purpose of bringing him to emuna. He came to my lecture to thank me. Can you imagine? Hashem is bringing people closer to Him by having them kidnapped!

My student Rabbi Lazer Brody told me that he heard the same exact story from a banker's wife in Johannesburg, South Africa, who came close to Hashem after having been kidnapped. Hashem wants emuna to spread! If people read emuna books and listen to emuna CDs, they won't need tribulations to bring them back to Hashem.

In the following pages, we present a series of stories about "I said thank You and saw miracles" from the Breslev Israel website at www.breslev.co.il:

171. A Few Little Words

Shalom!

Avigail, Hodaya and Shir-el are three gifts, cherished souls that Hashem gave me for safekeeping.

Then it happened. After three childbirths, I found myself suffering from depression. I could barely lift my head or speak. All joy in life eluded me, as if I had to climb up a glass wall to the heavens in order to find happiness again. I could barely function. I felt immobilized. When my husband would come home from work, I'd do into my room until he put the girls to sleep. Only afterward, I'd come out.

The tears and the depression enslaved me, body and soul. I had pains in my chest and I harbored the worst thoughts. My husband encouraged me to speak to a wonderful woman, our family doctor. She told me that this type of post-natal depression happened to many women, not just me. She gave me an anti-depressant prescription that I took with a heavy heart. I'm not the type to rely on meds and I never needed them, thank G-d. But my family was suffering…

Three months transpired and my drastic downfall crashed down on me – I received a referral to a psychiatrist.

When my appointment came, the psychiatrist asked me all kinds of questions. I tried to explain to her that my soul was trapped in a body that does whatever it wants. I'm a happy soul and I want to be happy, but my body refuses to cooperate. She didn't understand me at all; what connection does she have to souls? She wrote out a prescription and said, "Try this." I did, and nothing changed. When I returned to her for my next appointment, she had had me try something else. I was a guinea pig, a laboratory animal and not a human…

This time, I took the prescription but didn't buy the pills. I knew that something else was going on here, much higher and much deeper. A scream from way down inside me was waiting to be released. I found a place where I could be alone and screamed, "Please G-d, help me! Show me what's wrong with me and how to cure it for real." This scream could have wakened the dead, but that's all it took:

one scream and I saw salvation. The Creator sent me to a bookstore and the first book I took off the shelf was "The Garden of Gratitude."

In one of its chapters, Rabbi Arush refers to his CD, "Stop Crying" that became a life-changer for so many people. I was determined to obtain that CD. No sooner had that thought run through my head, when my girlfriend phoned me. She had purchased Rabbi Arush's CDs to distribute in memory of her parents and asked me if I would help her. I was glad to; among them was the CD, "Stop Crying."

I listened to the disc over and over. Rabbi Arush explains that this generation suffers from an exile of the soul that triggers all types of secondary problems like depression, anxiety, jealousy and anger. A person who wants a healthy soul must rid himself of ingratitude. He must thank Hashem for everything, the good and the seemingly otherwise.

The truth is that at first, it was hard for me to accept these concepts. But, I knew that I had to cast my intellect and logic aside like the CD says. "My way" lead to zero improvement in my condition. How could a few little words be so powerful? I started to say thank You: "Thank You, Hashem, for the chaos in my life and thank You that I'm fed up with it. Thanks you for the depression and all the useless meds." In order to be honest, I also thanked Hashem that I was not yet sincere in my thanks. But, Rabbi Arush said to do it and I listened to him. After two weeks of saying thank You, I started to see the light of truth.

I thanked Hashem for things I never thanked Him for – for our food, our income, our dishes, our home and for the chaos too. I thanked Him endlessly for our children, for the sky, the flowers, the molecules and the bacteria. I thanked

Him for my friends and relatives. All these expressions of gratitude redeemed my from my spiritual exile.

Rabbi Shalom Arush succeeded in doing what no one else did – he saved my life. He gave me tools to live my life. No wonder Rebbe Nachman said that it's a big mitzvah to be happy, for joy in life are the only accurate lenses to view the world through. Joy leads to more joy; I discovered that I was now expecting my fourth child. I received my first son, Sagi Shalom. Sagi means "great" and "Shalom" is in honor of Rabbi Arush, who is truly great.

No day passes anymore without my profusely thanking Hashem and for my getting to know Rabbi Arush by way of his books and CDs. May Hashem bestow him and his family with every imaginable blessing. I just wanted to send a gigantic note of gratitude.

172. The Only Address

Dear Rabbi Arush, I just wanted to thank you.

I'm from New York, married and a father to two wonderful children. Like you teach, everything I do, first I thank Hashem. Last November, you came here with Rabbi Lazer Brody and the Breslev Israel staff. Since then, my life has changed dramatically for the better. Thank you, Rabbi, for your CDs have changed my life. That's why I've began spreading your CDs to other people, my family, friends and people I do business with. There are many people suffering here – I know them from close up. I'm not talking about one or two, but many who need your wonderful advice and encouragement. Thank you!

Here's my story:

Five months ago, I was in speech therapy. I had some issues with my vocal chords and overall speech so I went to the therapist who treated my son for eating disorders. She was wonderful with my son so I figured she'd be good for me too. At any rate, she's a divorced woman in her sixties who used to be observant. Her children married out of the faith. Despite it all, I discovered that she's a happy, upbeat woman. One day, during treatment, she began telling me about some of the painful issues in her life, the main one of which is her children's marrying non-Jews. She was also suffering financially, because she was paid a modest hourly rate despite her seniority and experience. She had received advice from rabbis before but nothing seemed to work for her.

I gave her the disc that changed my life, "The Only Address" by Rabbi Shalom Arush. I told her to listen to it and that I was sure she'd see results. I told her to direct all her hopes and requests to the Almighty.

She looked at me like I was crazy.

I repeated what I said before and told her to direct all her hopes and requests to the Almighty.

"The truth is," she said while still looking at me in a weird way, "is that I never heard anything like that from a rabbi. Instead, they had all kinds of ploys for me to try."

"Put all that aside and move forward," I said. "Talk to Hashem all the time – on the way to work, at home, wherever it's comfortable – and tell Him everything. Ask whatever you want from Him, whatever you need."

She nodded and told me that she was willing to try.

During our next appointment, she told me that in a few days, there was going to be a board meeting of all the bigwigs in the clinic. Meanwhile, she had been asking Hashem every day for help in income. She entertained the idea of asking the bosses then for a raise and asked me what I thought.

"Don't ask a thing from them," I told her. Continue praying and Hashem will take care of your income. Just wait and see."

When I arrived for our next appointment, she was really happy to see me (I didn't know who was coming to whom for therapy). "You can't imagine what happened!" she exclaimed. "I was called into the board meeting and to be honest, I was thinking about salary. I didn't see that I had any other alternative than asking for what I need. But, before I had a chance to open my mouth, my boss said. "We've reviewed the wonderful job you do for is. We want you to be happy. We're raising you from $45/hour to $70 plus bonuses." I didn't know what to do with myself. I thanked them sincerely and left the room. Do you understand the magnitude of this miracle?"

I surely understood. It's just what Rabbi Shalom Arush promises in the name of Rebbe Nachman of Breslev all the time, namely, that Hashem wants to give us everything but we have to prepare a vessel for His magnificent abundance. That vessel is prayer.

I was overjoyed for the therapist. Nothing brings a person so close to Hashem as seeing his prayers being answered. The woman couldn't stop thanking me for the CD and all the advice I gave her. She now wanted to share this light with others.

My wife and I received much spiritual reinforcement from this story and we continue to spread emuna everywhere we go. We send Breslev Israel a giant hug. As for this letter, I hope it puts a smile on your face.

Thank you so much, dear Breslev Israel, for letting my wife and me share in your magnificent emuna distribution. It has been the biggest blessing in our lives.

173. You Won't Defeat Me!

Here's another story from our Breslev Israel website:

This week was my husband's birthday. He didn't make a big deal of it because since we have become observant Jews and parents, a lot of our secular ideas have fallen by the wayside. Yet, I felt the need to treat him with a gift.

I got the nerve to go to a mall that since seems to me to be a scary stronghold of the evil inclination. Yet, I wanted to buy my husband a pair of elegant trousers for Shabbat, so I figured it would be okay.

As soon as I passed the guard's booth where people get checked at the entrance, I knew I had made a mistake. But, I was inside the mall already. With my baby and with jittery legs, I went deeper into the mall.

It was a sound and light show. Dancing lights and brand names called out to you to come spend your money and buy them. It was like a big festival with loud music and tons of people. Empty folks were looking for "things" to stimulate them and fill their emptiness. I couldn't stand the din and the distractions. I focused on finding a men's store to purchase what I wanted for my husband.

Boy, was I distracted! While going up the glass-walled elevator, I saw three stores that I just "had" to check out before I left the mall.

I gave myself a half an hour, but the strong tides of the mall pulled and pushed me in all directions, just like a strong undercurrent at the beach. Things I never thought of called out to me, "You need me! Buy me!" I almost bought a pink "Hello Kitty" coat for my daughter but then I came to my senses – she'll love me just as much without the coat. Then, the evil inclination chimed in with, "What kind of mother are you? Don't you care about your daughter?"

All the materialism that engulfed me made my heart shrivel. Suddenly, Hello Kitty and Winnie the Pooh blurred because my eyes filled with tears. The mall was trying to convince my innocent soul that it was the solution to all my problems. What a liar! Money and things don't bring happiness. Money comes and money goes.

I felt weak and I now did whatever I do when I feel that way – I turned to my Father in Heaven. "*Heilige Tatte* – Merciful Father – have mercy on me and help me." That's all a person has to do to get a ray of Divine light to peek out from the dark clouds.

Then, I remembered the power of gratitude, so I started thanking Hashem. "Thank You, Tatte, for my husband, and for the additional healthy year You have given us together. Thank You for our sweet children who give me endless joy. Thank You for our home, our food and our income. We don't deserve any of Your marvelous gifts…" Suddenly, my normal breathing returned to me. Hello Kitty and Cinderella faded away; it was as if Hashem had stuck a pin in all the mall's balloon of illusions.

I continued thanking Hashem as I hurried out of the mall and was so delighted to see the sunshine and breathe the fresh air outside. Today, I know that no quantity or quality of materialism can bring happiness to a person. This is the knowledge that enables a person to tell the evil inclination, "You won't defeat me." I thank Hashem for the tools of prayer and gratitude that have enabled me to change my life for the better.

The important moral of this story is that when a person is happy and thanks Hashem for everything, he lacks nothing.

174. Hello, Emuna!

Here's what a student of ours from New York wrote us:

During a routine checkup, the doctor asked how I feel.

"Terrible," I answered. "I feel chronic fatigue and as if I'm enveloped in a cloud of sadness. I can't concentrate and the simplest task is difficult for me to do."

"You've got clinical depression," the doctor said, and gave me a prescription for Prozac.

The doctor's diagnosis didn't surprise me. I was recently fired from a job I had loved. I was vice-president for international marketing; foreign investors bought my bosses out and came in with their own staff. We were politely given the boot.

So what do I do now, with a wife and six children to support? My severance pay helped a little bit, so did unemployment benefits, but they disappeared a few weeks later. I need an income, a fulltime job. Just then, there was a terrible economic slowdown in the USA. No doors of opportunity were opening to me. I was faced with a rocky path of dim prospects.

Despite all of this, I fought the depression, but it just got worse. I felt that I was drowning. Ever since my doctor gave me the Prozac prescription, I carried it around in my wallet; I had never purchased the pills. I figured that I need to consult someone more specialized that a family doctor. I visited a well-known psychotherapist. Here in the waiting room were other embarrassed people like me. My turn finally came.

The psychotherapist wanted to know if I heard noises coming out of my nose or if the media tells me what to do. His routine questions were so weird to me. I told him about my worries and anxieties and how I didn't know where the next mortgage payment was coming from. I said that I have a wife and six children to feed. Like a judge banging his gavel, he too said, "Clinical Depression" and gave me a prescription for Prozac.

The Prozac did help me function better but they had a side effect – they made me feel like I was locked in a telephone booth. There was a thin line between the real me and the Prozac-me. It was so frustrating that oftentimes I simply refused to take the pills. I suffered tidal waves of anxiety and depression. My wife couldn't stand me. I was on a roller coaster of Prozac-no Prozac.

I finally found a good-paying job but I was still depressed and dependent on the pills. Then, one of my friends gave me :The Garden of Emuna" by Rabbi Shalom Arush.

I read the book three times. Only then, bright lights flashed in my head. Before reading the book, I thought that I had emuna. Of course I believed in Hashem! But after reading the book for the third time, I realized that I didn't have emuna at all. Now, I saw the world in an entirely different light. Hashem is G-d, there is no one but Him! I now realized that everything is the product of His magnificent Divine Providence. Everything He does is for the good of my soul, even if it's outside of my comfort zone. Hashem's Divine Providence is like a tailor-made suit; it's an exact fit for my soul. No one can help me or hurt me unless Hashem sanctions it.

I finally realized that my lack of emuna was the source of my depression. What's more, I hadn't been thanking Him for the blessings I had!

I was depressed because I wanted to control everything – what a fantasy. "The Garden of Emuna" introduced me to truth, a new reality: neither I, nor the investors who fired me nor my new employer controls the world; only Hashem!

I understand that Hashem alone did, does and will do everything. He is the source of everything. I also realized that life's difficulties are soul corrections and tests of emuna, to bring us closer to Hashem. Personal prayer (thank you, Rebbe Nachman) has replaced the Prozac. My depression hasn't returned since. I can imagine that I am only one of many who have substituted meds for emuna.

Thank you so much, dear Rabbi Shalom Arush, for your amazing book (and to you, Rabbi Lazer Brody, for translating this book into my native tongue of English). Most of all, thank You, Almighty Father in Heaven, the source of everything!

175. The Thief Who Erased the Debt

Here's another story from our Breslev Israel website:

In Israel, an act of burglary happens every three minutes, according to the Israeli Police. Someone who suffers a burglary becomes another statistic. The bored cops ask with indifference, "When did it happen? What did they take?" It's so impersonal and bureaucratic.

Hey, what about me?! I'm human! The crooks violated my private domain! Am I just another statistic? One more burglary is entered on Israel's national crime computer.

When you share your trauma with others, they tell you that you're not alone. That too is annoying. So you walk around feeling helpless and frustrated. You refuse to believe that thieves entered your personal domain, your soul! One shudders at the thought! Who has the right to violate my private territory? A person loses his self-confidence and joy in life. How else am I exposed? It's a personal tragedy, an earthquake.

So how do you deal with this? What do you do with the fear and anxiety? Well, emuna and trust have a great track record in the past. They've always kept my head above water. Thank G-d, we're believers. I turned to our sages for advice. I opened up Rebbe Nachman's "Aleph-bet" book and looked up *G'neva*, thievery. Rebbe Nachman says that this is the result of wasting time, among other hair-raising reasons. It's no simple matter when someone breaks in your home. Rabbi Shalom Arush – my rabbi – also helped me with the advice in his book "The Garden of Emuna." I reviewed the rules of emuna:

1.   Everything is from Hashem;

2.   Everything is for the best;

3.   Everything is for a reason, therefore there's a message for me in what happened. There are no tribulations without prior transgression.

I started to do some serious soul-searching, thinking all the time that everything is from Hashem and that He is infinitely merciful. I now decided to look at the burglary in a positive light, through lenses of emuna.

The lenses of emuna first of all filter out all the negativity of what you're seeing – I was no longer angry or embittered. Second, I started seeing the good in what Hashem (not the burglars) did. This sounds crazy to someone who doesn't cling to emuna, because emuna comes at the price of tears, tribulations and tons of prayer – but it's all worth it. Emuna always stood by my side during trying times – it didn't fail me now, either.

I didn't blame anyone anymore. I was only looking at Hashem and I was beginning to see the good in everything. Okay, the burglars stole my diamond wedding ring and the rest of my jewelry. Meanwhile, thank G-d, my husband and my two children are healthy. I was thinking how such a monetary loss beat medical bills and emergency treatments any day. Besides, the burglars had come in the late morning when the kids were at school and my husband and I were at work. What if the burglars were armed? What would have happened if they had had come at night and if my husband had confronted them? I shudder to think. I was seeing more and more Divine mercy in what seemed bad at a superficial glance.

One of Rabbi Shalom Arush's sayings echoed in my mind; "Hashem does a favor for a person and then collects the debt." Rabbi Arush explained this idea after Rabbi Yaacov Yosef osb"m died, explaining why Hashem took away the tzaddik. The world is in debt, so Hashem gives it the tzaddik; Hashem later takes the tzaddik back as the world's payment for its debt. On my level, I understood that Hashem gave me jewelry so that I could use it to repay my spiritual debts. In his mercy, Hashem was using silver and gold as payment instead of body and soul, Heaven forbid.

No one can comprehend Divine considerations, what and why. I'm not some righteous woman and I surely don't have a prophetic spirit. Nevertheless, I choose to lovingly accept everything Hashem does with simple, innocent emuna.

So Hashem, I thank You for the thief who erased my debt. This is much more than erasing America's twenty-trillion dollar deficit. Hashem's mercy is infinite.

176. Against All Odds

I woke up and I was so weak, still under the influence of the morphium. My wife told me that I was in an accident and that I had been unconscious for three weeks. But now, I'm in the hospital and everything's okay.

This must be a dream…

In the coming months after I came out of a coma, I tried to piece the puzzle together. Cognizantly, I remembered nothing. Friends told me that I rode my motorcycle on the way to university, and a speeding reckless driver sent me in orbit. I was thrown as high as a three-story building. The driver looked at me and fled the scene. Nobody caught his license number and he never got caught. On the Yom Kippur after the accident, I wholeheartedly forgave him.

Nobody gave me any chance of living. They all thought that I had reached my end. Most of my ribs were broken. My lungs were punctured. I had tubes in me just to drain the hemorrhaging. Both hips were broken. I had a tube draining my brain too. To make matters worse, I contracted a bacterial infection during my hospitalization.

Hashem rescued me and cured me!

After stays in two rehab hospitals and a third convalescent home, I came home, one big ball of pain. Eighteen months transpired and my wife gave birth to a son. I finished my university studies and began to work as a fulltime psychotherapist, listening to other people's problems.

But what actually helped my own rehabilitation? It was prayer, charity, and lovingly accepting everything that Hashem does.

At the time, I had not yet become acquainted with Rabbi Shalom Arush. I only discovered his books four years after my accident. I didn't yet know the power of gratitude as I was later able to learn in the "Garden of Gratitude". I merely relied on simple emuna. I only complained once, five months after I returned home, when the pain was unbearable. But I composed myself and started talking to Hashem, and the typhoon-level tribulation eased up a bit. I apologized to Hashem for not accepting the pain with love. After that, I felt a major soothing of body and soul.

Eventually, through eyes of emuna, I was beginning to realize that the accident was the best thing that ever happened to me. It gave me a new outlook on suffering. It helped me become a much better listener and a much more empathetic psychotherapist. It gave me a bold new look on priorities in life and on the purpose of life. It helped me understand that I am 100% in the hands of Hashem.

I love my life now, no matter how difficult it sometimes is. I love Hashem. I love inspiring people and bringing them to emuna. I hope that my letter has been an inspiration for you too.

177. A Time to Say Thank You

Shalom and blessings,

Two books led me to the teachings of Rebbe Nachman of Breslev: Rabbi Shalom Arush's life-changing book, "The Garden of Gratitude", and Rabbi Lazer Brody's book in English, "The Trail to Tranquility". I have learned that emuna and gratitude mitigate the sternest judgments that might be hovering over a person's head.

Gratitude brings more and more reasons to thank Hashem. By simply saying, "Thank You, Hashem", a person's life turns into paradise. Once a person learns to say thank You, he can't go for a minute without thanking Hashem for every little thing.

Not long ago, I found a small prayer of thanks that was printed on a wallet-size card. Feel free to share it!

Thank You, Hashem, King of Kings and Master of the World!

Thank You for the infinite times that You helped me, supported me, rescued me, encouraged me, cured me, guarded over me, and made me happy.

Thank You for always being with me.

Thank You for giving me the strength to observe Your commandments, to do good deeds, and to pray. Thank You for all the times You helped me and I didn't know how to say "Thank You".

Thank You for all the loving kindnesses You do for me each moment. Thank You for every breath I breathe.

And Thank You, Hashem, for all the things that I don't have, for my periodic difficulties, my occasional setbacks, and for the times when I don't feel happy, because everything is for my ultimate benefit, even when I can't see how it's all for the best...

Deep in my heart, I know that everything that comes my way is the very best for me and designed especially for me in precision and exacting Divine Providence, which only The King of Kings is capable of.

Thank You for the hard times in life, for they enable me to fully appreciate the good times; after having been in darkness, one can appreciate the light.

Thank You for the wonderful life You have given me.

Thank You for every little thing that I have, for everything comes from You, and from no one else.

Thank You for always listening to my prayers.

Creator of the World, I apologize from the bottom of my heart for all the times that I didn't appreciate what You gave me, and instead of thanking You, I only complained.

I am dust and ashes and You are the entire universe. Please, don't ever cast me away.

178. My Gratitude Notebook

Here's my story:

Rabbi Shalom Arush wrote a great book entitled, "Women's Wisdom." I never read such an astounding book in my life.

One of the gems of advice I gleaned from this book was the gratitude notebook. Rabbi Arush talks so much about the importance of gratitude, not taking any of Hashem's tiny favors for granted.

The problem is that it's not always easy to thank Hashem for painful things.

I struggled with this idea for many months. How can I thank Hashem for not yet having been blessed with children? How can I thank Hashem for the loneliness, or the fact that we barely scrape by financially? Rabbi Shalom Arush sends us a lifesaver in the chapter that deals with gratitude. He divides it into three stages:

Stage 1: Thank Hashem for all the abundance and blessings in your life, without even confronting the difficulty or painful issue that you're dealing with. Once you reach the level where you're truly grateful for your eyes, your heart, your lungs and all of life's other blessings, you can move on to Stage 2, but until you've completely rid yourself of the "victim" or "perpetual sufferer" syndrome.

Stage 2: Thank Hashem for all your difficulties in life. Once again, don't do this until you've resigned from the victim's club and returned your "official sufferer" membership card.

Stage 3: Once you've thanked Hashem, you may ask Him to illuminate your eyes as to the reason you incurred the suffering. Ask Him also how to do proper teshuva to rectify whatever needs rectification.

Why the above three stages? Any prayer that results from a feeling of self-pity is whining and not prayer. It's liable to make things worse. The above three stages rid of the victim and sufferer syndromes, enabling us to pray with joy.

I've tried this, using the three stages without asking for anything, just saying thank You. In addition, several weeks ago, I started keeping a gratitude notebook. Once you look for them, you find endless reasons for thanking Hashem. Wow, how many blessings!

The more I thanked Hashem, the more He gave me reasons to thank Him. I am now a mother – a trillion thank Yous! I have a wonderful husband – another trillion! I live in Israel and can go to the holy places whenever I want! Mindboggling!

Then, Hashem illuminated my eyes to make a separate gratitude notebook for all my challenges in life. This also helped me find the good in them. I'll give you an example:

I wrote, "Thank You, Hashem, that my business flopped two years ago." I then wrote eight reasons to sincerely thank Him for this and I began to see the silver lining of the cloud. My failed business had the following concealed blessings, which Hashem helped me realize:

1. It gave me more time to speak to Hashem.

2. It cured me of my workaholism.

3. It gave me more time for my family.

4. It improved our marriage dramatically.

5. My anxiety and tension levels went way down.

6. I started cooking, tending my garden and doing things I never had time to do.

7. It gave me the proper perspective of what's really important in life.

8. It helped me make genuine teshuva.

Little by little, my entire thought process changed. I was no longer seeing the negative in anything, only the positive. My mood and energy levels went way up.

Thanks to Hashem, I feel truly happy. I handle life's challenges much better. Life is so different ever since I resigned from the self-pity club.

Life does have its ups and downs. I admit that last month, I felt sad for several hours. My gratitude notebook bailed me out, together with an hour of personal prayer. Hashem helped me chase away the feelings of misery and being a victim.

If you really want to feel a change in life, invest a few shekels/cents and buy yourself a pocket-sized notebook. Right down all the reasons you have to thank Hashem. Don't stop saying thank You. From experience, it works!

179. Nonstop Smile

From our "Personal Stories" section on the Breslev Israel website:

My story starts five years ago. I had a great job in municipal government; I was married and a father of three, living in a gorgeous home in the suburbs. I had no problem paying my monthly mortgage of 4,000 NIS. My salary was great and I had money coming in from the side, too. My wife raised the kids with tranquility and everything was rosy.

Suddenly, a new supervisor replaced my old boss. Even though I was an outstanding worker, the new boss did everything to make my life miserable. Nothing I tried or did placated him, so I just tried to stay out of his way; that didn't work either. I asked to meet my boss's boss; the latter knew that I was an outstanding worker but he preferred to back up my boss and not me.

I felt that I had been dealt a severe injustice. I prayed to Hashem and I went to tzaddikim's gravesites trying to mitigate the severe judgment but nothing seemed to help. Two months later, I was fired. I took my severance pay and left. Now at age thirty, I was unemployed with my wife expecting child number four. We tried to tighten our belt but we were left with the problem of our high monthly mortgage payments. You can't tell stories to the bank – it's cash every month or else. They only understand numbers.

I went to the unemployment agency to see if they had anything suitable for me. The offers I received were not anything I could consider – menial jobs for minimum wage. Everyone seemed to prefer discharged soldiers, who the employers could get away with paying much less.

Meanwhile, my daughter was born and our financial situation became even more difficult. My one consolation is that I didn't have the expense of making a brit, a poor man's consolation…

My monthly unemployment check was a far cry from covering expenses, much less the mortgage. I borrowed money from my parents and from my brother. We started to think about selling the house and downshifting to something less expensive. The thought saddened my wife, but there was no apparent choice. The worst thing was that

I was losing my self-confidence. I felt like a loser after a year on unemployment checks. I'd wake up sluggishly for morning prayers and waste the rest of the morning scanning the want-ads. I felt lousy sitting at home so I'd read the newspapers at a local café. People who knew me looked at me with pity. From my senior position in the municipality, I was now a coffee-shop loafer. I couldn't smile anymore, so I started frequenting a café further away from my house where no one knew me.

I decided to read "The Garden of Emuna". It gave me the power to continue on, but reality would soon come back and slap me in the face. A whole year passed without my being able to find myself. My marriage was turning sour and I was starting to visualize myself living alone without my wife and children. The kids felt the tension and they too were losing their joy in life. I tried to hold on for them but I couldn't. My feeling of being a loser worsened from day to day.

In all fairness, I wasn't miserable 100% of the time. My baby girl always put a smile on my face. I noticed one thing: whenever I was happy, no matter why – whether it was from the baby's smile or a clever joke I heard – I functioned better. When you're down in the dumps, every moment of joy is a bright light. Even when I'd happily take the garbage out, it was an accomplishment for me. Unfortunately, the opposite holds ever so true. Any negative thought would paralyze me.

I was well aware of the ramifications of being happy or sad. I finally told myself that sadness is death and happiness is life. It doesn't matter why you're happy, you're alive! I decided to be happy at all costs. Whether I succeed or not, this was my new mission. Instead of looking for success, I searched for happiness, following Rebbe Nachman's timeless advice, be happy, no matter what! Sing and dance!

I decided to listen to music that I like. When my wife and kids weren't home, I'd dance, all by myself. The main thing was to be happy at all costs. Good jokes had a positive influence on me. I looked for sources of clean jokes. My wife saw the change that was happening within me. She certainly was pleased but she didn't understand why I was happy, for we were about to sell the house to pay off our debts.

"What are you so happy about?" she asked.

"What does it matter? I decided to divorce myself from sadness."

"But soon we'll be without a roof over our heads; that doesn't make you worry?"

"No big deal; we'll be able to purchase a high-quality family-size tent after we repay our debts," I smiled. "I always dreamed of living in a tent like a Bedouin. There won't be any mortgage or city taxes…"

She looked at me with pity but when she saw I was smiling, she smiled too. Sometime later, a good friend came to visit me. He would always console me. My other friends fell off the radar. He was surprised to find me in such a good mood. Instead of whining about my situation, I was throwing around ideas for having a good time. I asked him, "What do you think about the idea of starting a local weekly newspaper?"

My friend laughed. "I thought you had learned to be happy naturally; I didn't know that you're drinking something."

"No, seriously," I said, "I have a lot of experience in writing and editing."

"Do you have any idea what's involved?" My friend raised his voice when he saw that I wasn't just joking around. "It's not just pulling articles out of your sleeve, it's beating the pavement for every eighth inch of advertisement, accounting, employees, you name it!"

"Don't forget that I was a senior employee in the municipality and very abreast of what's going on in city hall. People want to know what's going on behind closed doors and where all the money they pay in municipal taxes is going."

"Yeh," my friend said skeptically, "but you've been out of the ballgame for a year. It's much more realistic that you buy a bicycle and start a newspaper route than open up your own newspaper…"

I let his put-down fly over my head. I was serious. My wife was shocked from the idea, but she saw that it infused me with a new vitality. She agreed to my exploring the idea further. Other friends tried to dissuade me, but they didn't succeed.

By virtue of my constant joy, good humor and perseverance, I began to take action. **I remembered that this was always my lifelong dream.** I started working at home. I found two great reporters and a woman who was very talented in editing various sections of the newspaper. Hashem sent me a great graphics artist and I embarked on the way.

I won't bore you with the details, but my local weekly has become a great hit. A year later, my staff consisted of forty people. All over the north of Israel, people read my newspaper. I barely have a free moment.

Today, people ask me what my secret is. I smile back and say, "It's the nonstop smile."

180. I'm a Different Person

Isaac Farine was about to receive his PhD in family counseling when he was fired from his job as a family counselor. He felt that his employers treated clients like numbers and not like human beings, which led to constant tension between him and his employers.

But, Hashem does everything for the best. Isaac was committed to finishing his PhD in this vital area, planning to incorporate the knowledge he had gleaned from Rabbi Arush's books.

Although Isaac is newly observant, he says that today, he is a different person, for he is now connected to Hashem. He has learned the magnificent power of personal prayer.

Talking about his dismissal from work, Isaac says, "When I was fired, I thought that I had weathered this challenge relatively well. I realized that it was Hashem and not the management who was firing me."

Today, Isaac has his PhD and a much more lucrative job. This happened exactly seven days after he finished reading "The Garden of Emuna." Since then, he has been spreading emuna books to family, friends and others. Isaac reads them over and over. He has attained tremendous success by applying the principle of "The Garden of Peace" to his marital counseling. He calls these books, "life-changers."

Not every person with a PhD in psychotherapy says that the love of his life is the Creator. He thanks Hashem incessantly for Rebbe Nachman and for Rabbi Shalom Arush. "I thank Hashem for the wonderful family He gave me, for the past-present-and future of the Jewish People, for Rebbe Nachman, for Rebbe Natan, for Rabbi Shalom Arush and for his student Rabbi Lazer Brody who so beautifully brought his teacher's lessons of emuna to the accessibility of English speakers. I pray that I can use my knowledge to help all those who seek my help."

181. Saying Thank You from a Young Age

We're now happy to present a series of stories that one of my students collected about children who have seen salvation by way of gratitude, so don't think that gratitude is just for grownups. Young children are pure of soul and readily internalize the way of emuna and gratitude. That way, they grow up to be wonderful human beings. We've brought a story or two to show how readily children learn emuna. This is an important message for parents and teachers – no age is too early to begin instilling emuna and gratitude in the hearts and souls of our children.

My name is Tamar and I'm nine and a half. My parents love me very much. I'm a good student, listen attentively in school, do my homework and listen to my parents. Last week at the Shabbat table, my father told a story from "The Garden of Gratitude" and said that if we thank Hashem for our difficulties, they become easier.

My father also said that even if it has been decided that a person must suffer, if he thanks Hashem, it will suffice that he won't feel any pain. He told us about a sad woman who was married for ten years but not yet a mother. She was jealous of all those girls that got married and had children a year later. Hashem had pity on her and sent her "The

Garden of Gratitude". After reading the book, she filled nine notebooks with thanks to Hashem that she didn't yet have children. Not long after, she had two babies.

Since then, I decided to start keeping a notebook for the unfavorable things in my life. On the first page I wrote, "Thank You, Hashem, that my father and my older sister went to the Kotel and they didn't take me." Or, "Thank You, Hashem, that I didn't get a present like my little brother did." Even though I don't understand why my father took my sister without me to the Kotel, or why my brother got a present and I didn't. I'll still thank Hashem. It's all surely for my benefit.

One day, I had a miracle. I want to tell you about it even though there are people who won't consider it a miracle. No one knows what my thoughts are and what's inside my head and what I pray to Hashem about. After I thanked Him for something hard, He made a miracle for me. This is the story I want to tell you about:

I have this big heavy bike that I received for an *afikoman* after Pesach. There are a lot of stairs going up to our apartment. Either my sister or my brother helps me carry the bike up the stairs when I come home from outside. One afternoon, I was all by myself, and I couldn't lift the bike up the stairs.

I was helpless. No one was around. I didn't know what to do until I remembered what my father taught me. I said, **"Thank You, Hashem, that I'm still too small and not strong enough to carry my bike up the stairs alone. Thank You that I'm sad about this. I know it's best for me, even though I don't know why."** Then, I understood that it was really Hashem Who was helping me carry my bike up the stairs but I never thanked Him. So I said, **"Thank You Hashem for all the times You helped me. Please send me someone now to help me."** Then, a miracle happened. Two high-school girls entered the lobby of our apartment building and asked if I need any help. I said, "Sure, thank you." They carried my bike up for me.

I always remind myself of this story and now thank Hashem for everything that's hard for me.

182. I Received Four Times More

I'm eight and a half and I live in Jerusalem. I'm a good boy. Another boy and I are the best students in our class and maybe that's why other kids are jealous of me. In recess, I'm always alone. Because I learned at home to behave, I don't hit other kids or pick on them. Kids take advantage of that and pick on me.

I love to learn Chumash and to pray. But, I started disliking school because of the kids that were picking on me all the time. I spoke to my father and mother and to my teacher but it didn't help much. Nobody likes to complain and tattle to the teacher all the time. My father taught me not to look at my friends but to look at Hashem, Who controls the world and everything that happens.

My father taught me to pray to Hashem, to thank Him and to say: **"Hashem, You don't want the other kids to play with me. I believe that it's all for the best. I understand that only You can help me. Even if I don't understand why the other kids pick on me, if You think that this is what I deserve, then fine – I believe in You, in Your goodness and**

that everything You do in my life is all for my best. I know that You want me to get close to You and to ask everything from You. So, I'm asking that You should help me and that the kids shouldn't pick on me and hit me all the time."

I prayed like this from the heart for several days. I spoke to Hashem. I even spoke in my own words like my father had taught me: **"Please Hashem, Father in Heaven, thank You that the kids in school beat me up because this gives me a reason to come and talk to You. Please help me."** Then, a miracle happened – in a few days, the kids stopped picking on me. The ones that used to hit me now wanted to be friends with me and play with me.

There's a game we play at school called "five rocks" (*a Chassidic children's version of "jacks"*). My father bought me a set of "five rocks", and Hashem helped me become the class champion. I even beat kids in the 4th and 5th grades.

How much better it is to go to Hashem than to cry to my parents or teachers, or to try and please the kids who were picking on me. Now thay all want to be my friends.

I wanted to tell you something else. Once I was jealous of kids in school who won better prizes than I did for getting good grades. I complained to my father that other kids always get the best prizes and I get the simple ones. My father said that Hashem was withholding the best prizes from me so that I would pray to Him. Not only that, but for anything else I need or want, I should pray to Hashem and ask from Him. I did. The next day, I won a battery-powered helicopter that I was really hoping for.

My father said, "Look how much Hashem loves you. Hashem wants you to talk to Him all the time. As soon as you do, everything in your life works out. Don't ever forget that – turn to Hashem for everything. He'll give you much more than you ask for."

It feels so good to see Hashem answering my prayers. He's right here with me!

183. Hashem is With Me

Dear Breslev Israel,

We live in a nice neighborhood with lawns and parks. The synagogue is right in the middle of the neighborhood. Everyone knows everyone else. I want to tell you a story from this past Purim.

I love Purim because everybody is happy. There's dancing and singing, tons of sweets, and costumes, which I also love. We have parties in school and everybody gives gifts to each other.

This year, I learned how to read the Megilla and was going to accompany my father to synagogue. He was going early and he said that he'd save me a seat. When I came to the synagogue, I couldn't find him anywhere. I looked all over. When I couldn't find him in the main shul, I went downstairs to the small minyan; he wasn't there either. I said down by myself and heard the whole Megilla reading. Funny, but I wasn't upset.

After the service was over, I waited for my father on the steps outside the synagogue. The firecrackers that kids were exploding were scary. A few minutes later, my father came and was happy to see me.

My father didn't understand why I didn't find him because he sat in his regular place; he simply said a long Amida prayer and his eyes were closed so he didn't see me. Yet, he was happy that I took the initiative to hear the Megilla on my own downstairs.

The next day, on Purim day, my father did an early personal prayer session in the forest. He asked Hashem what the message was in my not finding him the night before. Hashem illuminated his heart and let him understand that we don't find Him either because our eyes are closed. If we open up our spiritual eyes, we'll see that Hashem is right there with us.

I'm so lucky to have such a wonderful Father in Heaven and father on earth, who teach me so many good things, especially emuna.

184. On a Silver Platter

My name is Meir and I'm eight. Now it's Succoth and my cousins are here. They played with my big brother who is a year older than me. The game they play is "Tea Party"; if you don't know, you have to bring cookies, candy, Bamba or Bisli and we all have a party.

I wanted to play but they wouldn't let me. I was hungry, jealous and insulted.

I ran to my father in the Succa and told him that the cousins wouldn't let me play. He told me to go to a corner of the Succa and to ask Hashem to open their hearts to let me play with them. "But first," my father said, "thank Hashem that they won't let you play with them."

That's what I did. I said everything to Hashem that my father told me to say and I went back to them, but they still wouldn't let me play. I went back to my father and told him that it didn't work.

My father said, "Maybe you didn't pray enough? Say three more times what I told you to say then thank Hashem that they wouldn't let you play with them even after you prayed. Then go ask them again" I did that too, but they still wouldn't let me play.

I came back to the Succa and started to tell my father that his advice wasn't working. Meanwhile, my cousin came into the Succa and invited me to play. "This time," my cousin said, "We're going to play, 'Royal Tea Party' – you're the king and we're the servants. We're going to bring you everything – brownies, Bamba, chocolate and popcorn – on a silver tray."

They sat me down in the living room on a plastic chair that they covered with a silk and gold scarf that they borrowed from my mother – this was the throne. Then they served me everything – cakes, candies, snacks, fruit juice, nuts and fruit on a silver platter (Really a plastic tray covered with aluminum foil). My father passed by and saw me sitting like a king – he laughed.

"You see what happens when you pray?" My father smiled. From that, I learned that when you pray, you get much more than what you can get on your own.

The above stories show the power of educating children in emuna. This gives them wonderful tools for the rest of their lives, making their existence on this earth so much easier and more pleasurable. This is our main task, to teach emuna and gratitude to future generations.

185. Amazing Phenomenon

One phenomenon that never ceases to amaze me after every gratitude lecture I deliver is that people still come up to me after the lesson and ask for salvations. Where were they during the whole lecture? Didn't they hear that everything is from Hashem, for the best and for a purpose? I would have expected everyone to fly into their cars at the end of the lecture and rush to a park or a field where they can start thanking Hashem for their troubles and begin the process of rectifying themselves and seeing salvation. But no, none of that; they're still turning to me. Didn't I tell them repeatedly to start saying thank You and start seeing miracles?

Not only are they still whining and complaining, but they're justifying their "right" to be depressed. "Rabbi, no one has problems like I do. Give me a rabbinical dispensation to be sad, depressed and despairing and give me an exemption from prayer and Torah learning. You must agree with me that the only way to deal with my problems is to be depressed. I tell you such painful stories of my problems, and you tell me to thank Hashem?" His "solution" to his problems is to sever himself from Hashem...

As we've emphasized earlier in this book, a sad person indeed severs himself from Hashem. Our sages said that the Divine Presence hovers only in a place of happiness (Tractate Pesachim 117a). That's why Rebbe Nachman of Breslev (who was a blemish-free tzaddik), said, "Even if, Heaven forbid, I committed the worst sin, I would continue to be happy; then, I would repent." What did Rebbe Nachman mean by this? When a person is sad, Hashem is not with him. Therefore, *teshuva* –penitence – must be done with joy in order for a person's prayers and penitence to be accepted.

A sad person can't do teshuva because a sad person can't speak to Hashem, confess his wrongdoings or objectively assess himself. That's why joy is a tremendous mitzvah while sadness is a transgression. Sadness chases the Divine Presence away.

There's no justification for being sad. Imagine that someone's child is very sick. A neighbor asks the parent, "What are you doing to help your child get better?"

"I'm feeling sorry for myself," the parent answers.

How inane!

We must serve Hashem with joy, appreciating every chance to do a mitzvah and every mitzvah. We should all be keeping a gratitude notebook and writing down as many thanks as we can, ignoring nothing and appreciating every tiny act of loving-kindness from Above.

The reward for the tiniest mitzvah is worth more than all the treasures of this material world. People complain about all the obligations the Torah requires of them; that too is senseless. Rebbe Chanania be Akashiya says, "The Holy One blessed be He wants to bestow merit on Israel, so He gave them the Torah and its many mitzvoth" (Avot, ch. 1).

When the evil inclination tries to bring you down, tell him immediately: "Mr. Evil Inclination, with all due respect, have a look at my gratitude notebook; every day, there are a hundred thank Yous. I can't even write down all the mitzvoth Hashem lets me do every minute..." Now, the evil inclination is depressed, and not you.

As I wrote in "The Garden of Gratitude", gratitude is the basic character trait that the whole world stands on. Conversely, ingratitude is the basis of all evil in the world.

Any destruction in the world began with ingratitude.

Gratitude connects a person to the Creator, to holiness, to purity and to everything good. Let's begin saying thank You!

186. Needless Private Appointments

"Shalom to the Rabbi,

"We are a family with four children. My husband has very limited eyesight so we are entitled to a government-subsidized apartment. The problem is that there are hundreds of families like us waiting for an apartment, so the waiting line is years long. Meanwhile, we get rent support from the government and all we can afford is a hovel in a terrible neighborhood. There's no Torah educational framework for my children and I feel so alone.

"One day, someone gave me the book "The Garden of Gratitude" and my life changed right away. I devoured the book and started applying it right away. I thanked Hashem for not having an apartment and for stimulating me to get closer to Him. Within two weeks, Amidar – the government housing company – called to say that they have an apartment for us in a different neighborhood. This was no plain apartment but large, airy and remodeled in a great neighborhood. The children in the building are from good homes and well-behaved. I'm very satisfied. With my own eyes, I've seen the miracle of Hashem's Divine intervention and providence – I said thank You and saw miracles right away."

The above letter as well as the other stories in this book show that the whole concept of private appointments with me is needless. There are emuna and gratitude books, CDs and Gems pamphlets. Take them, start reading and start listening. There's no such thing that you won't see results. Our sages say, "You toiled and you found? Believe!" There are no instant solutions. Ask Hashem to give you the will and conviction to roll up your spiritual sleeves and to get to work on emuna and gratitude.

Learning isn't enough; one must implement what he learns. The way to implement and internalize is through personal prayer – the more the better. It's a fact! People who never met me before are witnessing tremendous miracles and salvations in their lives simply my taking the advice of the books, pamphlets and CDs and getting to work.

Here's my message to those with difficult marital problems: get "The Garden of Peace" and start learning it. Folks who never met me have turned the worst marriages around completely by doing so.

A person thinks that if he doesn't have marital peace with his wife, he'll have it with a different woman. To paraphrase the tuna advertisement, "Sorry, Charlie!" If you can't get along with your wife, you won't be able to get along with a different woman unless you rectify yourself. That's the good news – anyone who decides to work on himself will see results, no matter how acute the problem is. But, the harder the problem, the more a person must work on himself and pray, even devoting six consecutive hours to personal prayer if need be.

When I have private meetings with people who turn to me, I don't feel like a rabbi; I feel like a pharmacist. For whatever problem they have, I direct them to the appropriate book, CD or pamphlet. Are you looking for a solution, an address to turn to? I have a great address for you with 24/7 express mail service that doesn't cost you a cent – your Father in Heaven! You're His child! Go speak to Him and ask for whatever you need; this is the difference between a life of purgatory or paradise. Get to know the Creator and learn to believe in Him, for this is the purpose in life of every human being.

187. Delivered to the Front Door

One of my students tells the following story:

This was during the Gaza War in 2014 when Ashkelon and Ashdod were bombarded every day. Our teacher Rabbi Arush, who feels the pain of every Jew, sent his students to the south of Israel – the area under attack – to give out pamphlets, book and CDs for free, compliments of his "Emuna Outreach" organization. We went from house to house, knocking on doors and encouraging people. This is when the story starts.

A gruff looking man opened one of the doors we knocked on in an apartment building and said, "Whaddya want? To give me a book? I'm not interested."

We said, "The book is about joy and a worry-free life – it's surely not the other stuff you read."

"Forget it, I'm not interested."

We heard a woman calling from the background, "Who's at the door? The young men from the yeshiva? Give them a few shekels."

We told her, "Ma'am, we didn't come here for charity. We came here to spread the bright light of emuna and to help you rid yourself of worry. We want to give you some tools to successfully weather these tough times."

"Nu, how do you propose to do that?" she asked.

We showed her a copy of "The Garden of Emuna". She said, "This is eerie – just this morning a coworker of mine showed me the same book. During lunch break, one of the other women gave over some beautiful ideas from the book. Yes, thank you, I'll be happy to read it." She took the book and marveled at the Divine Providence that brought it to her front door…

This is the end of my student's narrative.

After one of my lectures, a man came up to me and said, "One of your students came to our town and brought me a book – it saved my life." I told him to tell them, for they don't realize the importance of their work in spreading emuna.

Without going into detail, that man was contemplating suicide four years ago. His whole life seemed hopeless. He was far away from Torah observance. He relates, "I saw this strange-looking book at my friend's house called 'The Garden of Emuna'. While waiting for my friend to finish something in the kitchen, I leafed through its pages; I decide to read this book, even if it did look a little weird…"

He didn't read the book – he gobbled it up and savored every word. He began learning emuna. A short time later, he met a great girl and got married. He took the book on his honeymoon. During the flight to where they were going, he was deeply into the book when suddenly, he heard screaming. Something had gone wrong and the pilot had lost control of the aircraft.

"What do we do?" asked his young bride, clutching his arm.

"We look at what's written in this book. I don't care about the plane or the pilot; Hashem will take care of everything!" Hashem did. Some four years later, they brought me their son for his "Challak'e" – his first haircut.

Don't let anything in the world scare you. Strengthen yourself in emuna! It's our solemn duty to share the light of emuna and gratitude with others, for only this will bring the *Geula*, the full redemption of our people, peacefully and pleasantly.

188. He Didn't Commit Suicide

I met a person after my lecture in Kiryat Ata who was a former police officer who was suspended from the police force because of a vicious libel against him. He suffered public humiliation for all the newspapers carried the story. He endured interrogations and hearings. His entire family suffered. He fell into deep depression to the extent that he contemplated suicide. Hashem had mercy on him and revived him from the dead. (The great tzaddik and holy Kabbalist Rabbi Avraham Chai osb"m would call "The Garden of Emuna", the "reviver of the dead"). A friend of his who knew what he was going through said, "Before you decide to do something foolish, read this book. The friend put a copy of "The Garden of Emuna" in his hand.

The suspended police officer began learning the book intensively and soon realized that it's not the false witnesses or jealous peers, it's only Hashem. All the toxic thoughts of revenge that corroded his soul like acid disappeared. He started to pray, to learn Torah and to be happy. Meanwhile, during his suspension, he was getting closer and closer to Hashem. Ultimately, the police disciplinary court discovered that the entire case was based on lying witnesses. He was soon reinstated.

After being reinstated in the police and embarking on an observant lifestyle that included Shabbat, kashruth and tefillin, he met a broken-hearted widow. She too wanted to commit suicide. He gave her "The Garden of Emuna". When he saw her a year later, she was smiling, in a wonderful mood.

The same police officer tells that he was in Eilat on a street that was always full of vendors carting their wares. The mayor decided that this was unsightly and that all the vendors would get small kiosks instead. One of the elderly vendors was so upset that he jumped into the Red Sea and committed suicide. The police officer overheard another vendor saying that he wanted to kill himself too. The police officer went into the local bookstore and bought a copy of "The Garden of Emuna", which he brought to the despairing vendor. "Read the book," he said, and left.

A year later, the police officer returned to Eilat and strolled down the same street. He saw the vendor who contemplated suicide standing in a small kiosk and smiling. They recognized one another. The vendor hugged him and said, "Thank you for the book that saved my life; it showed me that the mayor doesn't run the world – Hashem does!"

Can you imagine how important outreach is? By spreading emuna, everyone can save lives. What could be greater?

Know full well – there is no charity in the world that can

compare with emuna outreach – distributing emuna books, CDs and pamphlets! There's a big difference between twenty dollars and a million dollars. For example, if a person gives someone else a book that costs twenty dollars, or even a CD that costs two or three dollars; meanwhile, someone else donated a million dollars to charity. When they get to the next world, the person who gave out the book or CD will have a million times greater reward than the individual who gave the million dollars.

The million-dollar donor complains in the Heavenly Court: "Is this justice? I gave a million bucks and all the other guy did was give out a tiny booklet, some book, a 2-buck CD? What's the big deal?" They'll show him that the book or CD prevented a suicide, saved a marriage or brought a person back to Hashem. Not only the recipient's entire life changed, but the lives of his whole family. They started to believe! Not only that, but they were so grateful that they began to spread emuna too. His merit grows from day to day. But, you gave a one-time sum of a million dollars. You too have great merit, but it can't compare with the merit of twenty-dollars' worth of spreading emuna!"

No charity compares to the power of spreading emuna!

189. I Gave Out CDs and I Got Married

It's no wonder that spreading emuna mitigates all stern judgments.

A letter that the Breslev Israel Spanish-language website received from Mexico told about a man with a malignant tumor who was scheduled for an operation. Someone gave him the CD "Stop Crying" in Spanish and he loved it so much that he bought more CDs to give out to other people. When the time came for his operation, there was no longer need to operate – the sonogram showed that the tumor had vanished, thanks to Hashem! When he got that result, he ordered another 500 CDs.

In another letter, a young woman from Toronto who made Aliya writes: "For years, I couldn't find my soul-mate. Rabbi Shalom Arush gave a blessing that whoever gives out 100 CDs would see big salvations. I decided to do that, so I purchased 100 CDs to give out when I visited my family in Toronto. I got married exactly a year after that to the man of my dreams. Thank you so much for what you give to people every day."

It's amazing how a few emuna books and CDs can work such wonders. It makes sense, though – you bring other people closer to Hashem, and He brings what you need closer to you.

190. Concluding Stories: Emuna Outreach, the Greatest Act of Kindness

My student overheard two people talking; one said that "The Garden of Emuna" saved his life. The other one said that "The Garden of Riches" saved his – he owed millions and didn't know what to do. He followed the advice of the book and tore up his checkbook and credit cards. Just by doing that, he started seeing that his debts were decreasing.

He implemented the other gems of advice, including daily personal prayer, until he was no longer in debt.

A woman who suffers tremendous tribulations told me that she learns "The Garden of Emuna" daily. "Without it," she says, "I wouldn't be alive today."

Someone phoned me and told me that he had no connection at all wih Hashem until he received the CD, "Stop Crying". It changed his life and brought him to Torah, emuna and observant Judaism.

An American Jew came to me and told me that he was secular before receiving "The Garden of Emuna" and the CD "Stop Crying". That was it; not only did his life turn around, but he began spreading emuna to others. The prophet in Messianic times, the world will fill with spiritual awareness and knowledge of Hashem like the waters that cover the sea (see Isaiah 1:9). We therefore must fill the world with emuna books and CDs to spread this spiritual awareness and knowledge of Hashem.

One student heard the CD, "Stop Crying" and became so enthused that he now walks around campus giving out CDs: "Do me a favor", he says to people, "just listen to this CD then call me and tell me what you think of it." He said that the reactions are amazing.

I gave a lesson on the radio. A listener phoned in and said that she lives in a Charedi neighborhood. She was sure that her neighbors would say that they already have emuna and they don't need emuna books and CDs. She said to herself, "What can I lose?" She gave emuna books to a few of her neighbors. The reactions would soon come, like, "You have no idea what you did for me – this was just what I needed!"

I understand the phrase "You saved my life" in several languages, because so many people around the world tell me this. I'm talking about Jews and non-Jews, observant and non-observant; they all get a shot of encouragement and inner strength from these books and CDs. People are thirsty for the waters of emuna.

One man said, "I envy you, that you merited writing these books." I told him that his merit could be much greater than mine. He asked how. I told him to start distributing the books and CDs to people. It's not enough that I write them or that they collect dust on the shelves. Every book or CD that someone distributes earns the latter equal, if not greater merit, than what's due to the author.

Rabbenu Bachiya writes in "Duties of the Heart" (The Gate of Love, 5): "It is befitting that you know that the merit of the believer, even if he has arrived at the difficult destination of rectifying his soul before the Almighty, and even if his upright character resembles an angel...his merit is inferior to the merit of those who bring others to Divine service...for their merits are perpetually accumulating."

In the "Gate of Trust" of "Duties of the Heart", Rabbenu Bachiya writes explicitly that a person is not rewarded for his mitzvoth in this world, unless he brings others closer to Hashem, for the merit of all those people's good deeds is also credited to him.

The holy Zohar writes in Parshat Truma that if people knew the rewards that one gets for bringing others closer to Hashem, they would chase after this mitzvah their entire lives. The one who brings others close to Hashem ascends to a level where no one else can because he causes Hashem's Name to be exalted in the world.

The book "Chayei Moharan" says: "We heard several times from Rebbe Nachman about the power of bringing others close to Hashem…once on Motzaei Shabbat (Saturday night), we heard him scold a group of distinguished people for not doing enough in this area. He wanted us to go from town to town and from village to village to speak to people about emuna…"

There is no greater act of loving-kindness than emuna outreach, spreading emuna. Our sages said that this will save a person from the tribulations of Messianic times. Why? It's measure for measure: you save a person's life by bringing him close to Hashem, and Hashem saves your life. For sure, the people you spread emuna to will also testify, "You saved my life!" The Gemara in tractate Sanhedrin (37a) says that he who saves a life saves an entire world!

We must all strengthen ourselves in emuna and gratitude and believe that everything is for the best. Also, we must accept the solemn obligation of spreading emuna and gratitude to others. As our sages said, this is not only saving lives but saving entire worlds. Emuna and gratitude guarantee everyone good lives in this world and in the next.

Every contribution that a person makes in spreading emuna – whether he purchases emuna books and CDs to distribute or donates to our global distribution of emuna hastens the *Geula*. We have scores of stories from prisons all over the world, from the US Military in Afghanistan and in Iraq and from the most faraway places on the globe, like Hong Kong and rural Africa, of how the emuna books and CDs have literally saved people's lives. This global distribution of emuna is surely hastening *Geula*. What's more, it's the only chance for genuine peace on earth.

May the light of gratitude and emuna illuminate your personal path, singing and dancing all the way, to the *Geula*, the full and complete redemption, soon!

He who walks with the light of emuna and gratitude can say: "My Moshiach has already arrived." He who merits spreading this light can say: "I am doing the most cogent thing to hasten the merciful Redemption." You shall see with your own eyes how with gratitude, you'll see open miracles and the Geula, speedily in our days, amen!

The Prayer of Gratitude

Father in Heaven, benevolent King, merciful Father Who watches over us with constant Divine Providence, please, guard me against ingratitude and against taking any single favor You do for me for granted.

Please, grant me full emuna so I'll be able to believe that everything that happens to me materially or spiritually is all for my ultimate benefit.

Please, grant me the awareness that You don't owe me a thing and that everything You do for me is a free gift because You love me and You want my very best.

Master of the World, enable me to thank You from the bottom of my heart for everything.

Father in Heaven, thank You for the privilege of thanking You, for all my expressions of gratitude are nothing compared to my true obligation of thanking You, for everything is from You.

Thank You for all the things in the world that up until now, I have taken for granted and failed to thank You for.

Thank You for every breath, every heartbeat and for every part of my body that functions properly; thank You for my health.

Thank You for the magnificent world you created to serve me.

Thank you for all the messengers who do good for me.

He Who sustains every creature, thank You for the sustenance and the livelihood that You give me.

Thank You, King of the World, for each of my possessions and thank You for the things I lack, for everything is the product of Your Divine Providence for my benefit.

Thank You, Master of Emuna, for the emuna you give me, which is the greatest gift that a person can receive.

Thank You for the Torah, the mitzvoth, for Sabbath and for the festivals.

Thank You for our great righteous spiritual leaders and for the belief in them.

Thank You for giving me the heart, brain and power to do good: to serve You, to believe in You, to trust in You, to learn Your Torah, to fulfill Your holy mitzvoth, to learn upright character traits to praise and to thank You. Everything I do is only because You enable me to do so.

Thank You for Your helping me overcome the evil inclination and for helping me avoid temptation. Anything I achieve in serving You is a gift from You.

Thank You for my setbacks, failures and for the difficulties You give me. I believe that they are exactly what I need to truly get close to You.

Thank You for all the good You do for me every second of the day and for all the times You rescued me and guarded over me, encouraged me and made me happy.

Thank You for listening to and accepting all my prayers.

Master of the World, You certainly know that I lack the wherewithal of seeing how everything You do is for my very best; therefore, I ask Your forgiveness for all the times that I doubted You and failed to appreciate You. Instead of singing Your praise, I whined and complained. Beloved forgiving Father, I beg Your forgiveness for my discontent and complaining and for not having appreciated everything You have given me.

Glossary

Amalek (Biblical) – evil grandson of Esau; nickname for the Yetzer Hara, the evil inclination

Baal Teshuva (Hebrew) – spiritually awakened Jew

Bitachon (Hebrew) – trust in G-d

Brit mila (Hebrew) – ritual circumcision

Chassid (Hebrew) – literally "pious person", but alludes to the disciples of the Chassidic movement, founded by Rabbi Yisroel Baal Shem Tov in the early 18th Century CE

Chattan (Hebrew) – bridegroom

Chuppa (Hebrew) – marital canopy

Dinim (Hebrew) – the spiritual forces of severe judgments that are created by a person's misdeeds.

Emuna (Hebrew) - the firm belief in a single, supreme, omniscient, benevolent, spiritual, supernatural, and all-powerful Creator of the universe, who we refer to as God

Emunat Chachamim (Hebrew) - the belief in our sages

Epikoris (Greek) – skeptic, heretic

Epikorsis (Greek) – heresy, skepticism

Gemara (Aramaic) – The 2nd-5th Century CE elaborations on the Mishna, which serve as the foundation of Jewish law

Geula (Hebrew) – the redemption process of the Jewish people

Hashem (Hebrew) - literally means "the name," a substitute term for The Almighty so that we don't risk using God's name in vain.

Hitbodedut (Hebrew) – personal prayer

Kabbala (Hebrew) - Jewish esoteric thought

Kedusha (Hebrew) - holiness

Mishna (Hebrew) – The oral elaboration of the Torah as given from Hashem to Moses, finally codified by Rabbi Akiva, his pupil Rabbi Meir, and his pupil Rabbi Yehuda HaNassi, 1st-2nd Century, CE

Mitzvah (Hebrew) – a commandment of the Torah; good deed.

Mitzvoth (Hebrew, pl.) – literally, the commandments of the Torah; good deeds

Moshiach (Hebrew) – Messiah

Onaat Devarim (Hebrew) – a broad term for verbal abuse which includes several Torah prohibitions against causing anguish to a fellow human being

Pidyon Nefesh (Hebrew) – literally "redemption of the soul"; a monetary donation that is given to a tzaddik as atonement for a person's soul

Sandek (Hebrew) - godfather

Shabbat (Hebrew) – Sabbath, day of rest

Shalom Bayit (Hebrew) – literally "peace in the home", marital bliss

Shmirat Habrit (Hebrew) – literally "guarding the covenant"; male holiness in thought, speech, and deed, particularly the use of one's reproductive organs only in the performance of a mitzvah

Shmirat Eynayim (Hebrew) – "guarding the eyes," or refraining from looking at forbidden objects, particularly at a woman other than one's wife

Shulchan Oruch (Hebrew) – Code of Jewish Law, compiled by Rabbi Joseph Caro of Tzfat, late 16th Century CE

Tallit (Hebrew) – prayer shawl

Talmud (Hebrew) – Jewish oral tradition, comprised of the Mishna and the Gemorra

Tanna (Aramaic) – Mishnaic sage, 1st – 2nd Century CE

Tefillin (Aramaic) - phylacteries

Teshuva (Hebrew) – literally "returning," the term that refers to the process of atoning for one's misdeeds

Tefilla (Hebrew) - prayer

Tikkun (Hebrew) – correction of the soul

Tikkunim (Hebrew) – plural for tikkun

Tzaddik (Hebrew) – extremely pious and upright person

Tzaddikim (Hebrew) – plural for tzaddik

Tzedakka (Hebrew) – charity

Yetzer Hara (Hebrew) – evil inclination

Yetzer Tov (Hebrew) –inclination to do good

Yir'at Shamayim (Hebrew) – literally "the fear of Hashem," a term for sincere piety

Zohar (Hebrew) - the 2nd-Century C.E. esoteric interpretation of the Torah by Rebbe Shimon Bar Yochai and his disciples

WITH TREMENDOUS GRATITUDE
TO HASHEM

ON THE OCCASION OF
THE 1ST BIRTHDAY OF

JULIETTE TAYLOR ZOLNA

ZELDA BAS RIVKA

KAREN & PETER COOPER
RACHEL & JARED ZOLNA
DAVID COOPER

JUNE 2017   EASTON, PA.

Did you enjoy this book?

**Become a partner
in distributing emuna.**

Call:

972-52-2240-696

02-5812210

Dear reader!

The book You have just finished reading has changed the lives of many. Please note that this book is the outcome of a wonderful enterprise that is dedicated to the goal of spreading Jewish wisdom and emuna to hundreds of thousands of people around the globe.

We turn to you, dear reader with a request to become a partner in this enterprise by contributing to our efforts in spreading emuna around the world.
For your convenience please fill in the form on the back and send it to us.

With blessings always
"Chut Shell Chessed" institutions

⧉Chut Shell Chessed⧉
p.o. 50226
Bucharim mail box office
Jerusalem zip code: 91050
Israel

Support The Important Work of "Chut Shel Chessed"
Thank you for supporting "Chut Shel Chessed".

Recommended Operation
Support Levels:

$ 15.60 (30¢/week) ☐

$ 26.00 (50¢/week) ☐

$ 39.00 (75¢/week) ☐

$ 52.00 (1.00$/week) ☐

Other Amount: $ _____

Recommended
Support Levels:

$ 100

$ 250

$ 500

$ 1000

Please include your email address,
We will keep you informed about

E-mail address: _____

Name: _____

Street address: _____

City, State, Zip: _____

Phone: (_____) _____

Contribute by Credit Card:

Credit Card Type:

☐ Visa ☐ MasterCard ☐ Discover ☐ American Express

Credit Card #: _____

Expiration: _____ (Month / Year)

Cardholder Signature: _____

Contribute by check :
send a check to the address listed on the back of this card